The Campus History Series

ASHLEY HALL

ILEANA STRAUCH

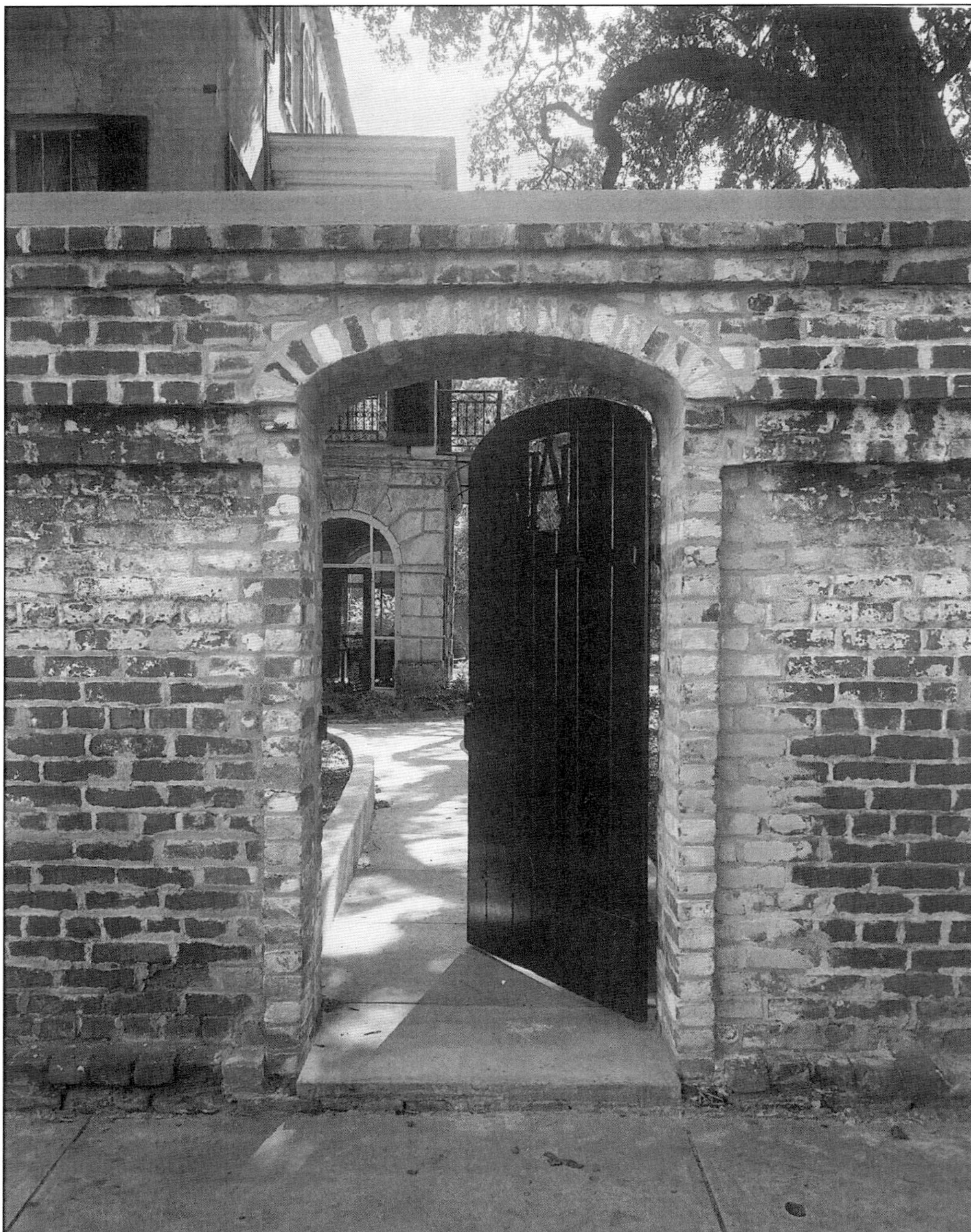

EMILY'S GATE, 1958. Mrs. Ashby Farrow (née Emily Ravenel, class of 1933) donated "Emily's Gate" to the school in 1958. As construction began on the gate, it was noticed that the entire old brick wall on Radcliffe Street needed reinforcing. Realizing the importance of this preservation, Mrs. Farrow also gave the money necessary for this. (Photo courtesy of the Ashley Hall Archives.)

The Campus History Series

ASHLEY HALL

ILEANA STRAUCH

ARCADIA
PUBLISHING

ISBN 978-0-7385-1564-9

Published by Arcadia Publishing
Charleston, South Carolina

Printed in the United States of America

Library of Congress Catalog Card Number: 2003108858

For all general information contact Arcadia Publishing at:
Telephone 843-853-2070
Fax 843-853-0044
E-mail sales@arcadiapublishing.com
For customer service and orders:
Toll-Free 1-888-313-2665

Visit us on the Internet at www.arcadiapublishing.com

To all of the faculty, staff, students, and friends at Ashley Hall who prompted me to write this book in order to help preserve the history and complete essence of the school where I experienced many of my fondest memories.

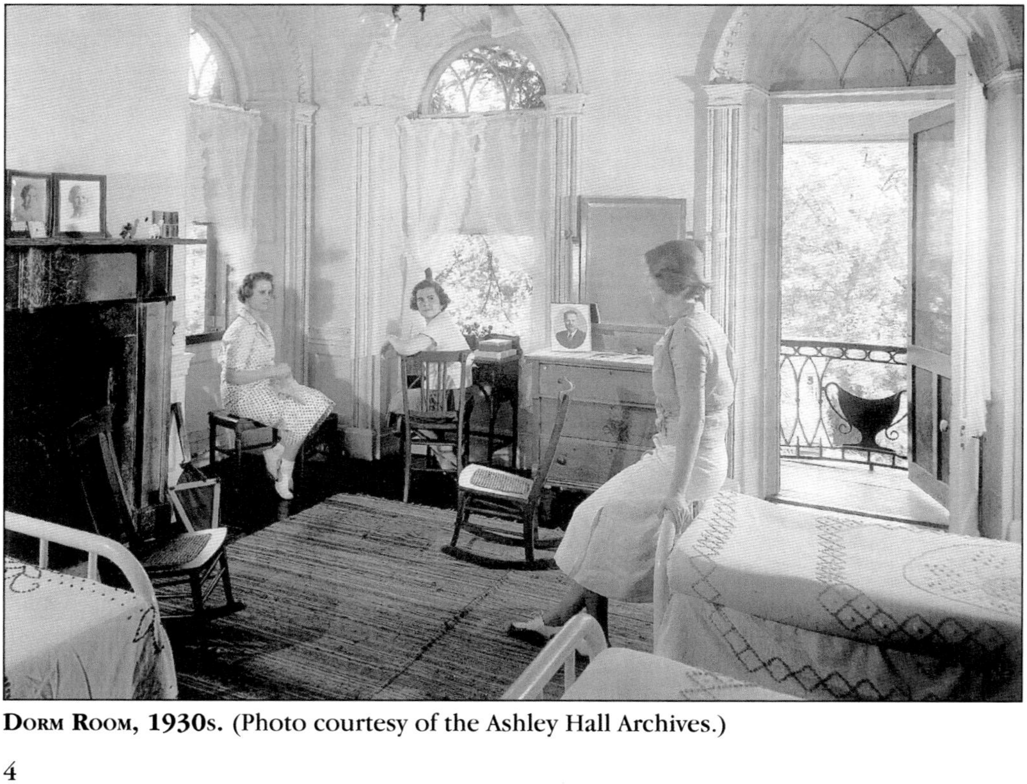

Dorm Room, 1930s. (Photo courtesy of the Ashley Hall Archives.)

CONTENTS

ACKNOWLEDGMENTS

My thanks to Margaret Tenney for her endless knowledge and tireless assistance and also to Margaret MacDonald for generously opening the resources of the Ashley Hall Archives.

Thanks to Jane Thornhill, Angie LeClercq, Beth Cole, Vereen Coen, Josephine Hutcheson, Elizabeth Puckette, Sally Dobbins, Patti Workman, Franny Slay, Katherine Orr, Ann Burger, Mary-Louise Rhodes, Ann Meredith, Abigail Van Alyn, Molly Gray, Daisy Leland, Rosemary Hutto, Carolyn Swan, and Caroline Haydock for their time and reminiscences.

And thank you to my family and friends for their support and patience during the writing of this book.

INTRODUCTION

Three tough days of placement exams to be accepted by Smith College taught Mary Vardrine McBee the vital importance of a certified secondary education. Even as a freshman she had declared a life goal of founding a school that would give Southern girls the college requirements equivalent to those given to girls in the North.

Upon graduation from Smith, McBee taught for a year at Fairmont, her former boarding school in Monteagle, Tennessee, and then earned her master's degree in history and education from Columbia University. She then moved to Charleston where she found the perfect site for her future all-girls school. The Witte house, built in 1816 by Patrick Duncan, had gone through many owners before McBee made her small offer of $25,000.

In September 1909, McBee's dream came true as Ashley Hall opened its gates to 45 young ladies. In 1911 three girls graduated, and in 1912, Mary Howden, a prize student, took the college entrance exams, which gave Ashley Hall the distinction needed to become a certified school.

McBee was not only the Headmistress, but she also took on the responsibility of the tracking the school's finances, maintaining an agreeable atmosphere on campus, and teaching history classes. Through the Great Depression and two World Wars, McBee ran the school with a firm hand and a soft heart. But as she aged, she realized that a foundation was needed so Ashley Hall would not perish at her death. In 1949, Miss McBee retired after 40 years of dedicated work and left her school to the Ashley Hall Foundation. McBee still lived on campus and took an active role in the school up until her death in 1965.

Mr. and Mrs. William Piper briefly ran the school from 1949 to 1954, followed by Caroline Pardue. Miss Pardue tried to keep the same traditions of the school, but in 1974 Ashley Hall closed its doors to boarding students, leaving only the day program. The number of day schools had increased all over the state, sharply reducing the need for parents to send their girls to Charleston.

Marian Bell Leland became Headmistress in 1979, succeeded upon her retirement by Margaret MacDonald in 1985.

Now the all-girls school, still located at 172 Rutledge Avenue, is the home to over 600 kindergarteners through twelfth graders. Known for excellence in sports, leadership, and education, the school continues to thrive. Boasting of college acceptances to such prestigious schools as Harvard, Washington and Lee, the University of Virginia, Rice, the University of Pennsylvania, and many others, it can safely be said that Miss Mary Vardrine McBee accomplished her dream of providing "young women of diverse backgrounds with a solid foundation to further their study of the liberal arts and sciences."

One

HISTORY

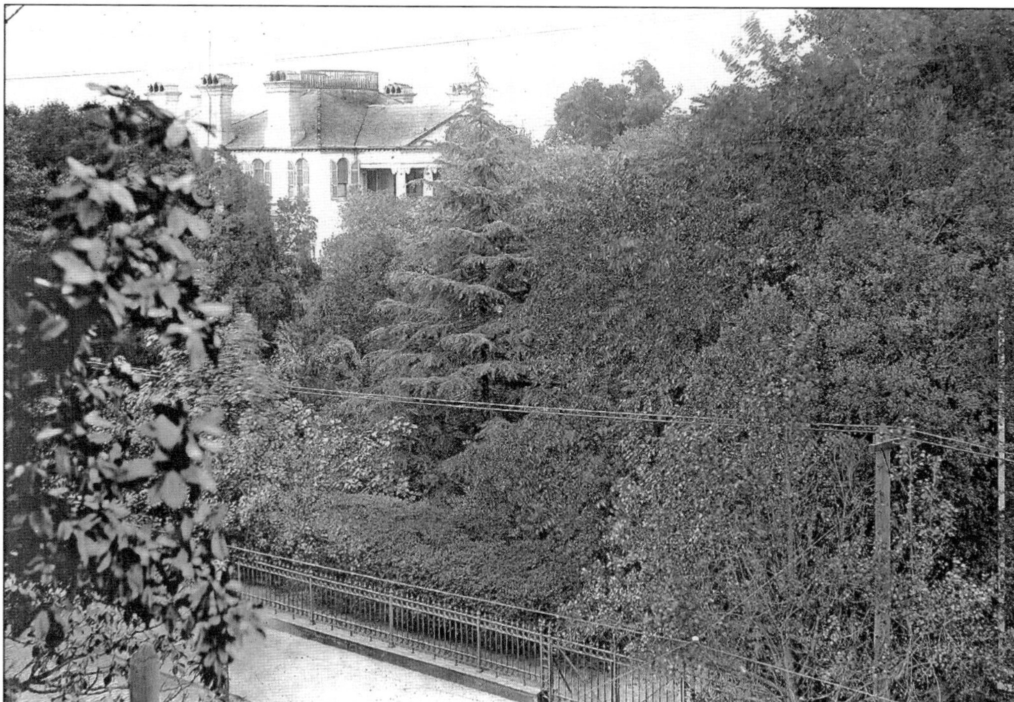

VIEW OF CAMPUS, 1920s. The Main House, renamed McBee House by the Alumnae Association after Miss McBee's retirement, on Ashley Hall's campus was built in 1816 by Patrick Duncan, a tallow chandler and factor. It is one of Charleston's best examples of suburban Regency villas. As seen in this photo, the land all around the campus was marsh, creek, and forests until more recent days. Duncan worked to make his land more elegant by planting gardens; the neighborhood around him was becoming a fashionable suburb of Cannonsborough. In 1836, the house was bought by James Reid Pringle, the leader of the Unionist Party in the Nullification Controversy. Pringle was also a well-known collector of Customs of Charleston from 1819 to 1840. (Photo courtesy of the Ashley Hall Archives.)

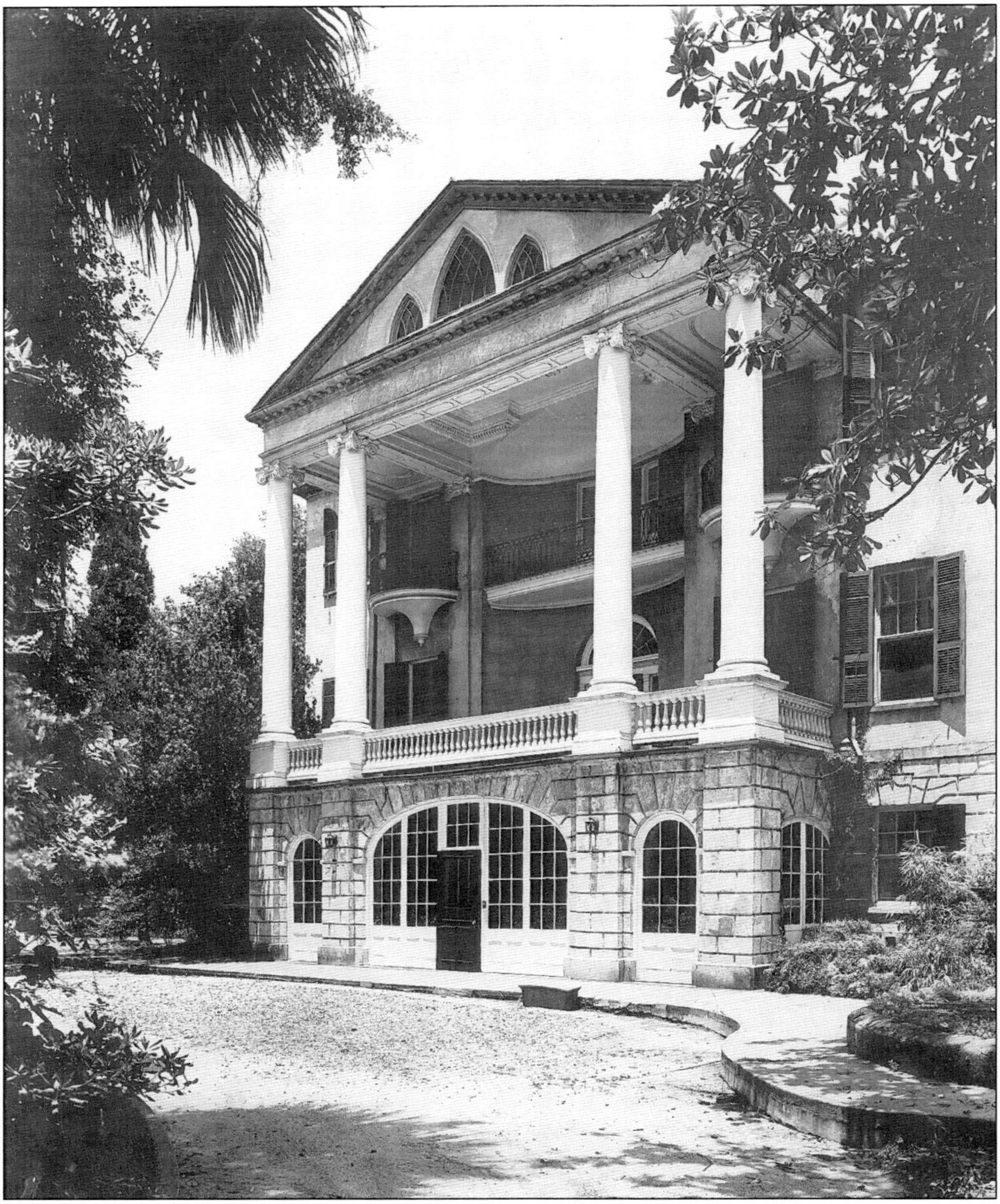

McBee House, 1920s. The McBee House was next bought for $18,000 by George A. Trenholm, a merchant, owner of blockade runners, and the last Secretary of the Treasury of the Confederacy. Trenholm was a man of charm and is rumored to be the man after whom Rhett Butler in *Gone with the Wind* was modeled. The heavy moldings and Victorian decorations were probably added to the house during his ownership. Charles Otto Witte, a cotton merchant and banker, next owned the house and takes much of the credit for landscaping the grounds. When Comings Creek, above Calhoun Street, was stopped up, Witte filled in the marsh at the east and added them to his grounds. Witte designed the grounds to conform to his preference for exotic plants and animals. The Shell House was an aviary for his exotic birds, and the Bear Cave, or grotto, was added for his pet bear. (Photo courtesy of the Ashley Hall Archives.)

MARY VARDRINE AND ESTELLE MCBEE, LATE 1800S. Mary Vardrine, born September 2, 1879, in Lincolnton, North Carolina, is pictured at right with her older sister Estelle, born in 1878. The girls were the daughters of Mary Estelle and Silas McBee, a well-known layman of the Episcopal church, architect, and editor of *The Churchman*. After the death of their mother, the two girls and their brother, Silas McBee Jr., were sent to live with an aunt in Philadelphia. The clothing of the girls here was very representative of the time. Laura Witte Waring, daughter of Otto Witte and former occupant of 172 Rutledge Avenue, recalls in her book *The Way It Was in Charleston*, "Mother Hubbards had come into style, dresses made with guimpes, sailor suits with box-pleated skirts, fluffy, embroidered, frilly party clothes, and always sashes. The sashes were of wide ribbon worn flat, like a plaster in front with a brooch pinned exactly in the center and a big bow in the back." (Photo courtesy of the Ashley Hall Archives.)

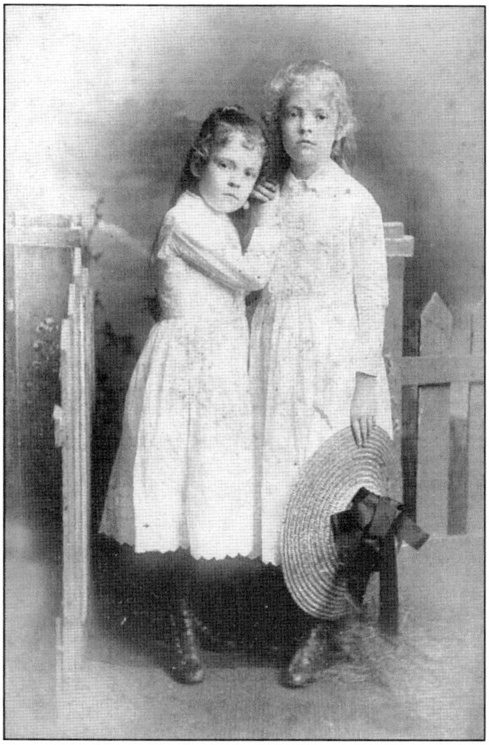

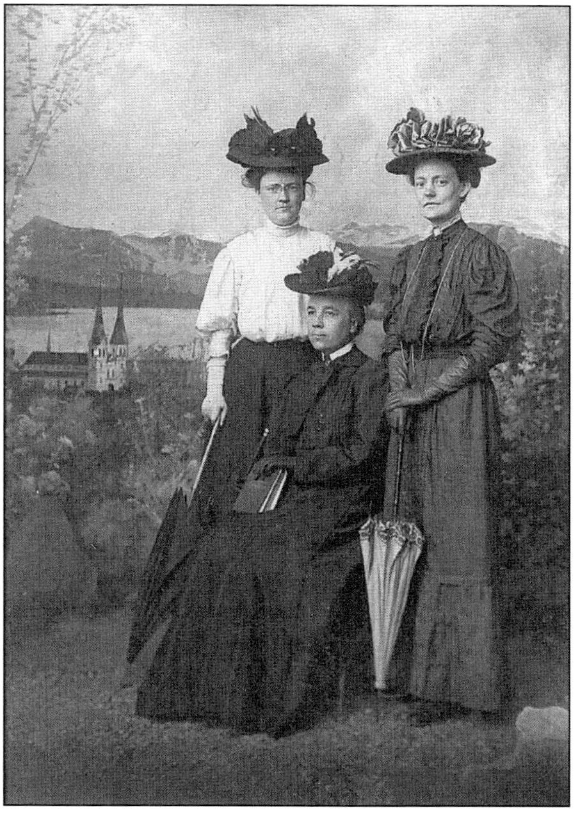

MARY VARDRINE AND ESTELLE WITH THEIR STEPMOTHER LOUISE POST MCBEE, 1908. Around 1900, Silas McBee married Louise Jaggers Post of Long Island, and Mary Vardrine was part of a complete family again. The children referred to their new mother as "Mother Louise" and went on memorable trips together to Europe during the summer. These trips abroad are more than likely the reason that Mary Vardrine decided to study at the University of Jena in Germany for a year. (Photo courtesy of the Ashley Hall Archives.)

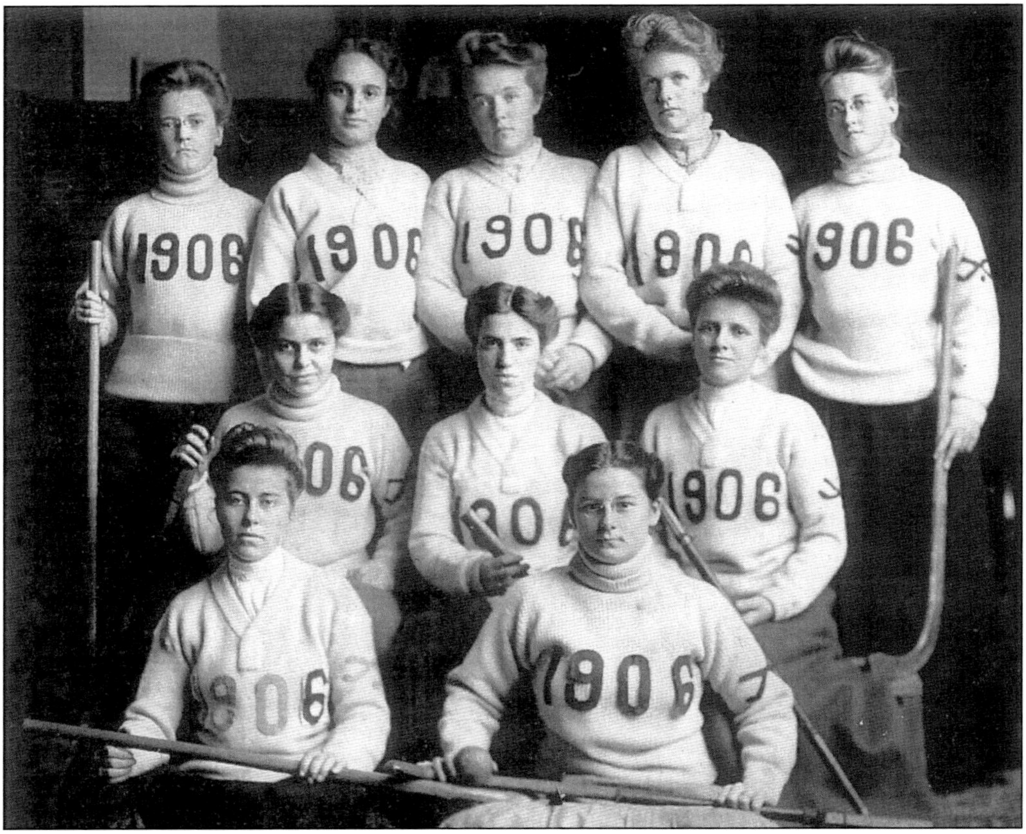

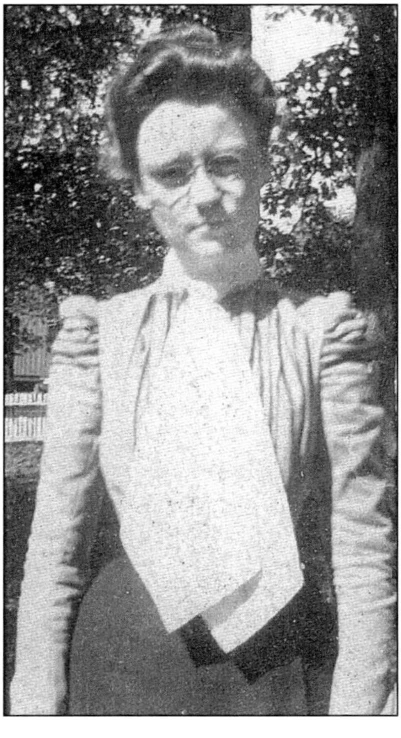

SMITH COLLEGE, GIRLS FIELD HOCKEY TEAM, 1906. McBee's boarding school—Fairmont in Monteagle, Tennessee—lacked certification, so it was necessary for her to pass college entrance exams to be accepted by Smith College. After the arduous experience, McBee decided she would start a school for Southern girls with the college preparatory requirements given to girls in the North.

Smith, in Northampton, Massachusetts, was founded in 1871 and became one of the famous "Seven Sister Schools" to the Ivy League.

Field hockey was a classic girls' school sport of the time, a descendent of the Irish game of hurley. (Photo courtesy of the Ashley Hall Archives.)

MARY VARDRINE MCBEE, 1910s. After graduating Smith with an A.B., McBee went on to teach at Fairmont. She then went to Columbia University where she obtained a masters in history and education. Her uncle, bishop Alexander Guerry, advised her to meet with the clergy of South Carolina who desired to start a church school. So, she came to Charleston. (Photo courtesy of the Ashley Hall Archives.)

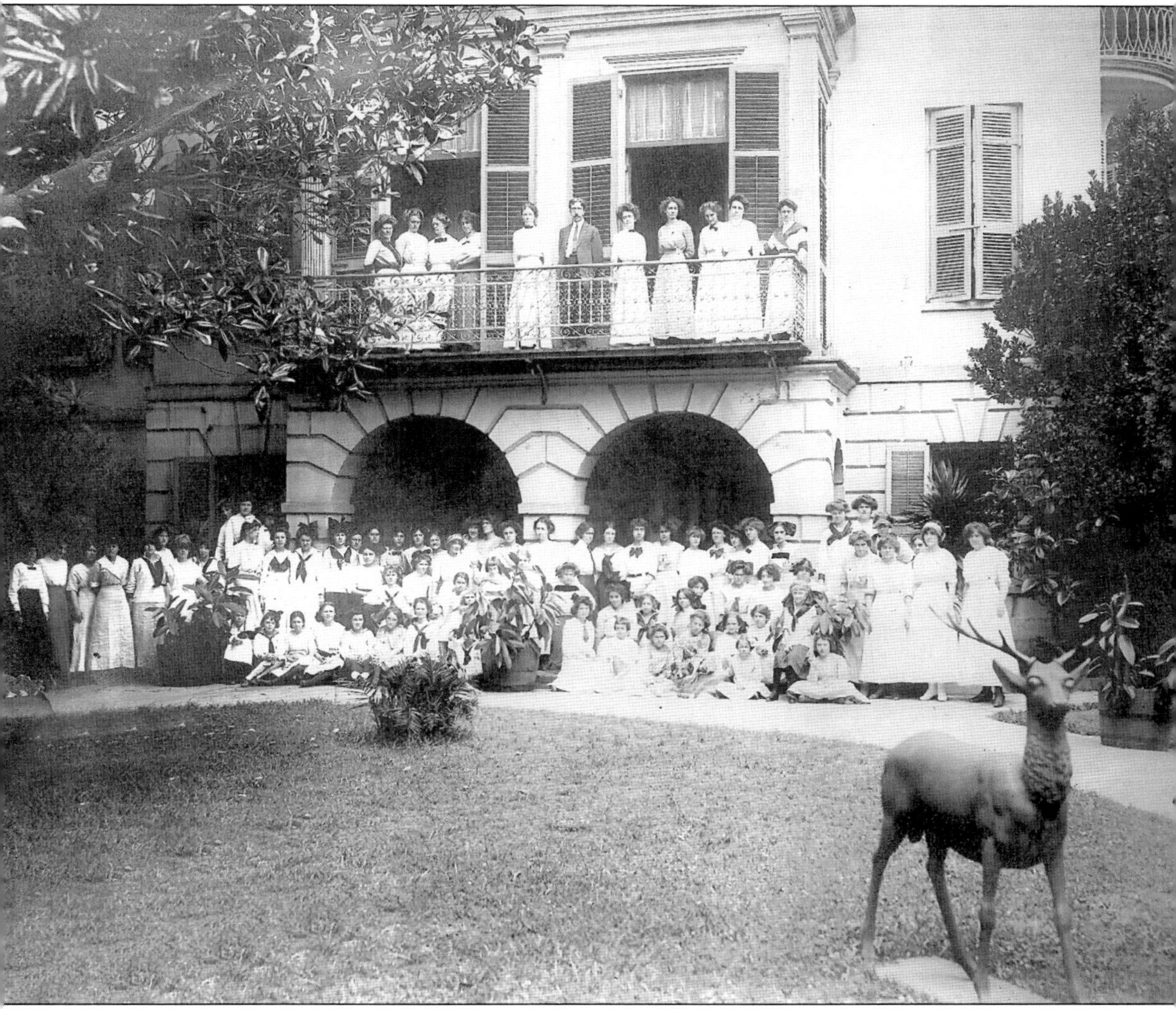

Entire School, 1912. The meeting did not end with McBee starting her own school, but it left her more determined than ever. A few years later she traveled to Charleston again in search of the perfect house for her school. She came across the Witte's House and made such a small offer she was sure the family would refuse. As fate would have it, Otto Witte had six daughters of his own and wanted the property to become a girls' school. So in 1908 he sold the estate for $25,000.

The life-sized bronze deer in the foreground was a favorite of the girls, and they used to fight to sit on it. (Photo courtesy of the Ashley Hall Archives.)

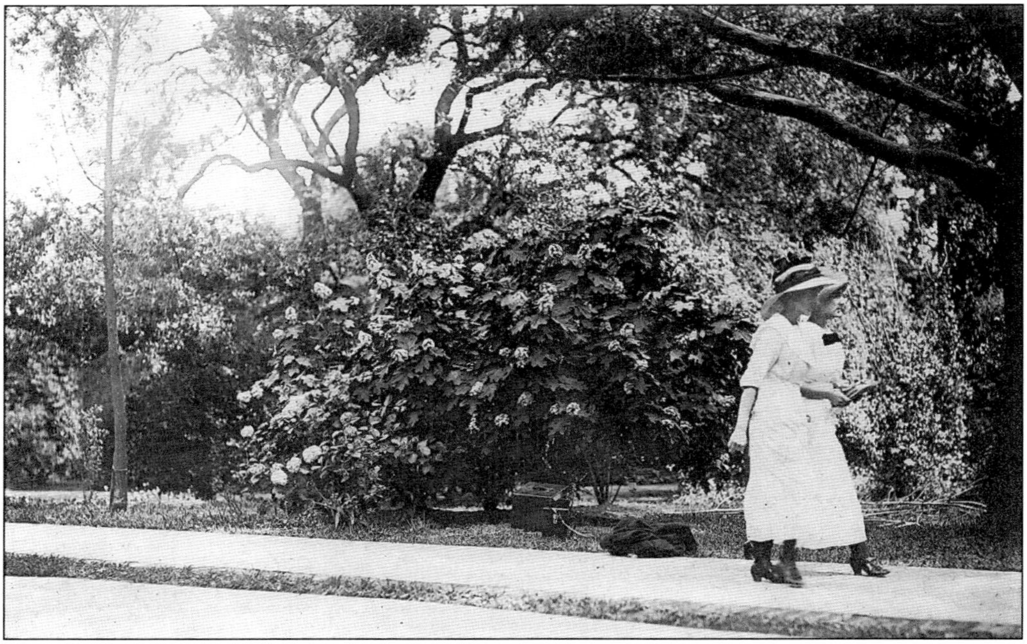

Girls on Campus, 1910s. After the house was bought, McBee still had to furnish it and find teachers and students to make her dream come true. She persuaded teachers from Fairmont and Columbia to leave their schools and come teach at Ashley Hall. She advertised for students, ordered text books from the North, and planned an appropriate curriculum. (Photo courtesy of the Ashley Hall Archives.)

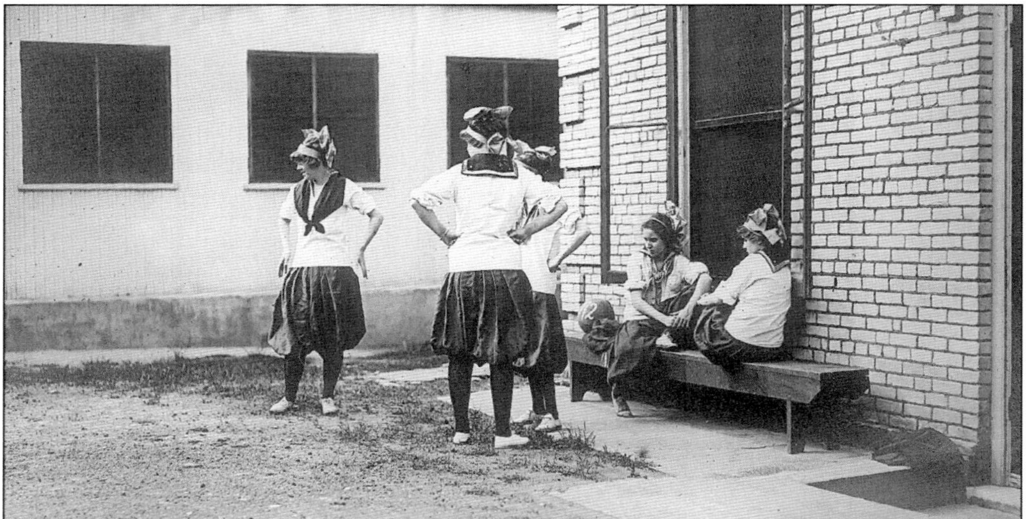

Girls in Physical Education Clothes, 1910s. In September of 1909, Bishop Guerry blessed the school as it opened its doors to 14 boarder and 30 day students. Josephine Pinckney was the first day student and Pauline Sanders was the first enrolled boarder. There were no graduates the first year, but in 1911, Lucille Lebby, Katherine Paul, and Ethel Thrower became the first graduates of Ashley Hall. The next year, a star pupil, Mary Howden passed the first college entrance exams and gave Ashley Hall the title of a certified school. (Photo courtesy of the Ashley Hall Archives.)

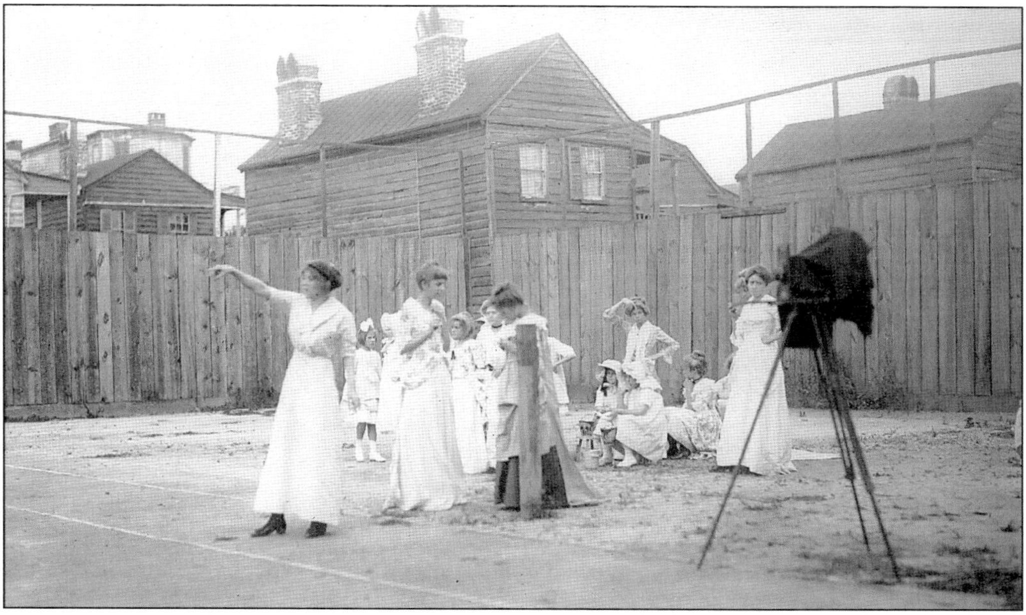

Preparing for a Photo, 1910s. Because there was only one building on the campus, all classes, meals, and rooms for boarders were in the McBee House. Understanding the importance of a well-rounded education, McBee believed her students should be exposed to music and physical exercise. She hired Miss Marie Baker to teach piano and violin, and the first building added to the campus was a gym so the girls could participate in athletics. Built in 1909, the gym later became an auditorium, which was then renovated and renamed Burges Auditorium. (Photo courtesy of the Ashley Hall Archives.)

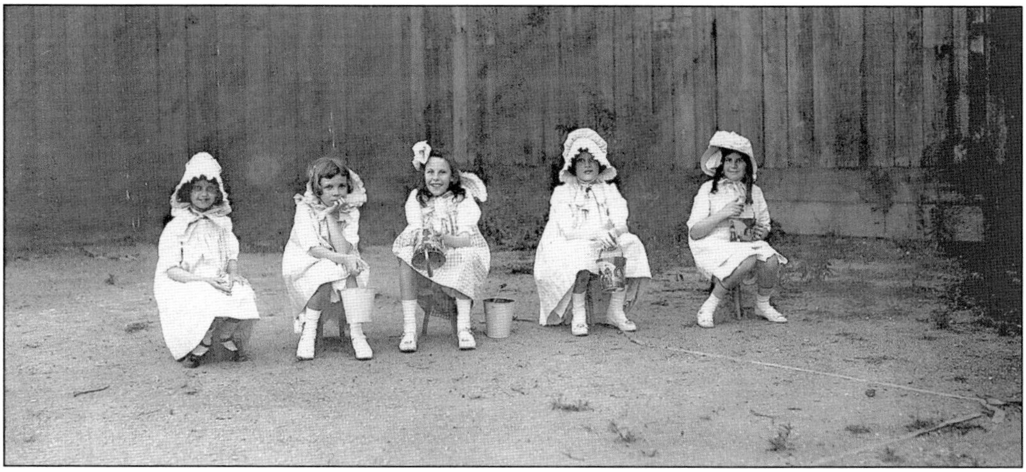

Young Girls Posing for a Picture, 1910s. A normal school was established in 1923 to provide young women with courses in kindergarten and primary school training. The idea was for Ashley Hall to encourage other schools around the South to participate in Progressive Education, a rapidly growing trend among educators. Miss Adeline Babbit was the first head of the department and the following year Miss Mary C. Jacobs took over the position. In later years, Louise Hanahan, a graduate of the Normal School became the head of the Ashley Hall kindergarten. The Normal School was closed in 1932 as Miss McBee wished to focus more on preparing girls for higher education. (Photo courtesy of the Ashley Hall Archives.)

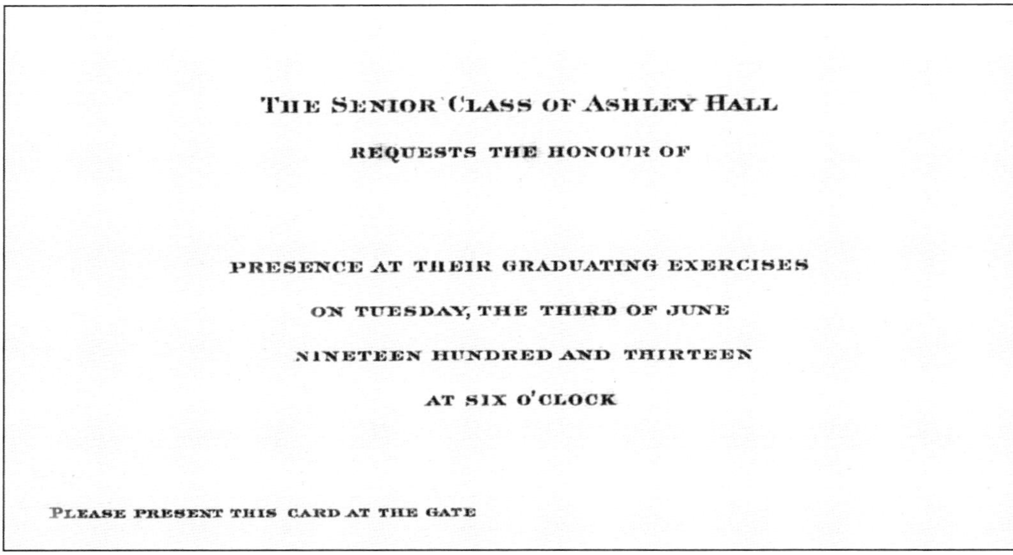

THE SENIOR CLASS OF ASHLEY HALL

REQUESTS THE HONOUR OF

PRESENCE AT THEIR GRADUATING EXERCISES

ON TUESDAY, THE THIRD OF JUNE

NINETEEN HUNDRED AND THIRTEEN

AT SIX O'CLOCK

PLEASE PRESENT THIS CARD AT THE GATE

GRADUATION INVITATION, 1913. Miss McBee took on every responsibility of the school, acting as the financial adviser, overseeing daily problems, maintaining a conducive atmosphere for learning among faculty and students, and teaching her own history classes. The school grew and somehow managed to survive through the hard years of depression and war. As the 1940s approached, McBee realized she was getting older and needed to start making plans for the school when she passed away. Not wanting to close the school, she decided to leave it to a foundation in order to secure its existence in the future. (Photo courtesy of the Ashley Hall Archives.)

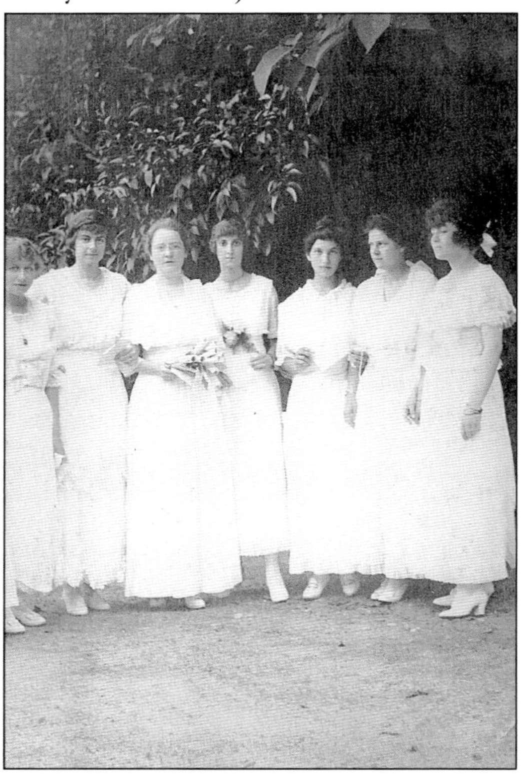

GRADUATION, 1916. A Board of Trustees was made up of Charleston citizens sincerely concerned with the future of the school. In 1949 Miss McBee retired but lived in a restored house with a garden that connected to the campus. McBee lived with her father, Mr. Silas McBee, affectionately known to the students as the "grandfather of the school," until his last days. Mr. McBee was well-known to the girls on campus and one of the favorite commencement speakers. Miss McBee stayed involved and extremely interested in the affairs of the school until her death in 1965. (Photo courtesy of the Ashley Hall Archives.)

Two

Traditions and Events

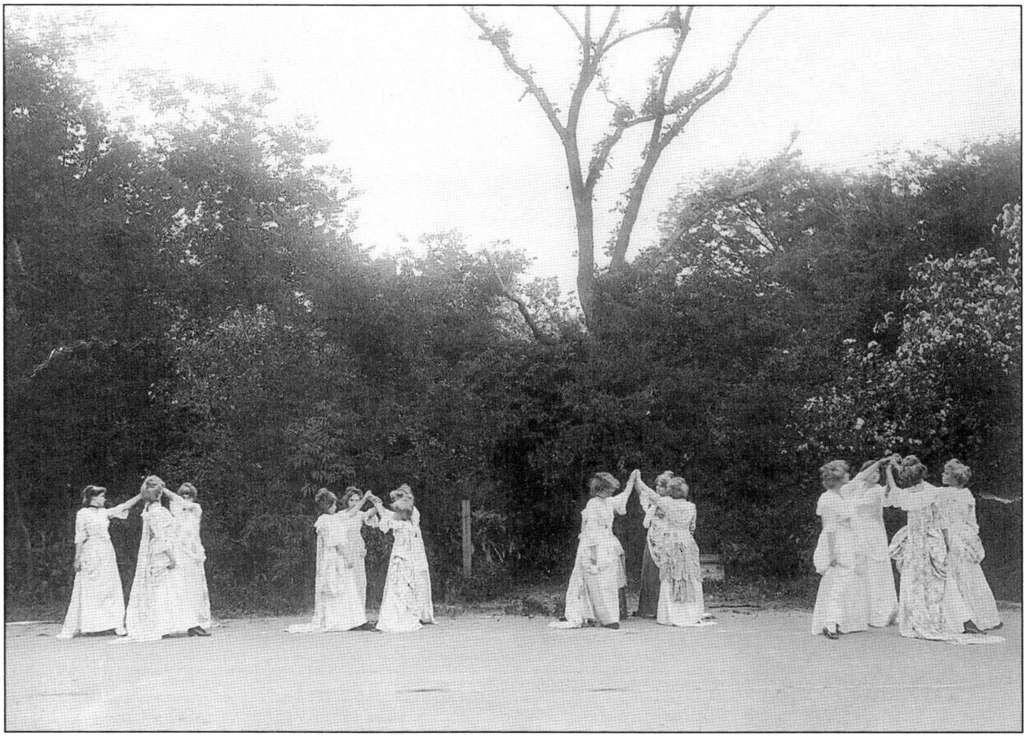

The Minuet, 1910s. The minuet, dating to 17th century France, was a dance performed annually during the field day events. It was a graceful dance in three-fourths time with forward balancing, bowing, and toe-pointing. (Photo courtesy of the Ashley Hall Archives.)

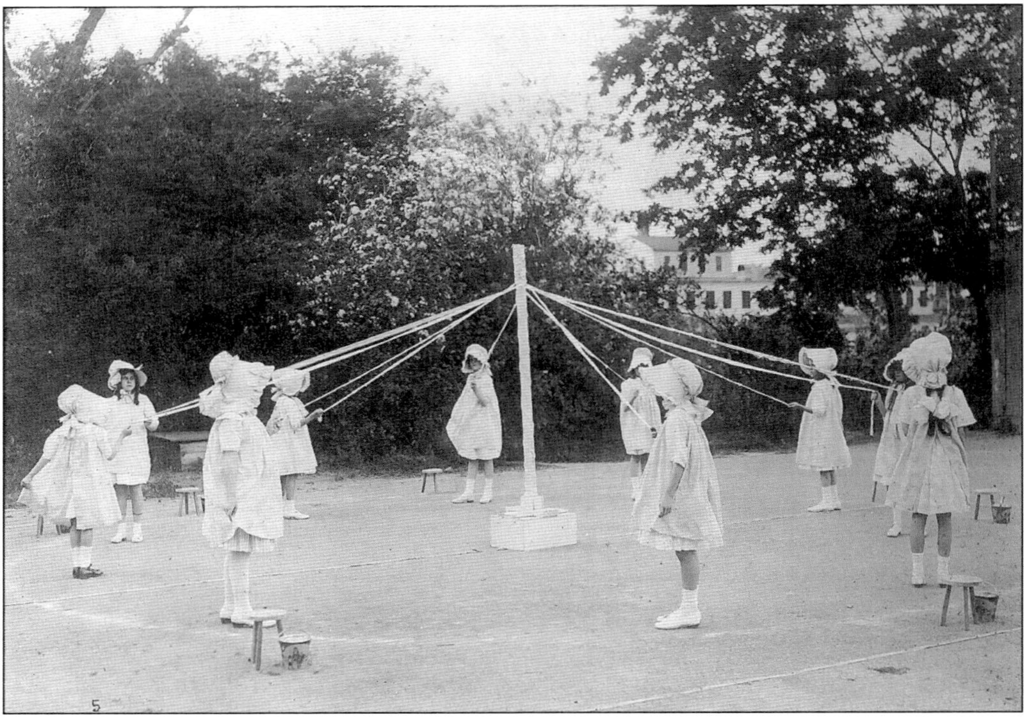

Dance Around the Maypole, 1910s. The dance around the maypole was another traditional dance performed at field day by the younger grades. The dance dates to the rural May Day customs of Medieval times when women would entwine ribbons around a pole as entertainment for the May Queen. (Photo courtesy of the Ashley Hall Archives.)

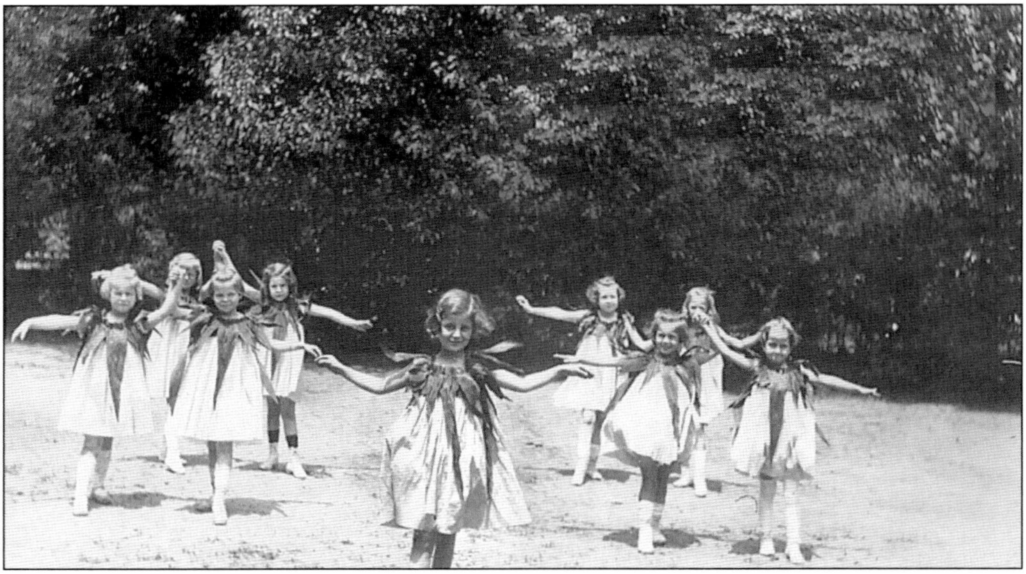

Field Day Dance, 1920s. This dance was performed by the younger grades at Ashley Hall during field day. Representative of a May Day dance, the girls dressed in colorful costumes and resembled little fairies as they jumped and danced around. Preparing took a substantial part of each day as the girls practiced for their big moment in front of the entire school. (Photo courtesy of the Ashley Hall Archives.)

FIELD DAY PLAY, 1910s. Plays, dances and games were the main events at field day. This photo shows a play performed one year. Each girl was dressed as a country, and a patriotic script was written. England, France, and America are featured in this picture. (Photo courtesy of the Ashley Hall Archives.)

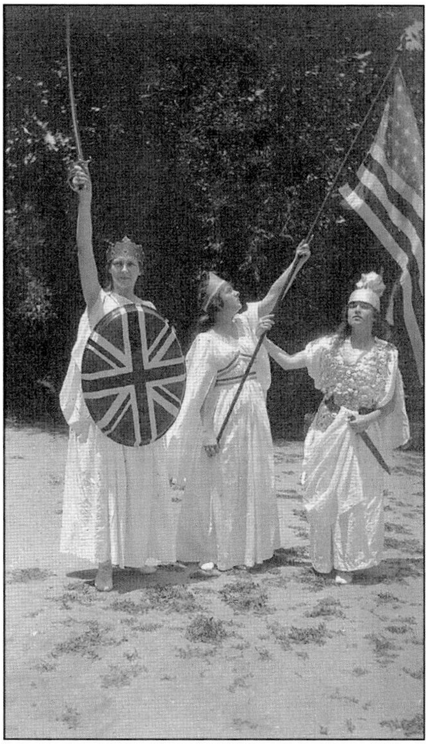

EARLY FIELD DAY, 1920s. A firm believer in daily exercise, Miss McBee organized an annual field day in which girls from every grade could compete in physical activities. All of the girls were split into two teams, Purple and White, the school colors. Then they would compete for a silver cup. Notice the gym uniforms; the long bloomers and the scarf around the neck like a sailor's uniform are representative of the time period. (Photo courtesy of the Ashley Hall Archives.)

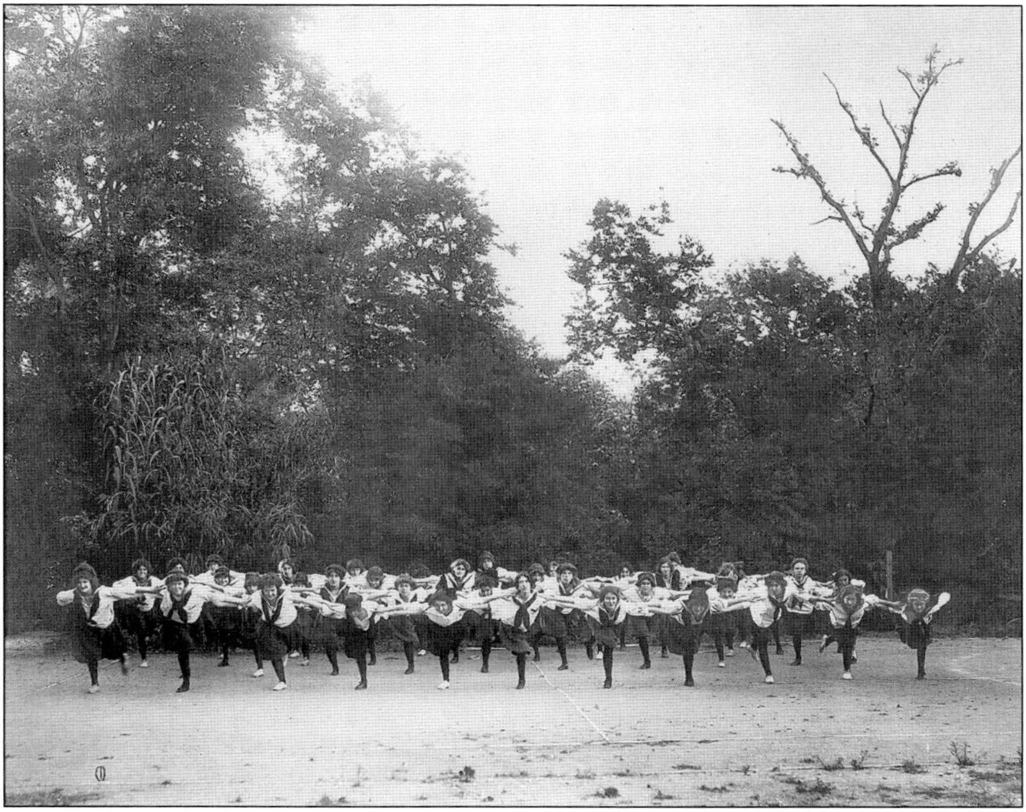

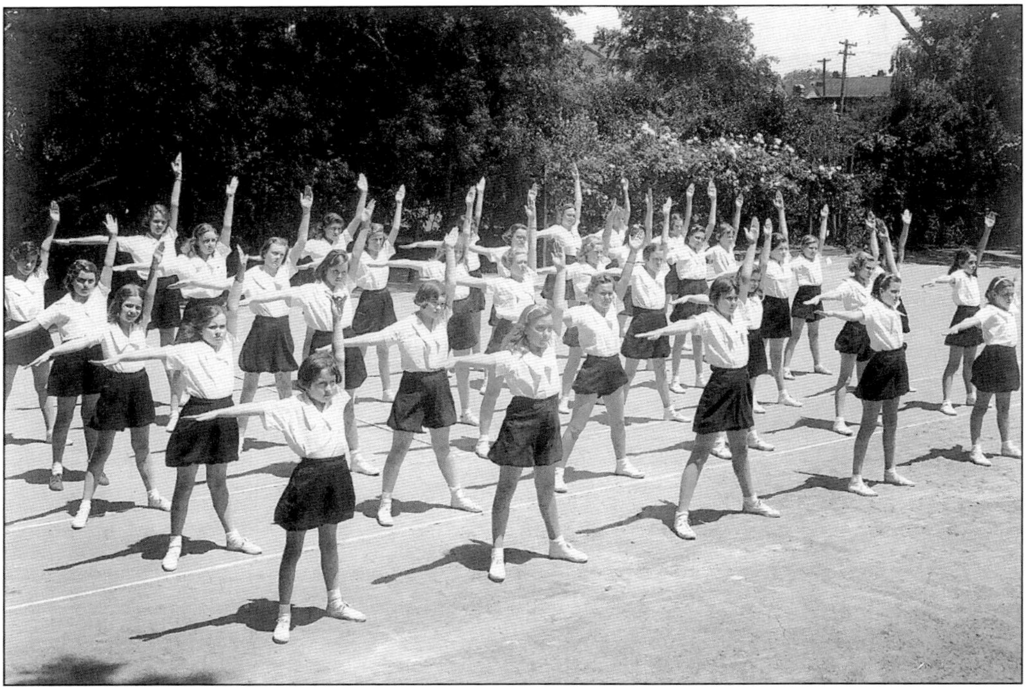

Lower School Field Day, 1930s. A 1935 *Cerberus* excerpt reads, "The Purples won the Field Day Cup. The gym team exercises were only part of the interesting program represented by the gymnasium classes of the whole school." The Purple and White memberships are considered so important that a girl is assigned the color of other family members who went through Ashley Hall to prevent friction within the family. (Photo courtesy of the Ashley Hall Archives.)

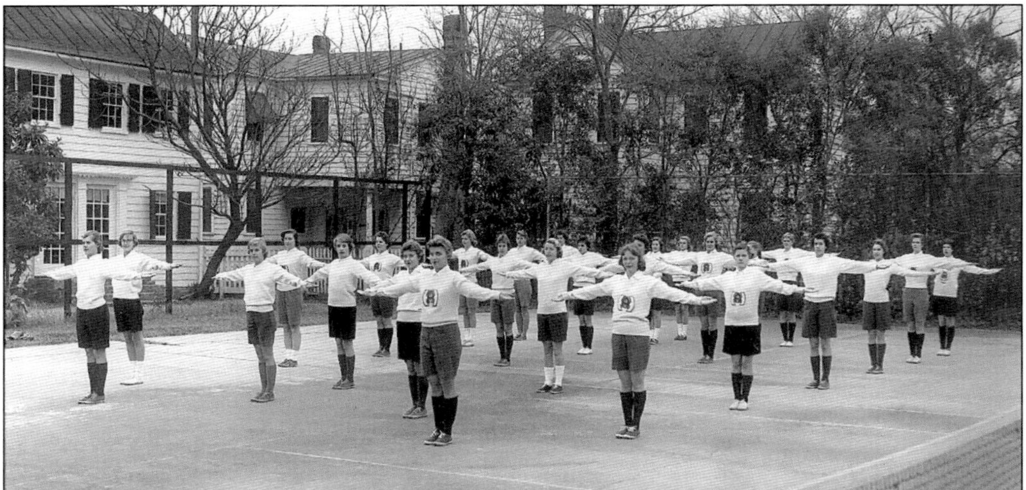

Drill Team, 1959. Today this event in the annual field day is known as Drill Team. This is just one of the major events in which the Purples and Whites compete against each other for the cup. The different teams can acquire points through participation in clubs and sporting events, the academic bowl, and field day. Drill Team is led by the captain of each color and judged by faculty based on difficulty of performance, simultaneous formations, and overall enthusiasm of the girls. (Photo courtesy of the Ashley Hall Archives.)

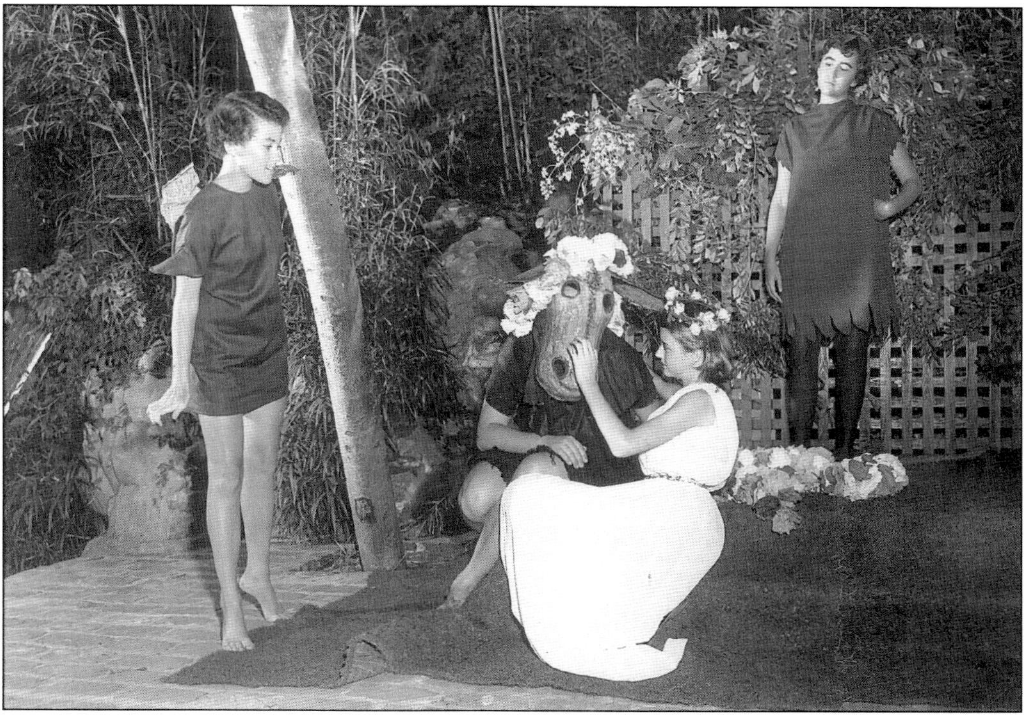

***A Midsummer Night's Dream*, 1950s.** Shakespeare's plays were performed nearly once a month in front of the grotto or Bear Cave and other locations. This was training in speaking and stage presence. The girls both acted and directed the performances. *A Midsummer Night's Dream* is shown here. (Photo courtesy of the Ashley Hall Archives.)

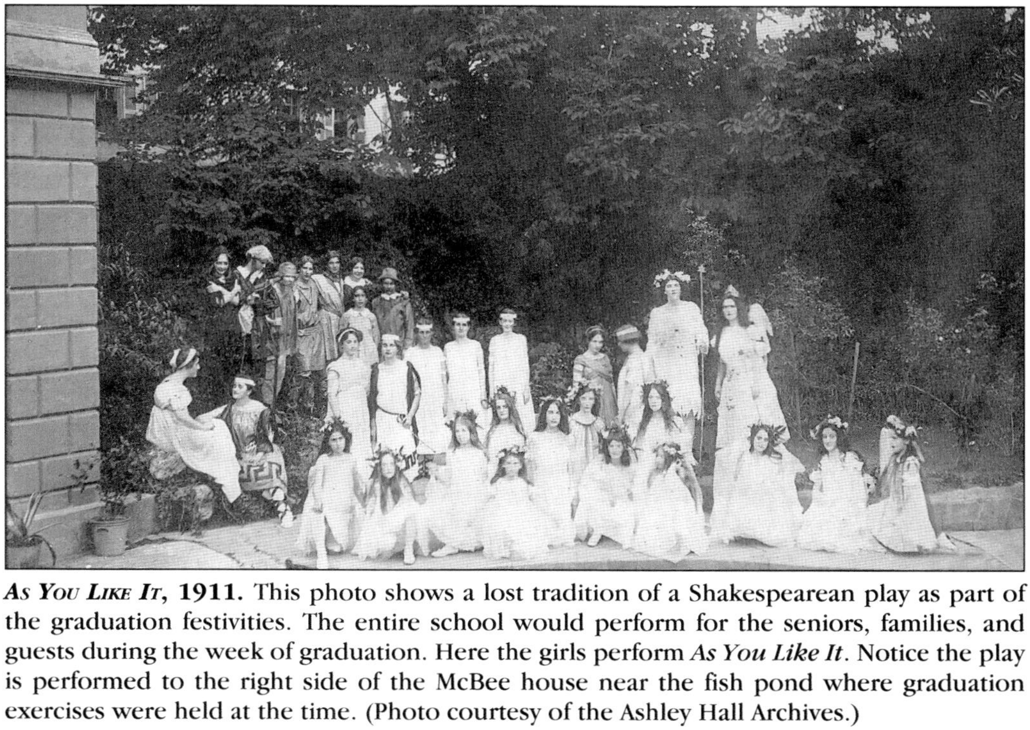

***As You Like It*, 1911.** This photo shows a lost tradition of a Shakespearean play as part of the graduation festivities. The entire school would perform for the seniors, families, and guests during the week of graduation. Here the girls perform *As You Like It*. Notice the play is performed to the right side of the McBee house near the fish pond where graduation exercises were held at the time. (Photo courtesy of the Ashley Hall Archives.)

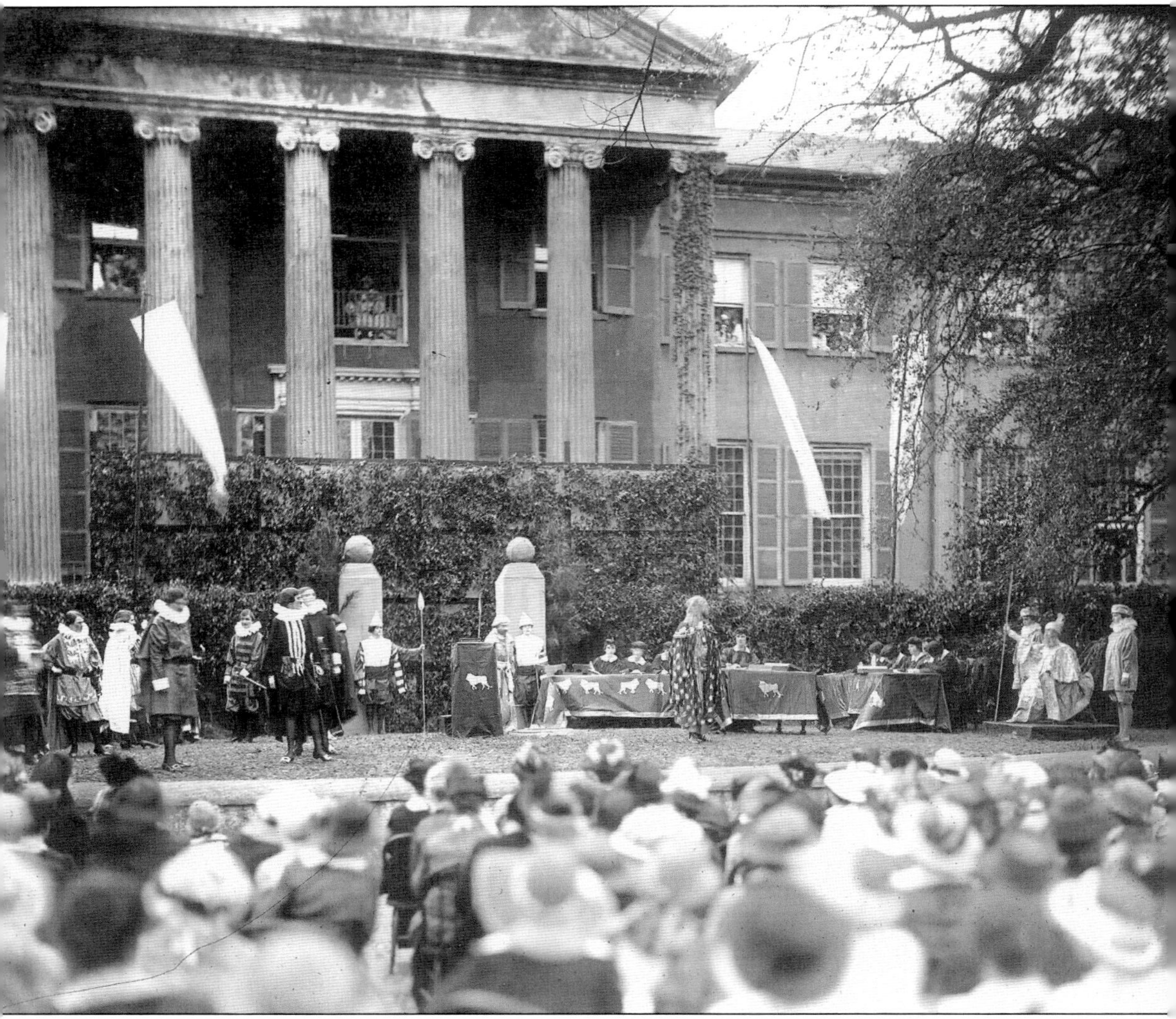

College of Charleston Shakespeare Festival, 1916. Because Ashley Hall was so well-known around Charleston for its excellent productions, the school was invited to perform in the College of Charleston's Shakespeare Celebration. The girls above are doing the trial scene from *The Merchant of Venice*. The Cistern and Randolph Hall of the College of Charleston are easily recognizable in the background of the picture. (Photo courtesy of the Ashley Hall Archives.)

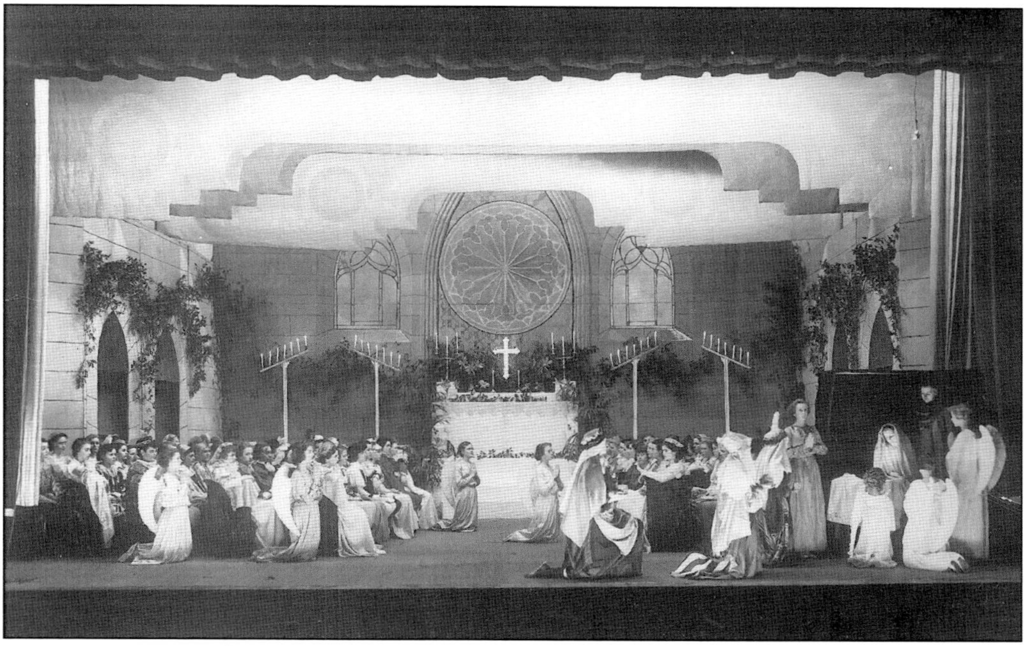

Christmas Play, 1941. The Christmas play was started in 1923 and has been an annual tradition of Ashley Hall ever since. Starting with *Why the Chimes Rang*, the production evolved into a "miracle play," a Medieval custom from the 12th century and a revival of our English cultural heritage. (Photo courtesy of the Ashley Hall Archives.)

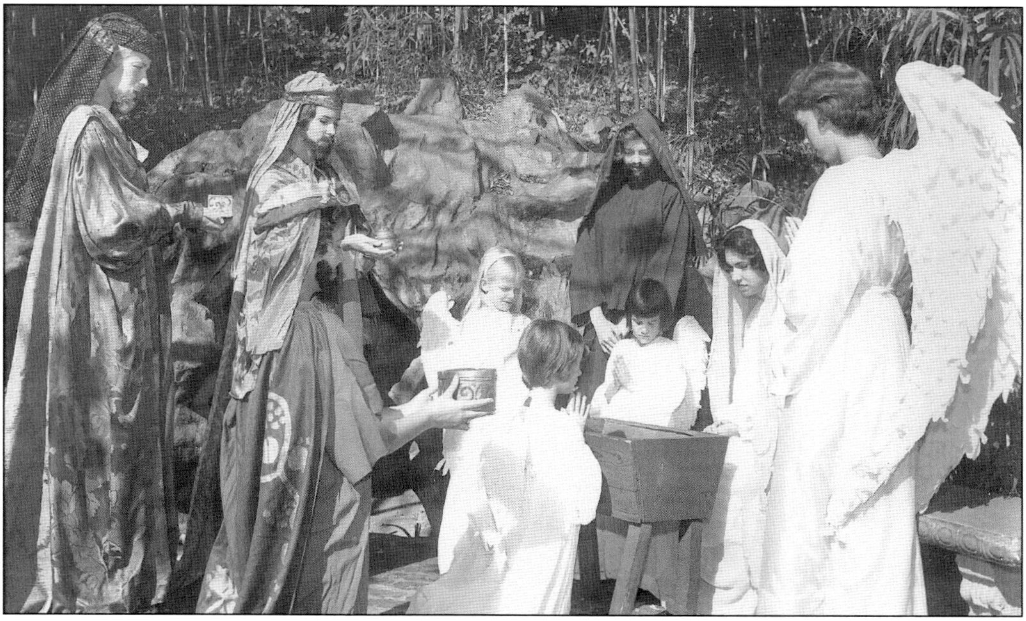

Christmas Play, 1958. In this photo, the Christmas play is being performed in front of the grotto. Over the years, the play was performed at Memminger, the Victory Theatre, and Davies Auditorium, when it was built in 1966. As the audience grew, it was necessary and more fitting to move the play to a church. Currently, the play is performed at the Cathedral of St. Luke and St. Paul on Coming Street, a church built in 1811 and probably attended by previous owners of the Ashley Hall property. (Photo courtesy of the Ashley Hall Archives.)

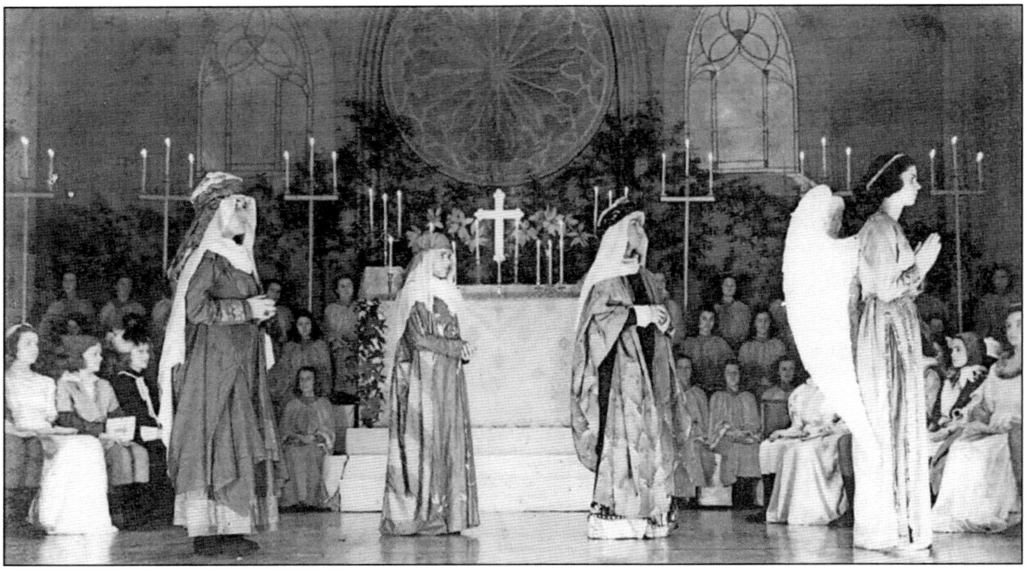

CHRISTMAS PLAY, 1939. The Christmas play production involves almost every student at Ashley Hall. The Red Choir sings each year, as well as the middle school choir. The upper school students play the major roles, and even a few of the lower school girls play little angels. A "congregation" of students dressed in ornate, Medieval costumes processes into the church and there are student ushers to seat the guests. (Photo courtesy of the Ashley Hall Archives.)

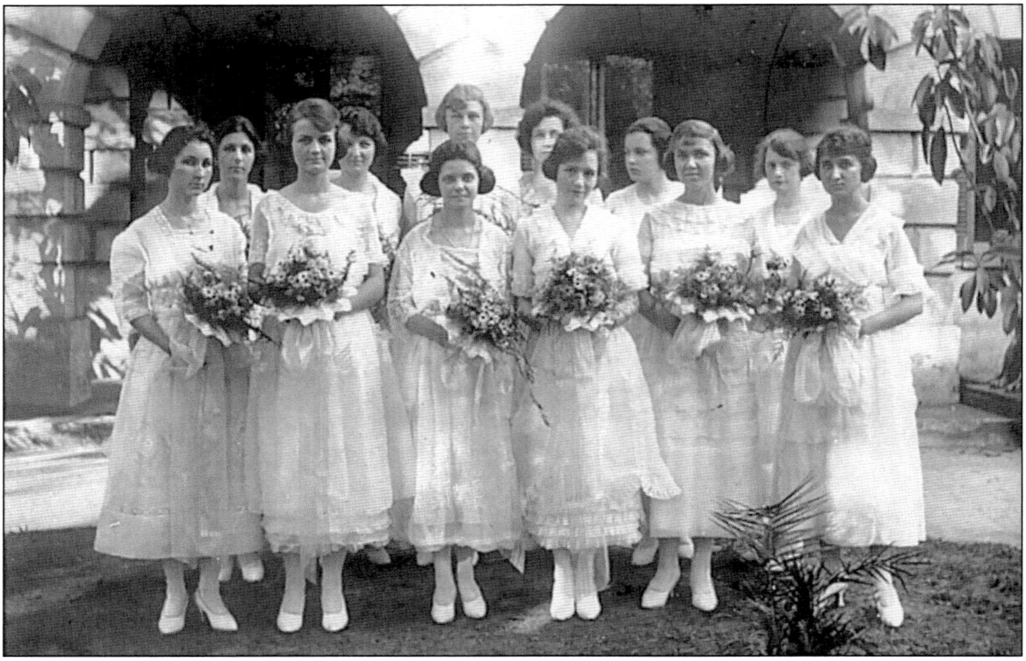

CLASS OF 1921. The class of 1921 illustrates the tradition of graduating seniors wearing all white dresses and carrying flowers at commencement. With 12 students, an observer can see the growing class sizes from the beginning days when only three girls graduated at a time. Notice the haircuts and dresses of the period. (Photo courtesy of the Ashley Hall Archives.)

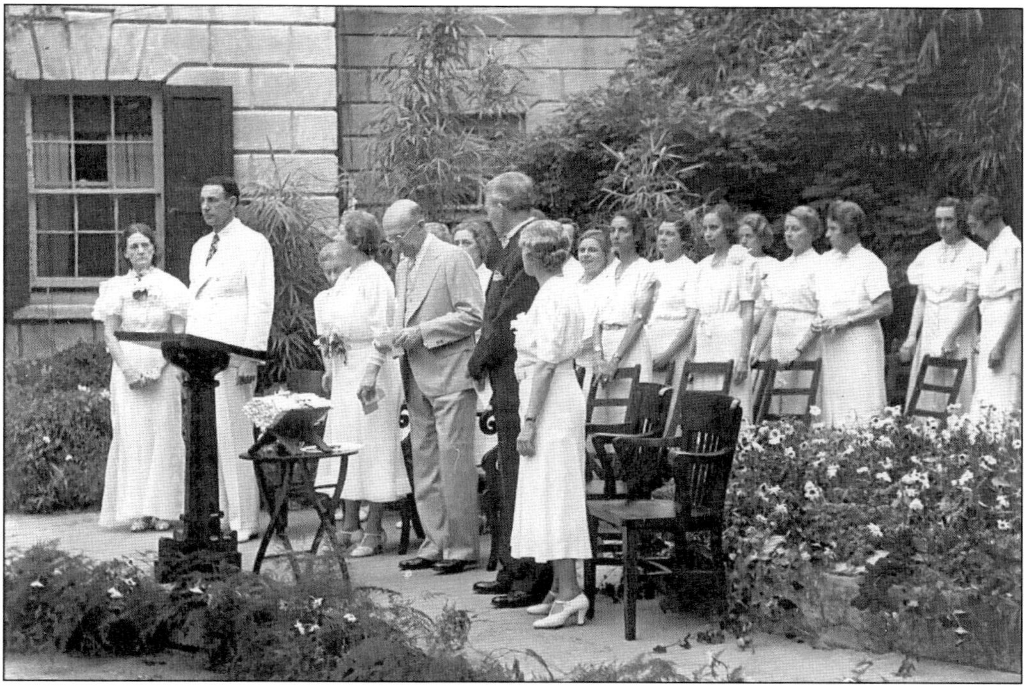

GRADUATION CEREMONIES, 1939. This photo displays the tradition of the faculty also wearing all white during commencement ceremonies. Miss McBee (to the right of the podium) and Miss Estelle (to the left of the podium) stand out. Also shown in this picture is the spot to the right of the front of the McBee House where graduation used to be held before the classes and audience grew in size. (Photo courtesy of the Ashley Hall Archives.)

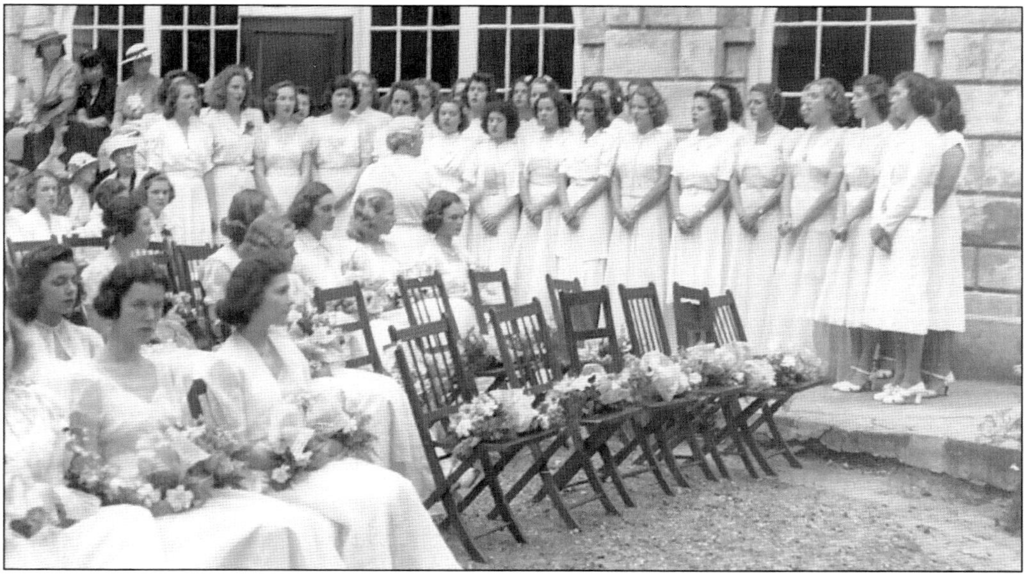

GRADUATION, 1939. The group of girls in this picture looks as though they are being conducted in song by a woman in the middle of the semi-circle. This is a tradition still carried on today by the seniors in the Red Choir. The a cappella piece once performed at graduation is now sung during a Baccalaureate service held the morning of graduation. (Photo courtesy of the Ashley Hall Archives.)

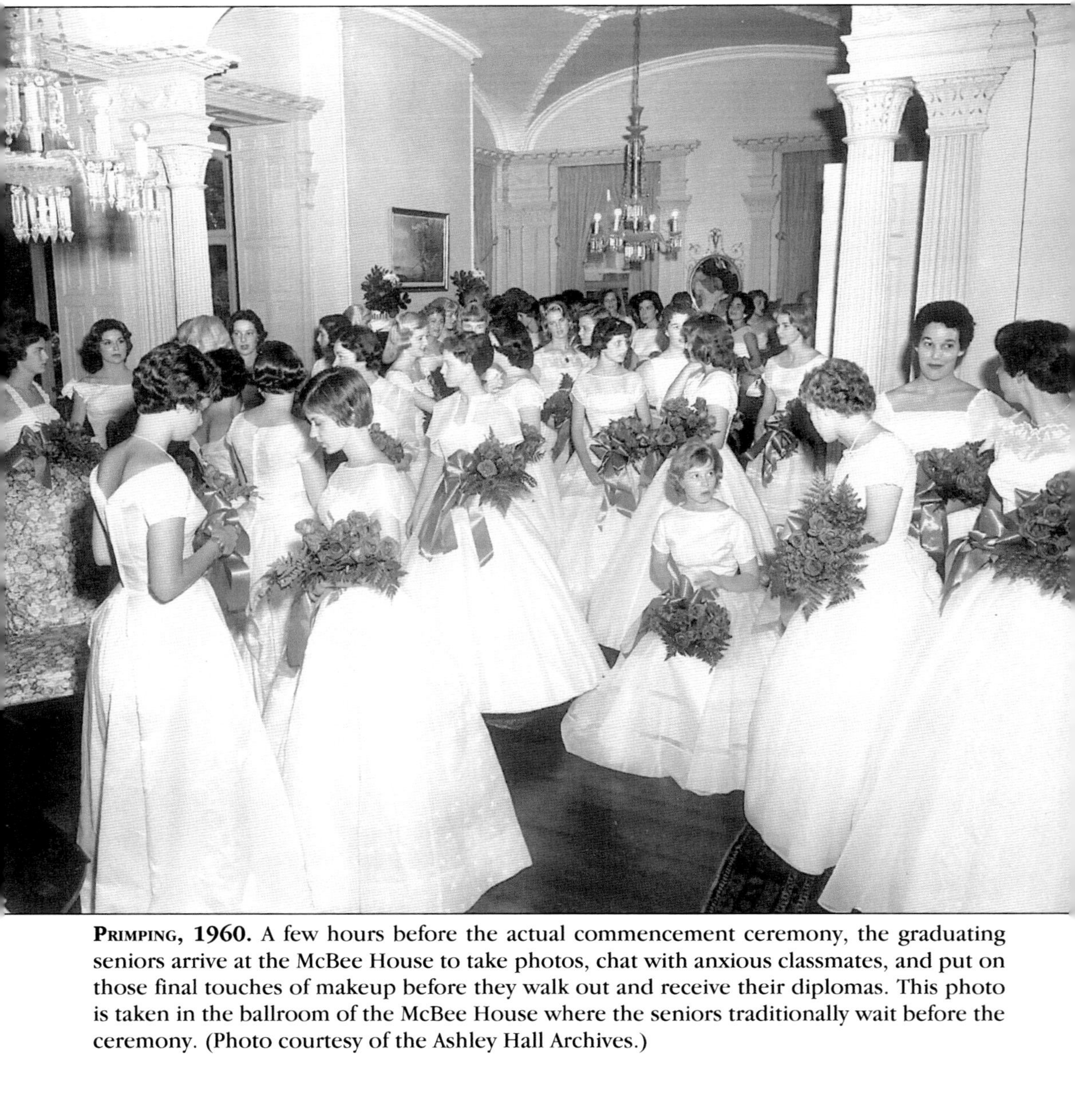

PRIMPING, 1960. A few hours before the actual commencement ceremony, the graduating seniors arrive at the McBee House to take photos, chat with anxious classmates, and put on those final touches of makeup before they walk out and receive their diplomas. This photo is taken in the ballroom of the McBee House where the seniors traditionally wait before the ceremony. (Photo courtesy of the Ashley Hall Archives.)

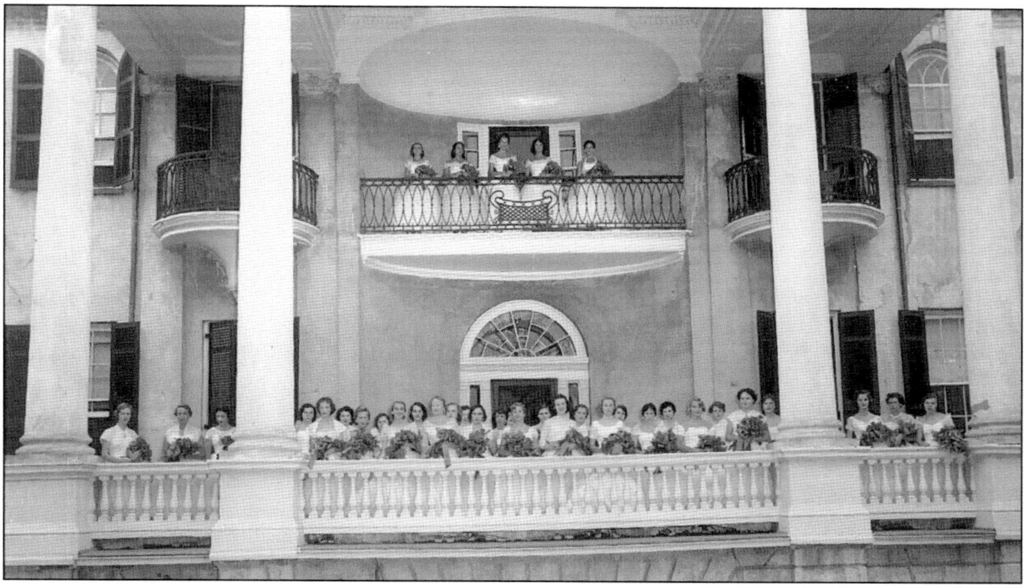

Class Graduation Picture, 1950s. Shown here is the tradition of the final class photo just before the commencement ceremony. With 36 girls, this is a large class. The class officers are standing on the top-most balcony on the third floor. Seniors still go out on the second floor balcony to take their individual graduation pictures. (Photo courtesy of the Ashley Hall Archives.)

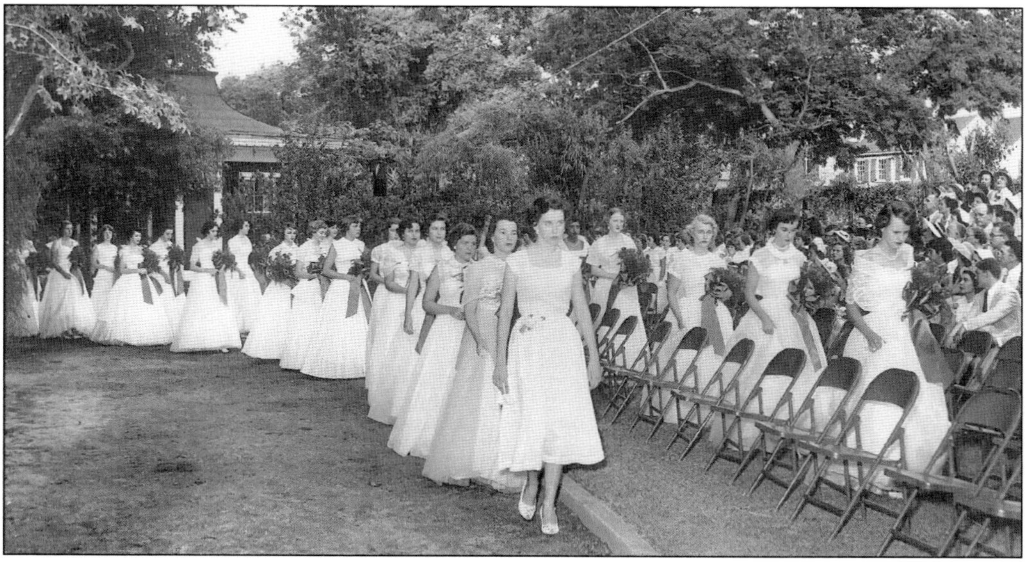

Commencement, 1951. This photo shows the spot, in front of the grotto, where graduation is held today. Graduation is always outside unless there is rain and the school has been known to post-pone graduation for a few hours to wait for rain to pass; the grounds of Ashley Hall are still so beautiful that seniors pray there will be no rain, so they can have the traditional outdoor ceremony. The seniors process out, one at a time, led by the class officers, and are seated in the front of the audience facing the grotto. The names of the girls are called out at random, selected from a silver bowl, to receive their diplomas. There is always a guest speaker and speeches by the first and second honor graduates. (Photo courtesy of the Ashley Hall Archives.)

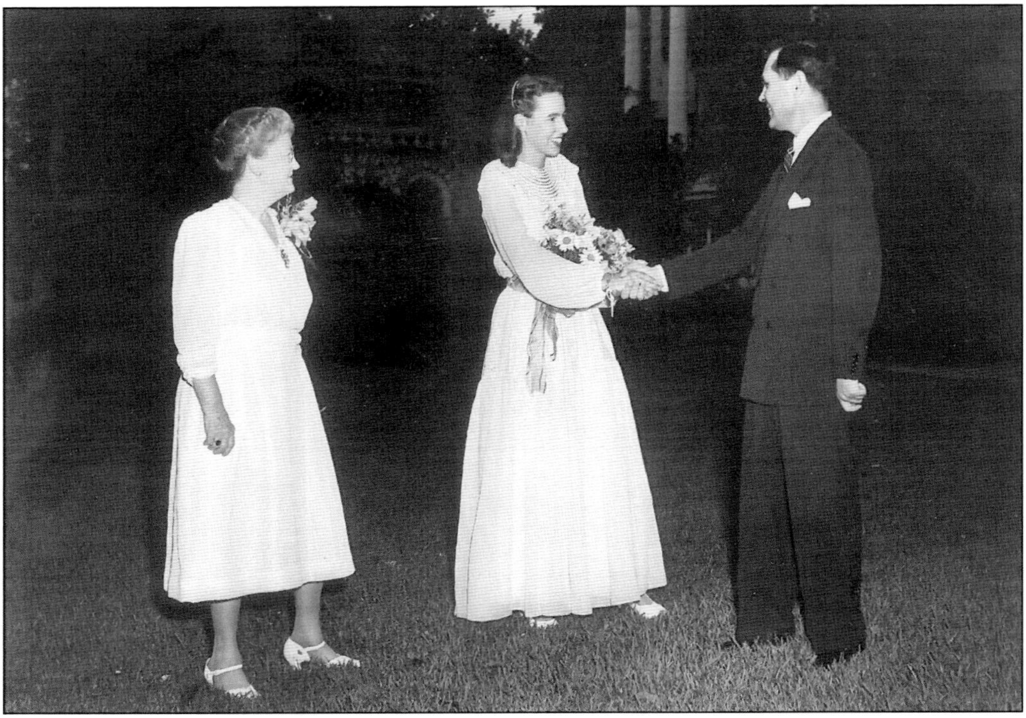

Presenting the Senior Gift, 1946. Isabella Dickson, the Senior Class President, is shown here shaking hands with the guest speaker of 1946, Mr. P. Clemenceau. Miss McBee is standing to her right. The senior class president also presents the class gift to the school during the graduation ceremony. (Photo courtesy of the Ashley Hall Archives.)

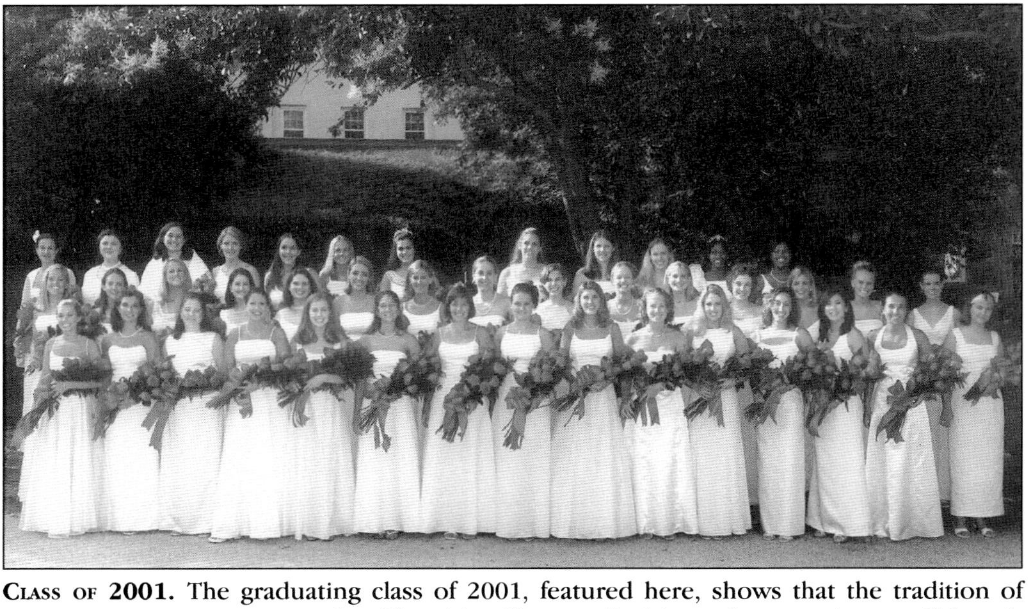

Class of 2001. The graduating class of 2001, featured here, shows that the tradition of commencement continues today. The girls still wear all white and carry red roses. Although the commencement weekend play is no longer performed, there are many other weekend festivities, such as Baccalaureate, a service added in 1917, on the morning of graduation and a party after the ceremony. (Photo courtesy of the Ashley Hall Archives.)

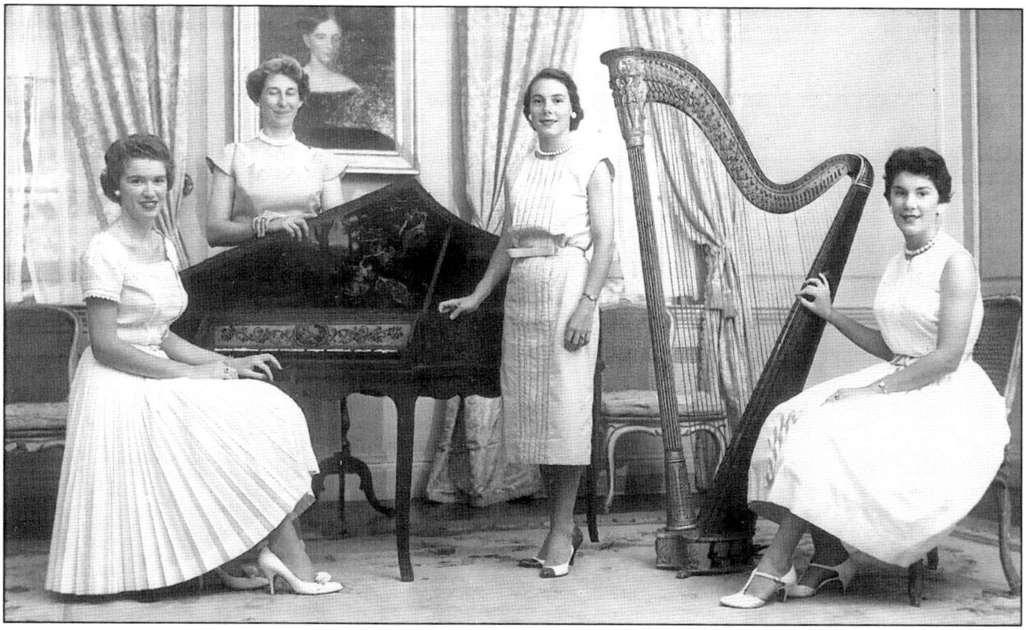

ALUMNAE TEA, 1950S. Mrs. Farrow began a tradition of inviting seniors and their parents to her garden at the Williams Gibbes House for a reception and tea. Although no longer at the Williams Gibbes House, the reception has continued to be a part of the graduation week festivities in which the seniors first experience what it means to be an Ashley Hall Alumna. (Photo courtesy of the Ashley Hall Archives.)

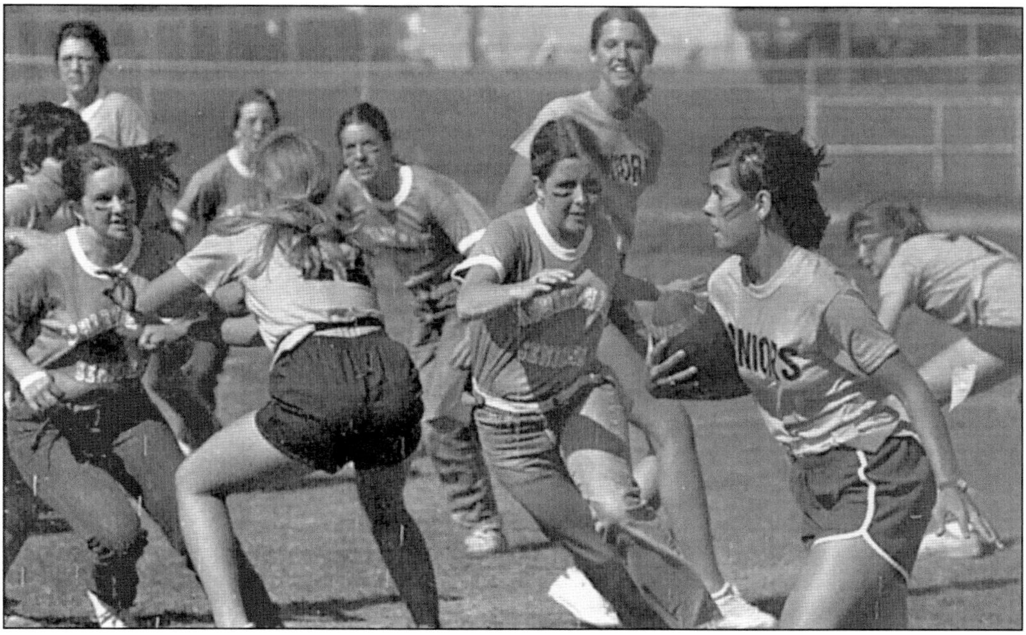

POWDER PUFF, 1978. One of the greatest advantages of an all-girls school is the small class sizes, which allows the girls to get to know all of their classmates extremely well. The junior and senior classes especially have fun, interactive events each year. The year this photo was taken, the senior class of 1978 lost a powder puff football game held at Porter Gaud to the junior class. (Photo courtesy of the Ashley Hall Archives.)

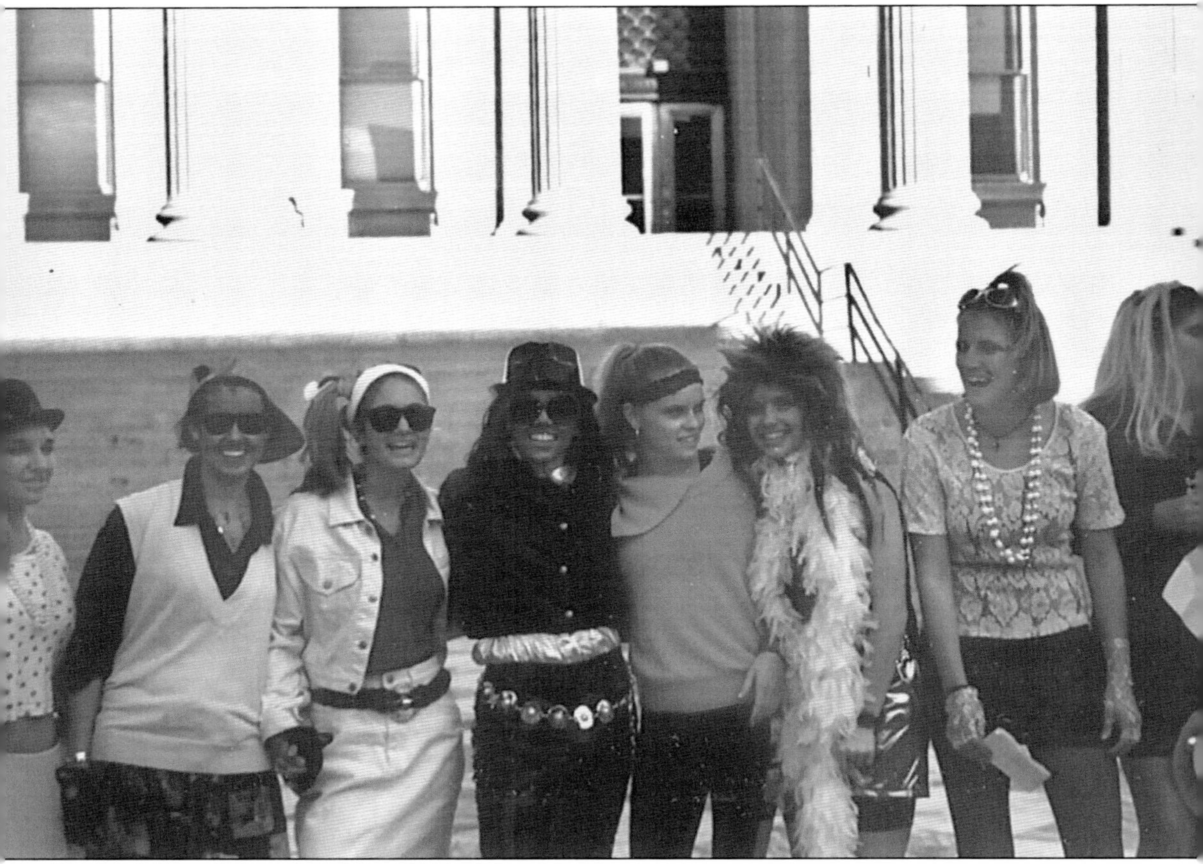

Kidnap, 1999. Known as "Kidnap," this tradition is a more recent one among the junior and senior classes. Each senior has her own junior whom she "kidnaps" by surprise, dresses up in an embarrassing costume, and forces to perform on the steps of the Federal Customs House. The theme for the year above was "Woodstock '99," and the girls are dressed as famous rock singers. All of this is done in good fun between the two classes and has become a very popular event as students and parents from Ashley Hall and other schools watch. (Photo courtesy of the Ashley Hall Archives.)

PROGRAM

INVOCATION .... Dolly Myers

WELCOME .... Sue Ottimer, Pres. Junior Class

TOASTMISTRESS .... Mitzi Lyons

Toast to Miss McBee .... by Anne Kahrs

Response

Toast to the Seniors .... by Marilyn Stevens

Response .... by Evelyn Lyons, Pres. Senior Class

Toast to Miss Mazyck .... by Patricia Robertson

Response

Toast to Mrs. Jervey .... by Marian Birlant

Response

Toast to Miss Estelle .... by Barbara Caplan

Response

Toast to Ashley Hall .... by Mitzi Herrin

Response .... by Sally Thrower
Pres. Student Council

Junior/ Senior Banquet, 1949. This clipping from 1949 shows the program from the junior-senior banquet held at the Fort Sumter Hotel. The traditional junior-senior was a weekend without boys where each junior would ask a senior to be "her date." The juniors would pick up their seniors and take them to a banquet with a large dinner and live entertainment. The entertainment consisted of skits, songs, and toasts all written and prepared by the junior class.

The tradition continues with some variations today as junior-senior weekend. Seniors throw prom for the juniors on Friday night and the juniors hold a banquet in honor of the senior class on the Saturday night. The places for the weekend events are always kept secret. Toasts are still given in honor of the faculty and a nice dinner is served. After the meal, the juniors put on a skit poking fun at the seniors in retaliation for the Kidnap experience. The evening ends in songs written by the juniors to let the seniors know how much they will be missed when they graduate. (Photo courtesy of the Ashley Hall Archives.)

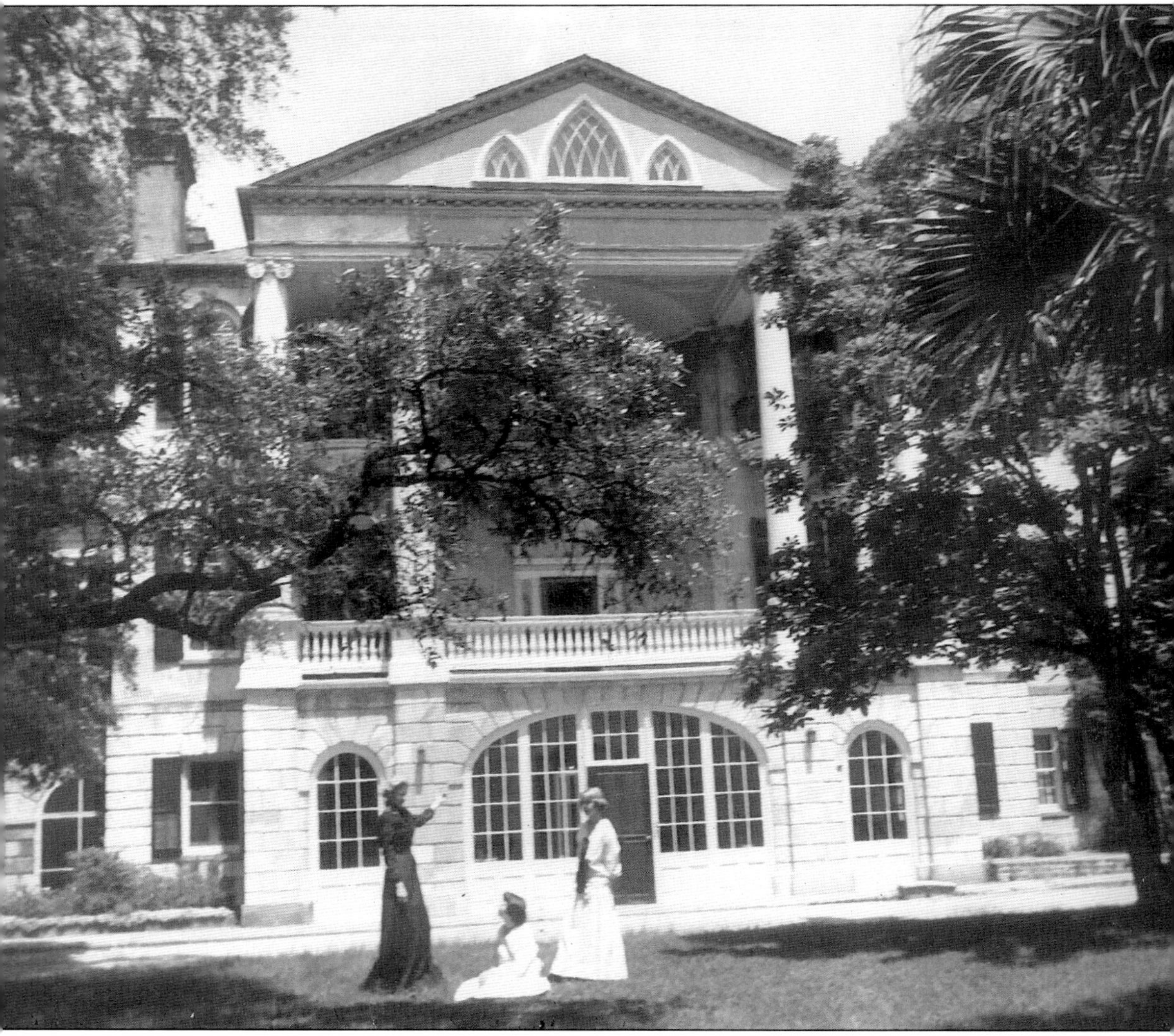

50th Celebration, 1959. In 1959, Ashley Hall had a huge celebration to honor the 50 wonderful years the school had been in Charleston. This picture shows girls dressed in clothes of the period of the founding of the school (1909) standing in front of McBee House. Many photos were taken as the girls reenacted a scene of Miss McBee (the girl dressed in black) talking to her students (the other two girls). Their dresses and hairstyles along with the historic main house accurately portray the founding of the school. (Photo courtesy of the Ashley Hall Archives.)

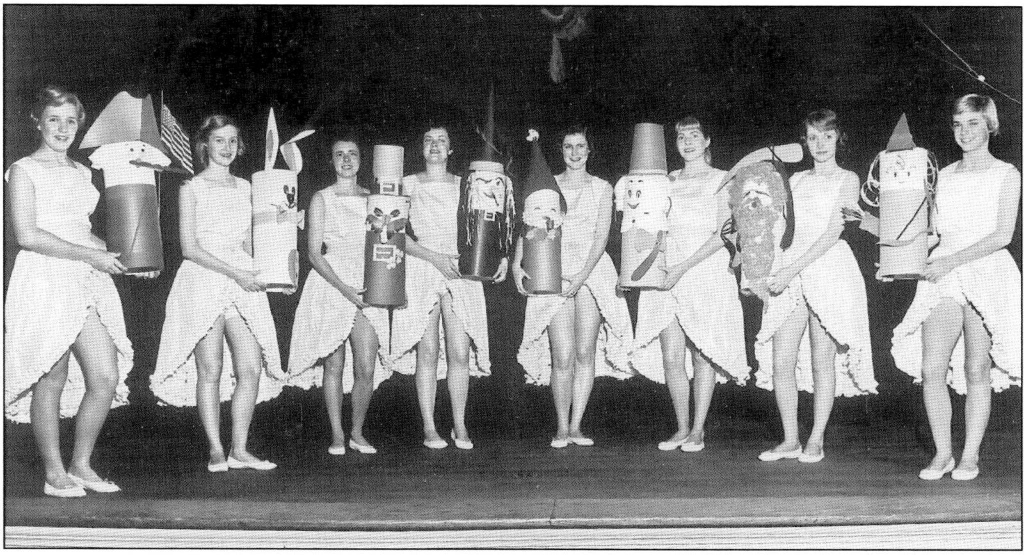

50TH CELEBRATION REVIEW, 1959. As part of the 50th celebration the school had a review, which included dancing, singing, and funny sketches. It was held in Burges Auditorium because the larger auditorium, Davies, had not yet been built. Burges Auditorium was originally built as the first new building on Ashley Hall's campus and served as a gym to the girls. Later, a new gym was built, but the old auditorium still exists today and is used as a middle school auditorium for morning announcements and small presentations. (Photo courtesy of the Ashley Hall Archives)

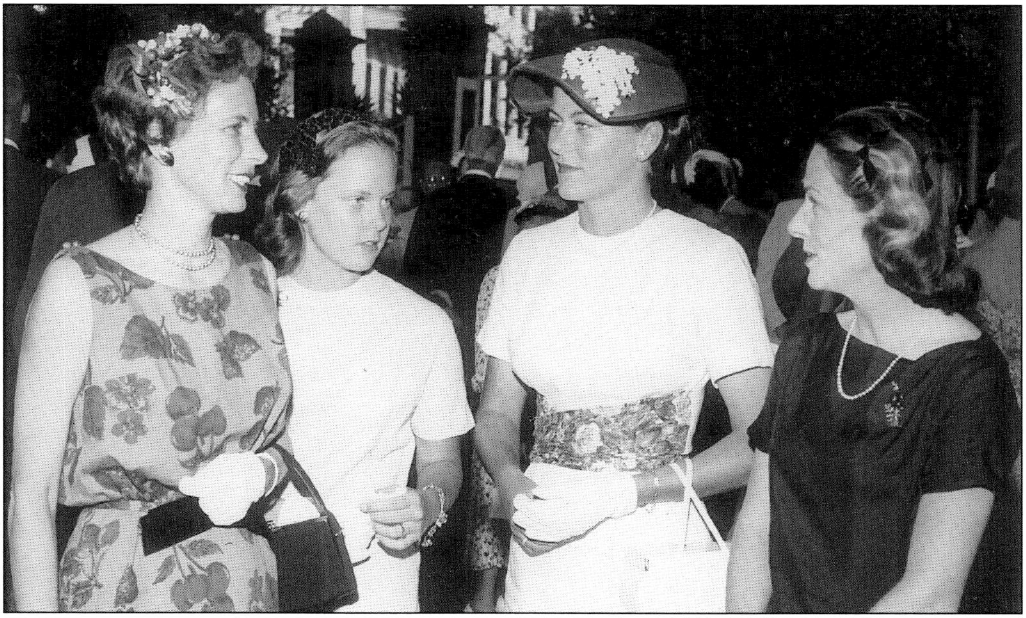

MOTHERS' MORNING, 1958. This photo shows the annual tradition at Ashley Hall of Mother's Morning. Each year in the spring time, the students of Ashley Hall invite their mothers to attend school with them to see their classes and everyday routine. Usually it is a half day, filled with fun activities, opportunities for teachers to get to know the mothers, and an afternoon tea. This event continues today among girls of all grades. (Photo courtesy of the Ashley Hall Archives)

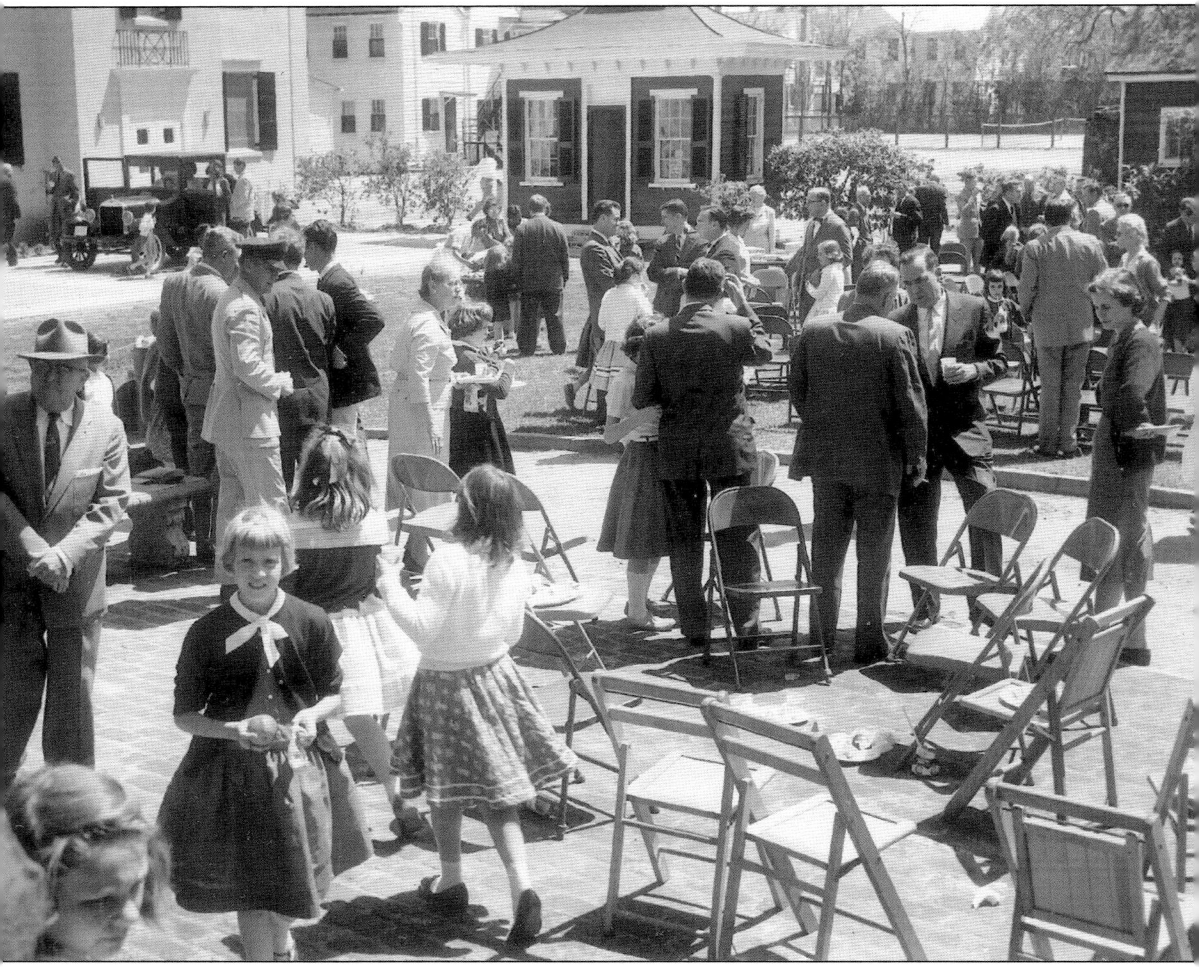

Fathers' Morning, 1960. These students milling around the senior lawn are celebrating Fathers' Morning. Like Mothers' Morning, it is an opportunity for fathers to see the daily activities and class schedules of their daughters. This year there is an old car visible in the background that was donated by Hugh C. Lane to auction off and raise money for Ashley Hall. Notice Lane Hall had been built, so this car was much older than 1960. On alternating years on Fathers' Morning, the senior quilt—a quilt with a square decorated by each senior—is auctioned to raise money for the school. (Photo courtesy of the Ashley Hall Archives.)

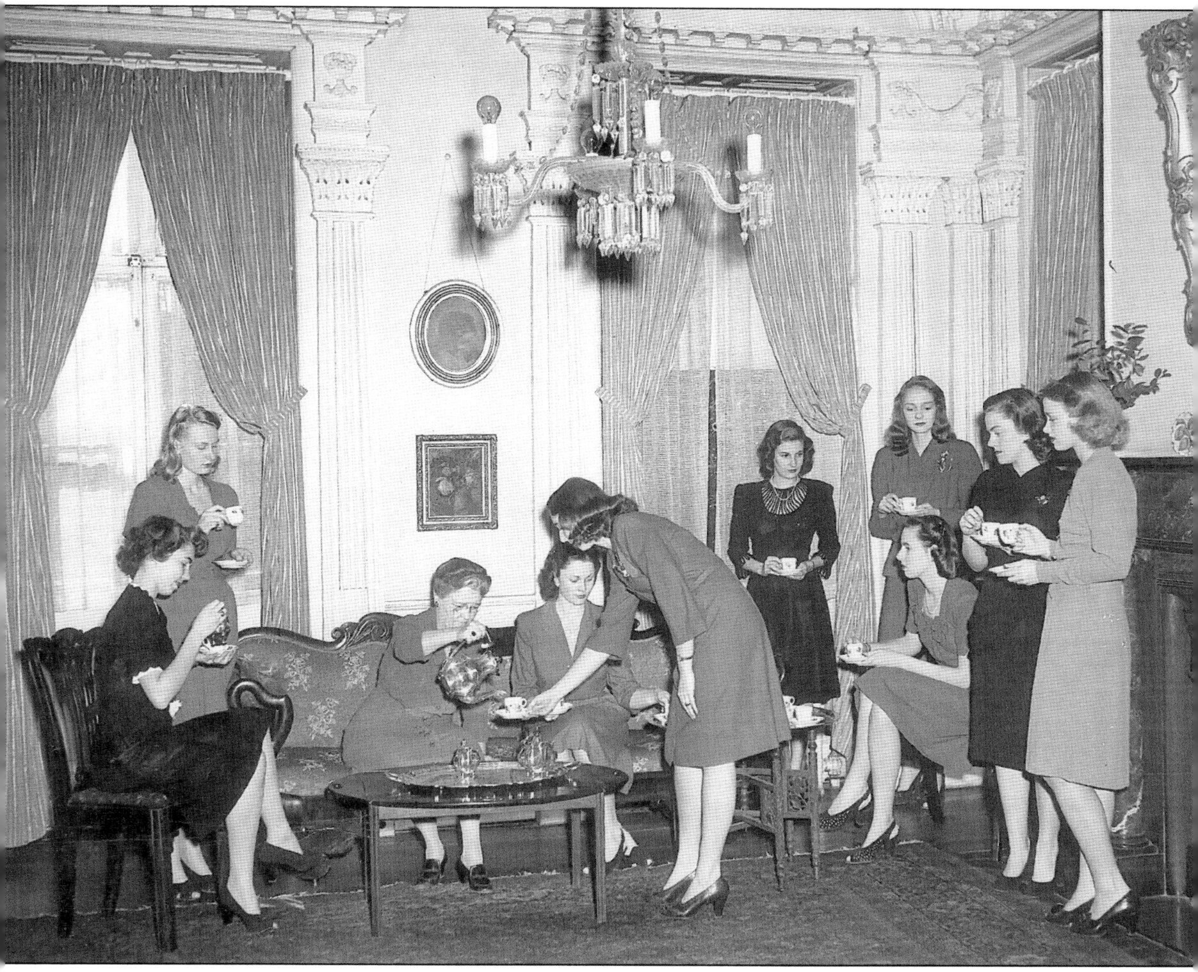

WEEKLY TEA, 1946. Evening tea with the Headmistress was once a weekly event that was lost due to increasing class sizes and the loss of boarders. Usually after Sunday night dinners, the boarders would have tea with Miss McBee in the drawing room. This tradition continued until the 1960s, when the faculty would have coffee together in the drawing room every night after meals. (Photo courtesy of the Ashley Hall Archives.)

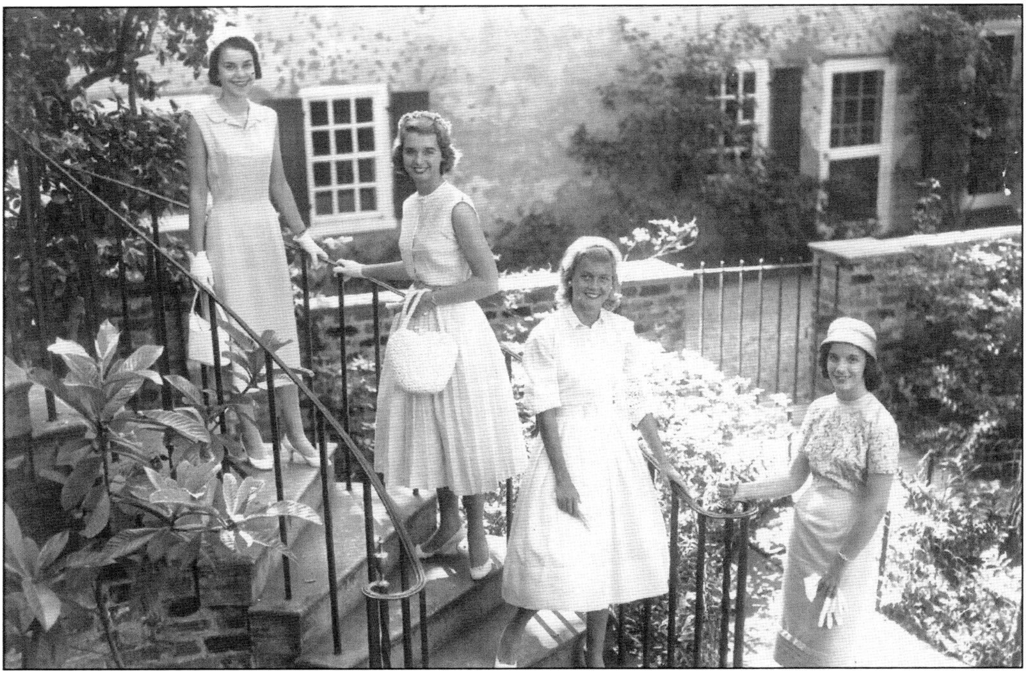

Almost Alumnae, 1958. Anne Clay Blanton, Dottie Henderson, Dargan Fishburn, and Linda Strickland, all graduates of 1958, pose here for a photo during the annual alumnae tea at the Williams Gibbes House. The graduating seniors and their families were guests of Mrs. Ashby Farrow. A few years later the senior class of 1963 came up with a fund-raising idea for their class gift. They convinced Ashley Hall parents and alumnae to open up their homes for an annual house tour. (Photo courtesy of the Ashley Hall Archives.)

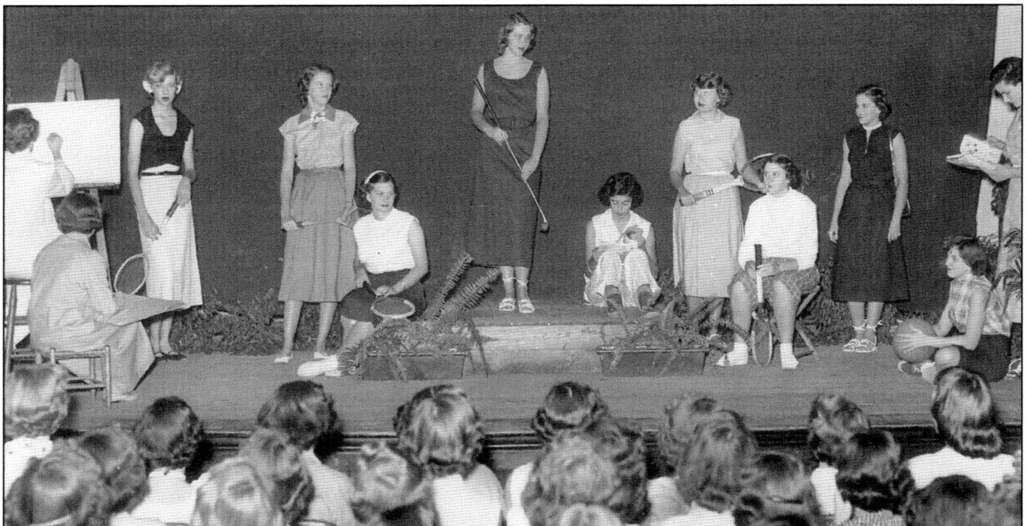

Sewing Class Fashion Show, 1950. Each year the sewing class held a fashion show displaying their savvy stitching to the school and the city of Charleston. The show was given in Burges Auditorium usually as part of the Mothers' Morning assembly. Sewing class was an optional class, and some girls did not take it due to the extra money required for more than just the core courses. (Photo courtesy of the Ashley Hall Archives.)

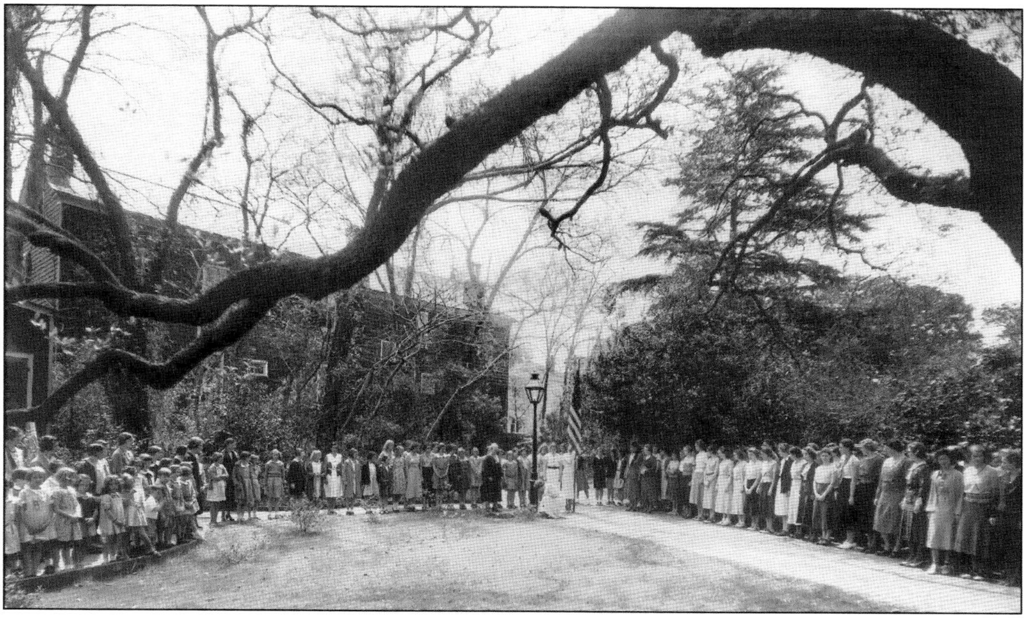

Planting of the Washington Oak, 1932. In this all-school event, a seedling from the oak that George Washington planted on Mount Vernon was planted on campus. Virginia Porcher, an alumna, was on a committee to help restore Mount Vernon, which had fallen into sad decay from years of neglect. She brought back the seedling as a gift to the school. (Photo courtesy of the Ashley Hall Archives.)

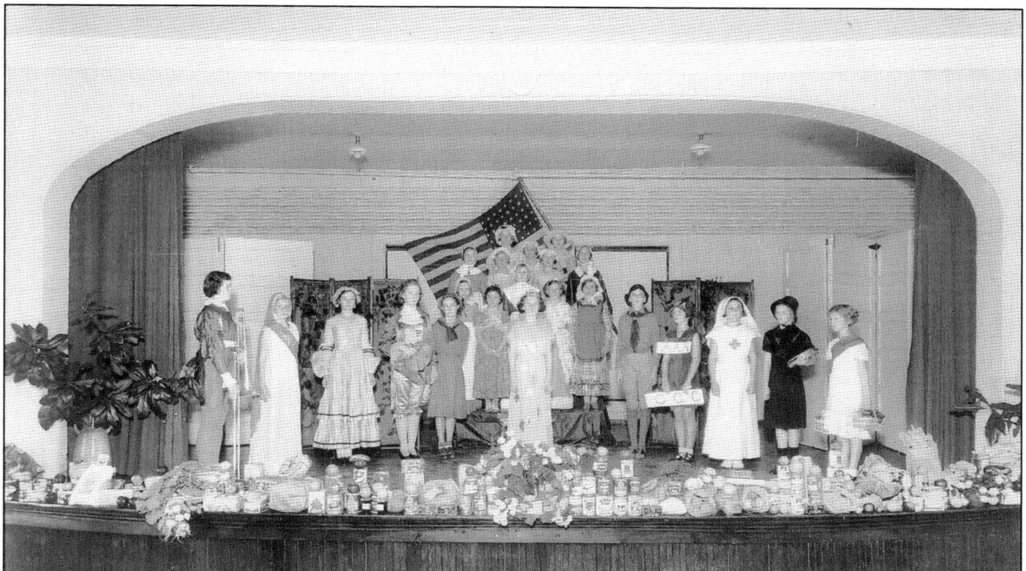

Food Drive, 1920s. This lower school play, performed in Burges Auditorium, doubled in entertaining an audience and aiding the community as the food in the front of the stage was donated to a local charity. Each audience member was asked to bring a can of food as an admission price. Still understanding the importance of giving to the community, Ashley Hall has annual fund-raisers throughout the school year and especially around Christmas time. Each class gives a gift to the school or the community, and the clubs and organizations have their own philanthropic events. (Photo courtesy of the Ashley Hall Archives.)

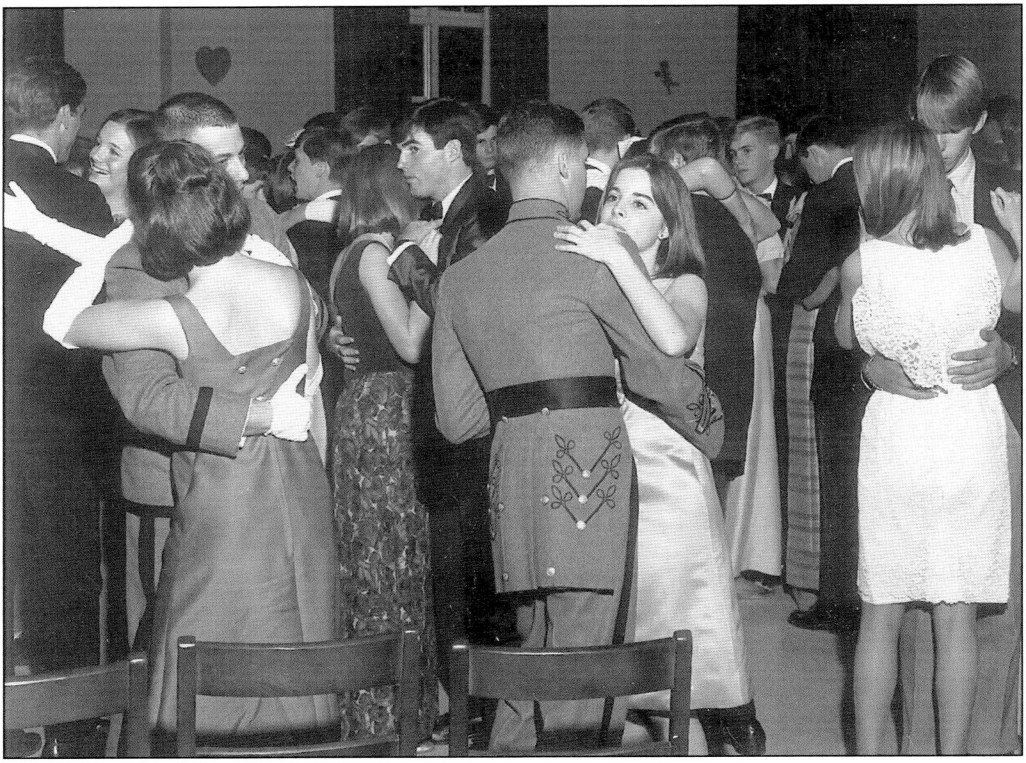

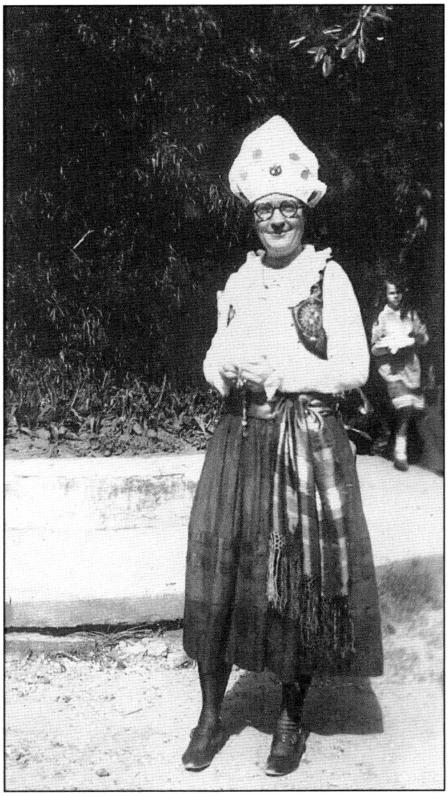

UPPER SCHOOL DANCE, LATE 1960S. Dances have long been a tradition of the Upper School. The boarding students had frequent teas and dances with the local boys' schools, Porter Military Academy and The Citadel. Weekly tea dances at the Citadel were important occasions for the girls who spent that afternoon getting dressed up. Coca-Colas were served, and records played as the girls danced in a room above the canteen at the Citadel. (Photo courtesy of the Ashley Hall Archives.)

"GENIE MCBEE," 1910S. Miss McBee is dressed as a genie in this photo taken at one of the school's first fund-raising events. Kettledrum, a fund raiser to build the school pool was so named because it sold everything from kettles to drums. Everyone dressed in costume and paraded around campus competing for a prize. There were fortune telling booths and other carnival type events. (Photo courtesy of the Ashley Hall Archives.)

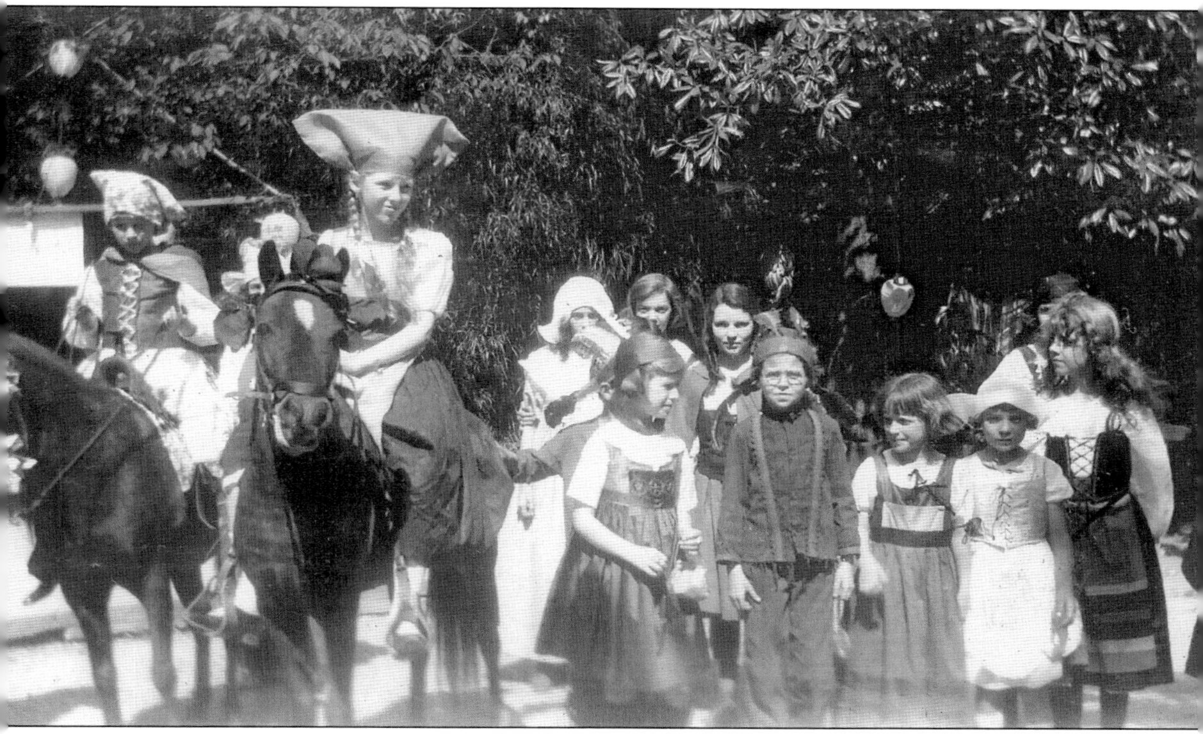

Kettledrum, 1910s. After the money to build the pool was raised, Kettledrum was discontinued until being started up again in the 1940s. The events were more spectacular than ever and included a petting zoo, water ballet show, and a surprise parcel pick-up. In many ways Kettledrum is similar to the Halloween carnival held annually today. Different clubs and organizations, such as the Athletic Association and the Alumnae Association, have fun booths. Money earned by each booth goes towards that organization's treasury. (Photo courtesy of the Ashley Hall Archives.)

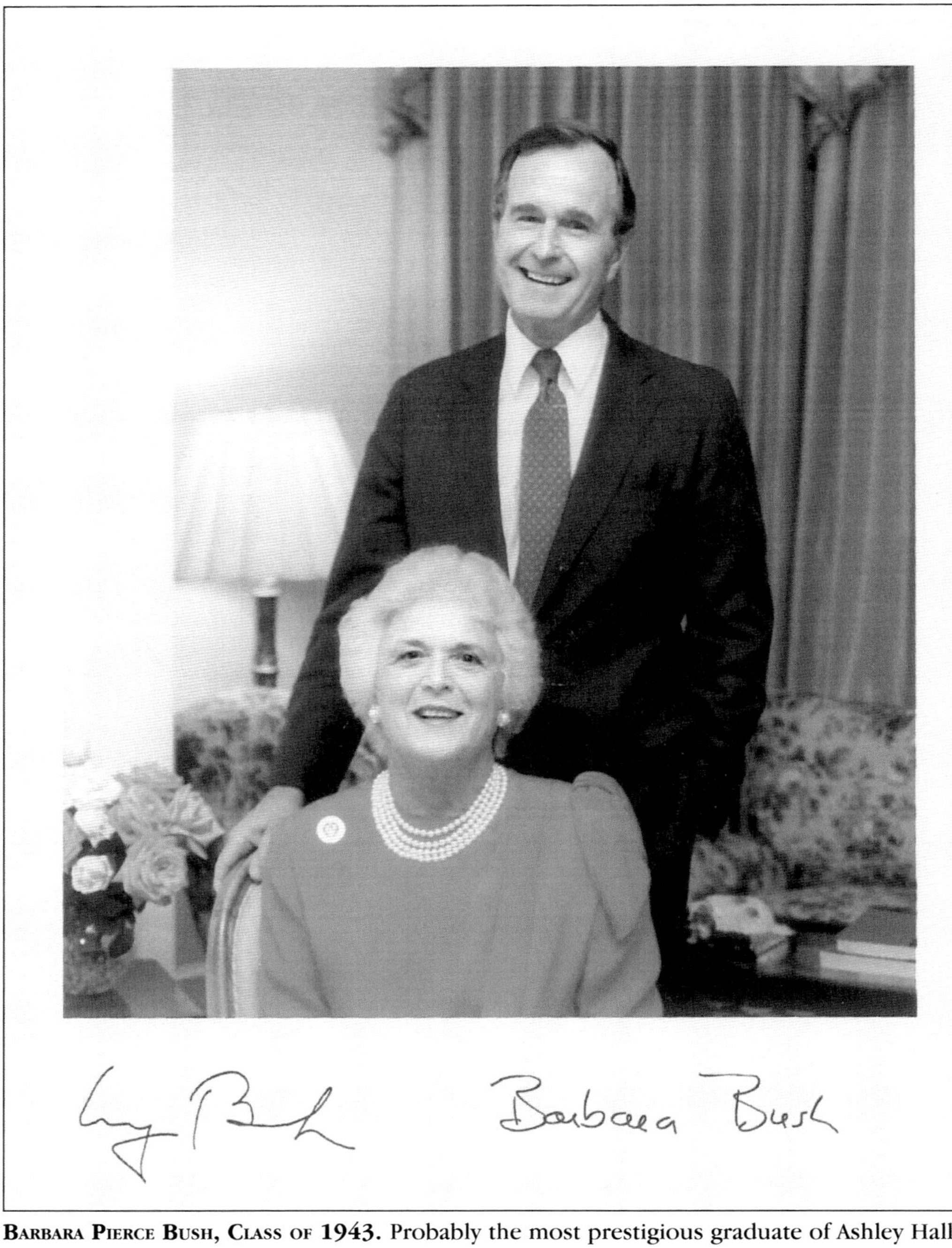

Barbara Pierce Bush, Class of 1943. Probably the most prestigious graduate of Ashley Hall, Barbara Pierce Bush, class of 1943, spoke to the school during her class reunion. Mrs. Bush, the First Lady of the United States for four years, attended Ashley Hall as a boarding student in high school. For years while she was in Washington D.C., she welcomed the visits of the Ashley Hall middle school during their annual trip to the country's capital. A classmate, Mrs. Jane Thornhill (née Jane Lucas, class of 1943), describes Mrs. Bush as being "fresh, vivacious, and a pleasure to know" during her years at Ashley Hall. During the reunion, Ashley Hall students had the pleasure of hearing Mrs. Bush speak on her years at Ashley Hall and her life after school. (Photo courtesy of the Ashley Hall Archives.)

Three

Campus Views

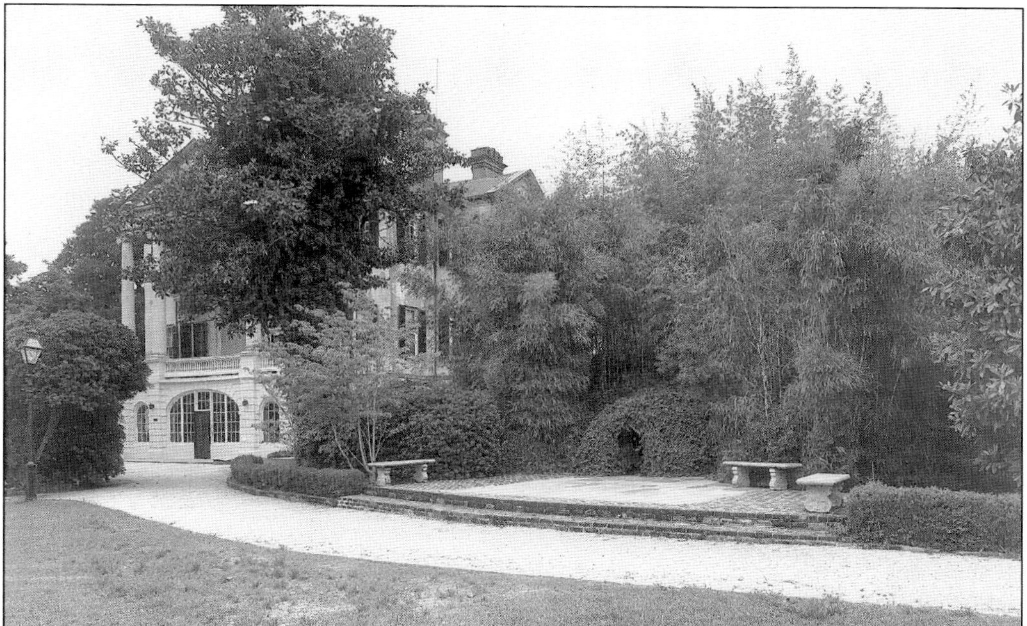

Ashley Hall Campus, 1930s. The name of the school was determined when Miss McBee decided the main building was large enough to be called a "hall." Then she chose to include the name of the closest river, the Ashley River. Hence the school's name became "Ashley Hall." It was not until some years later that Miss McBee learned of the first Ashley Hall, a plantation on the Ashley River many miles from Charleston. (Photo courtesy of the Ashley Hall Archives.)

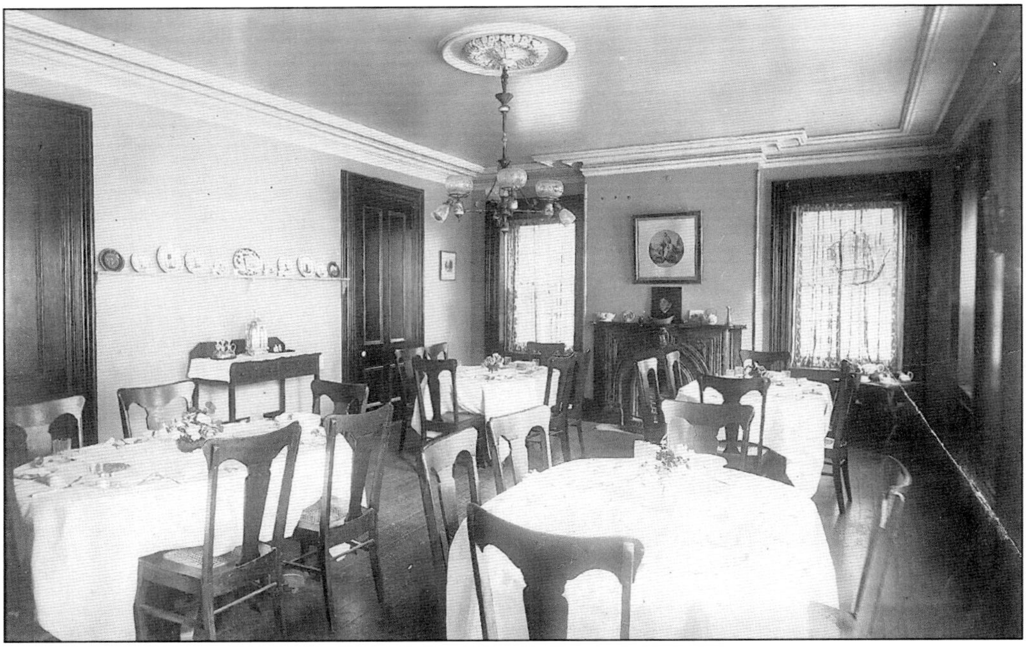

Dining Hall, 1910. In the very beginning of the school, everything was located in the main house, later named the McBee House by the Alumnae Association. This three story house contained the bedrooms for boarders, classrooms, and the dining room pictured here. This dining room, located on the first floor, was the Headmistress's office in 1982 and is now the business office. (Photo courtesy of the Ashley Hall Archives.)

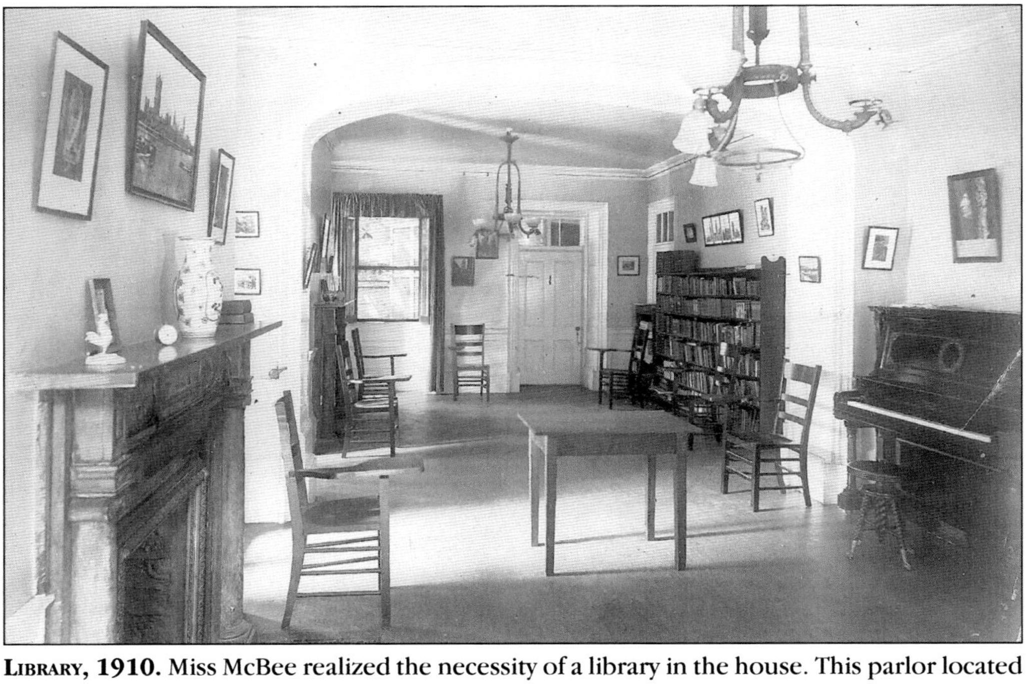

Library, 1910. Miss McBee realized the necessity of a library in the house. This parlor located on the first floor to the left of the spiral staircase was the admissions office and is now the office of the Headmistress. In 1910, best-selling novels were *Howards End* by E.M. Forster and *Prester John* by John Buchan. (Photo courtesy of the Ashley Hall Archives.)

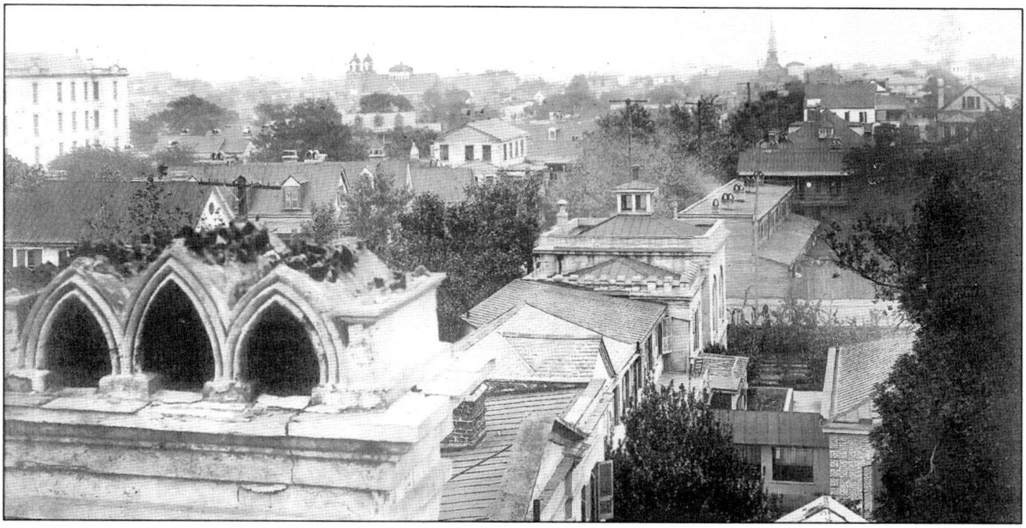

ROOFTOP VIEW OF CHARLESTON, 1920s. "The building in Charleston which most resembles [William] Jay's work is No. 172 Rutledge Ave, now Ashley Hall school for Girls. A Regency villa, it was built when the area was still suburban. It has a riot of curved lines, the curved rooms and curved doors characteristic of his houses, an oval staircase and an apse under the portico. Its exact date has not been determined. The first owner, Patrick Duncan, bought the land in 1798, added a strip to the south in 1807, and was listed in the directory as living on 'Pinckney St. cannons' borough (the present Rutledge Avenue) as early as 1806. . . . Tradition credits this building to 'an English architect,' and this belief was stated as a fact by an architectural writer, C.R.S. Horton, in 1902. The best argument, however, for this dwelling's being of Jay's design is the dwelling itself."—*Architects of Charleston* by Beatrice St. Julien Ravenel on the architect William Jay (1769–1853). (Photo courtesy of the Ashley Hall Archives.)

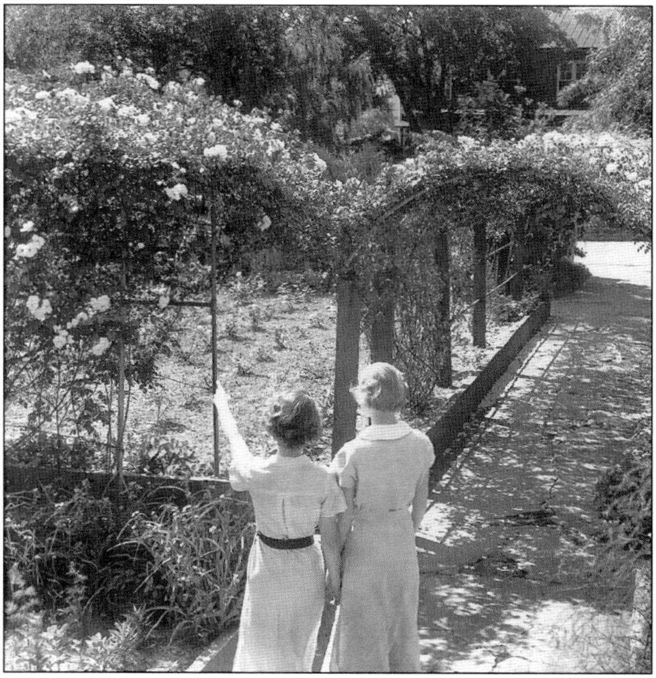

CAMPUS GARDENS, 1930s. Otto Witte, who sold the property to Miss McBee, had planted exotic plants and trees. Due to her love of growing things, Miss McBee kept and expanded the extensive gardens. At one point the entire grounds of Ashley Hall were filled with beautiful gardens and fantastic floral walkways. (Photo courtesy of the Ashley Hall Archives)

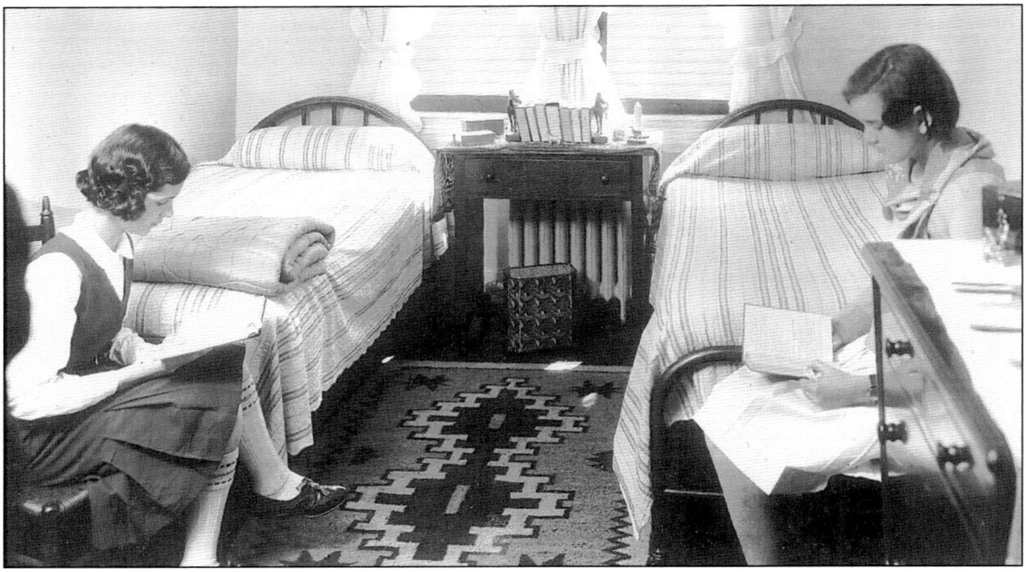

Dormitory, 1931. More buildings were added to house the out-of-town boarders as their numbers increased. This dorm room, located on the second floor of what is now the edge of the Art Center, is a great example of what the living quarters for boarding students looked like.

It was a terrible year of world-wide financial panic and depression. The girls were not untouched by this, but they were girls all the same. "Mood Indigo," "I Don't Know Why I Love You Like I Do," and the first version of "Love Letters in the Sand" were popular songs. (Photo courtesy of the Ashley Hall Archives.)

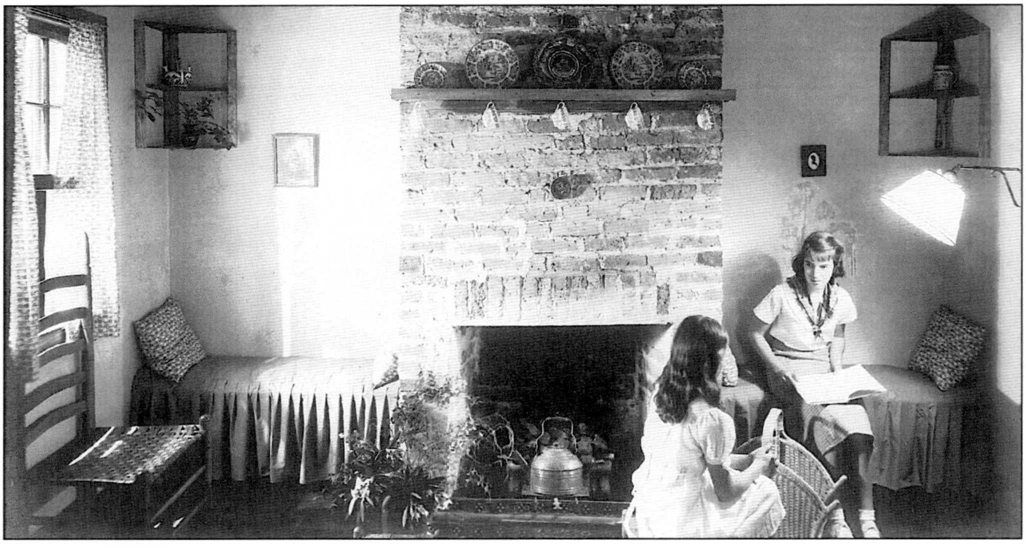

Cozy Living Quarters, 1930s. Many small buildings around the neighborhood were bought by the school to accommodate the growth in the number of students. Here is another dorm room. Notice the fireplace; it may be odd to students today to think about living in a room without central heating and cooling, but building a good fire was a well-known skill at the time of this photo.

The 1935 *Cerberus* jokes: "Sign on a girl's room—'Studying—if you come in don't wake me up!'" (Photo courtesy of the Ashley Hall Archives.)

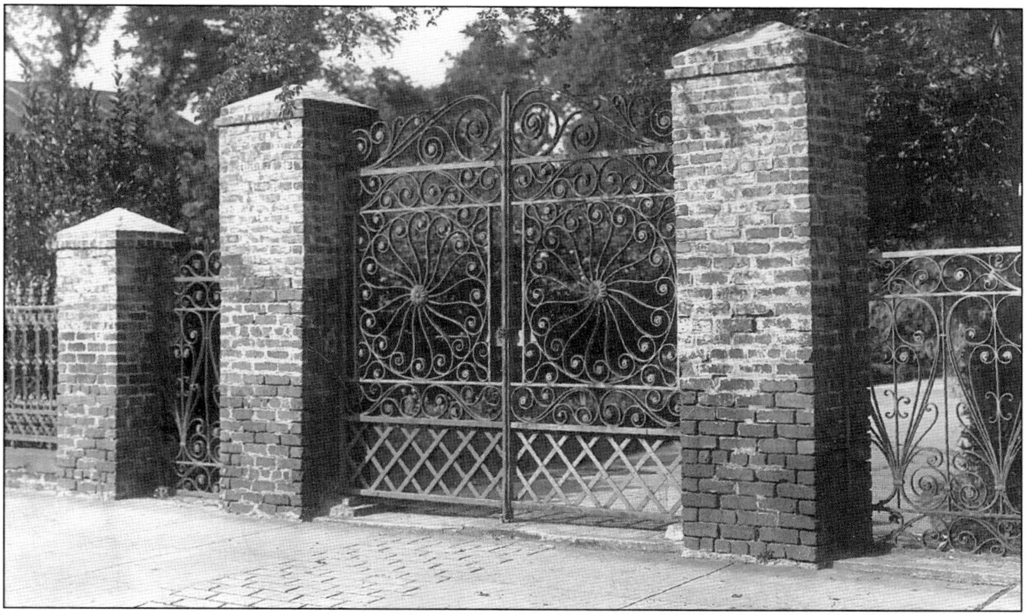

Back Gates, 1920s. Charleston is known for its extraordinary and unique iron work. Originally serving as the back entrance to the school, these wrought-iron gates no longer exist. In more recent years, gates with a similar design were given as a senior class gift to the school and act as the entrance on the Smith Street side of campus. (Photo courtesy of the Ashley Hall Archives.)

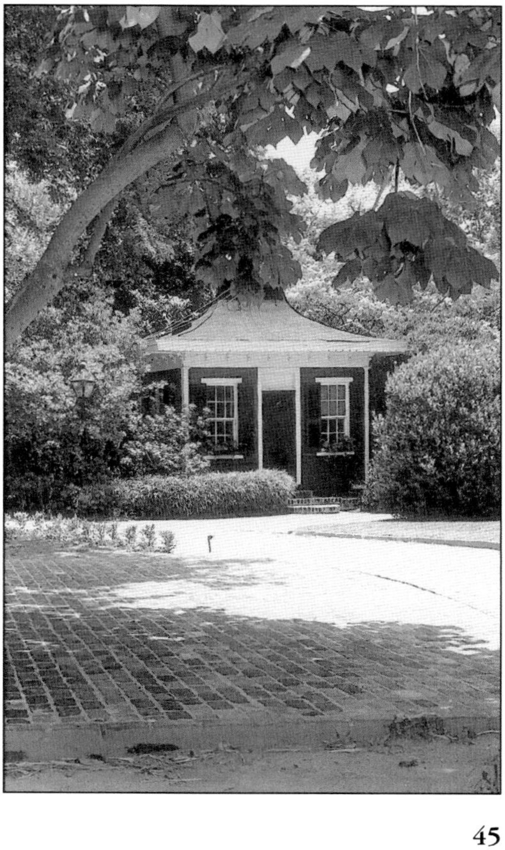

School Store, 1920s. This building is easily recognized today as it is still in use as the school store. It is speculated to have been storage space for the owners of the property before Miss McBee purchased the land. While the Wittes owned the property, many exotic animals lived on the premises. Laura Witte Waring writes in her book *The Way It Was in Charleston*, "Prairie dogs at one time occupied a little concrete, dome-shaped house and a yard, with a large tank sunk underground so that they could not burrow out . . . silver and gold pheasants had houses with yards . . . usually one or two peacocks, which walked around the grounds and roosted in a tree at night. . . . In the large bird house: cockatoos, macaws, parrots, love birds, Java sparrows, parakeets . . . alligators and cooter lived in the fountain, near the front fence; gold fish in a pond, a part of the grotto . . . turkeys, chickens, and ducks were kept in a yard in the back, near the stable, and when I was a child, there was always a cow." (Photo courtesy of the Ashley Hall Archives.)

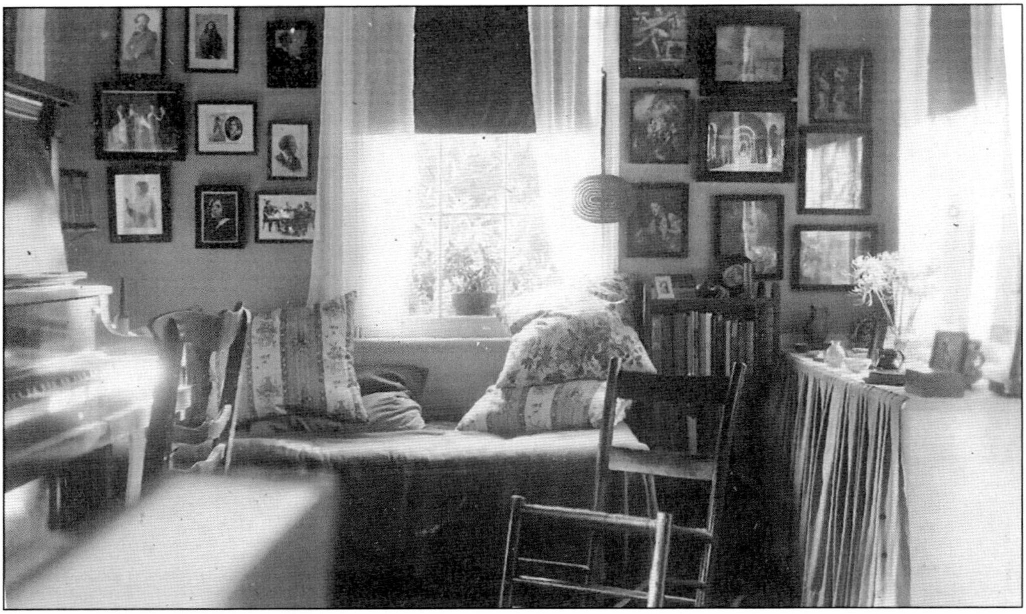

Miss Baker's Studio, 1920s. Miss Marie Baker, a teacher of music and a tutor of violin and piano, lived in this tiny studio on campus. She would hold lessons here for any students from Ashley Hall, the Citadel, Porter Military Academy, and others around the city who wished to learn and improve their music skills. Miss Baker was a member of the Charleston Symphony Orchestra and served as the concert master for many years. (Photo courtesy of the Ashley Hall Archives.)

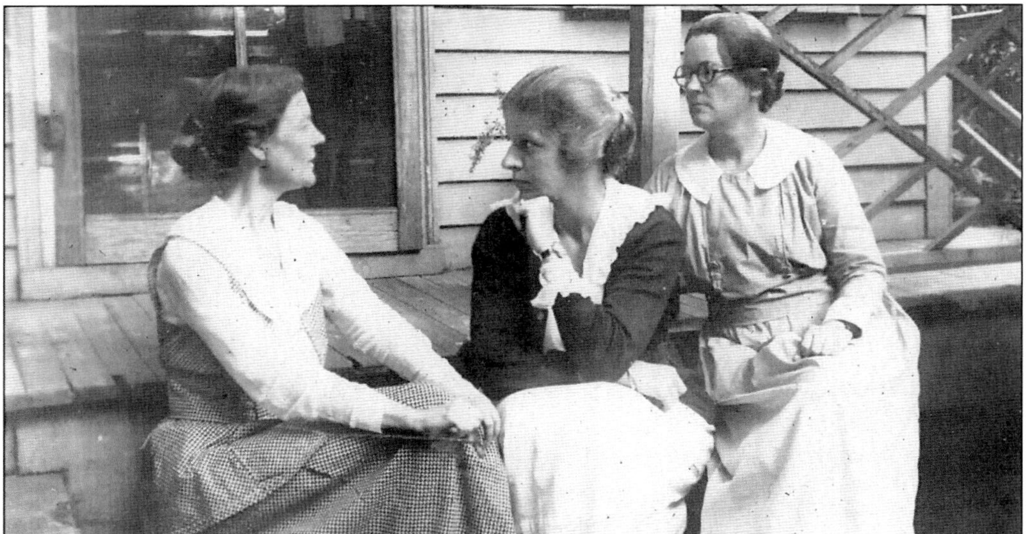

Best Friends, 1920s. Estelle McBee, Marie Baker, and Mary Vardrine McBee sit outside Miss Baker's studio and chat about the day. Marie and Estelle were two of the first faculty members to come to Ashley Hall to assist Miss McBee. A teacher of music for many years, Miss Baker also served as the choir instructor, lower school French teacher, and school librarian. She was also the chaperone for "*Le Verre D'Eau*" club, a charitable organization at Ashley Hall. The three women remained close friends for the remainder of their lives. (Photo courtesy of the Ashley Hall Archives.)

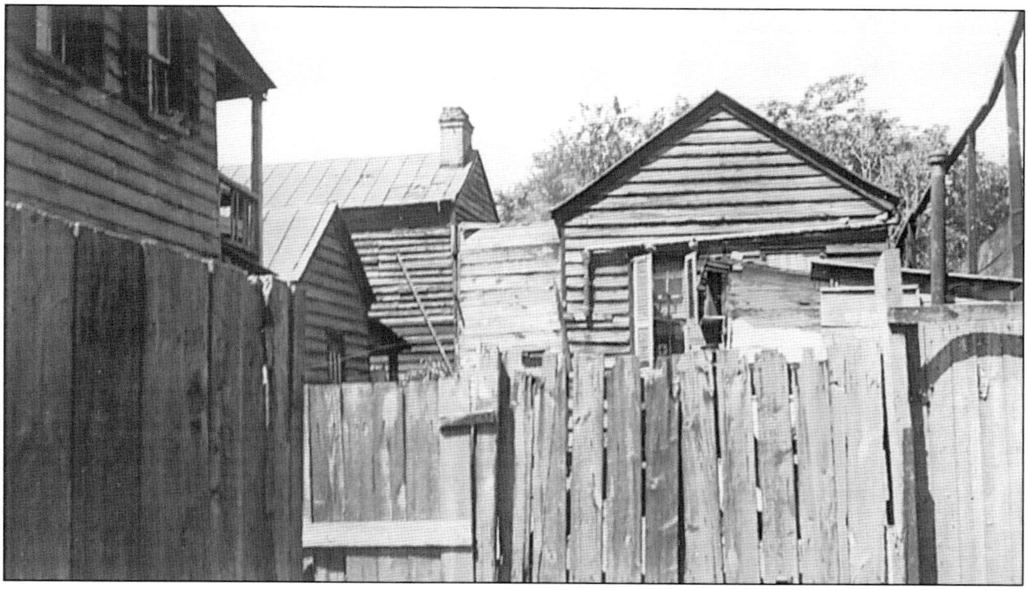

Site for Future Lower School, Early 1900s. This picture shows the neighborhood surrounding Ashley Hall. These houses were in complete shambles until they were bought by Miss McBee and converted into lower school classroom buildings. (Photo courtesy of the Ashley Hall Archives.)

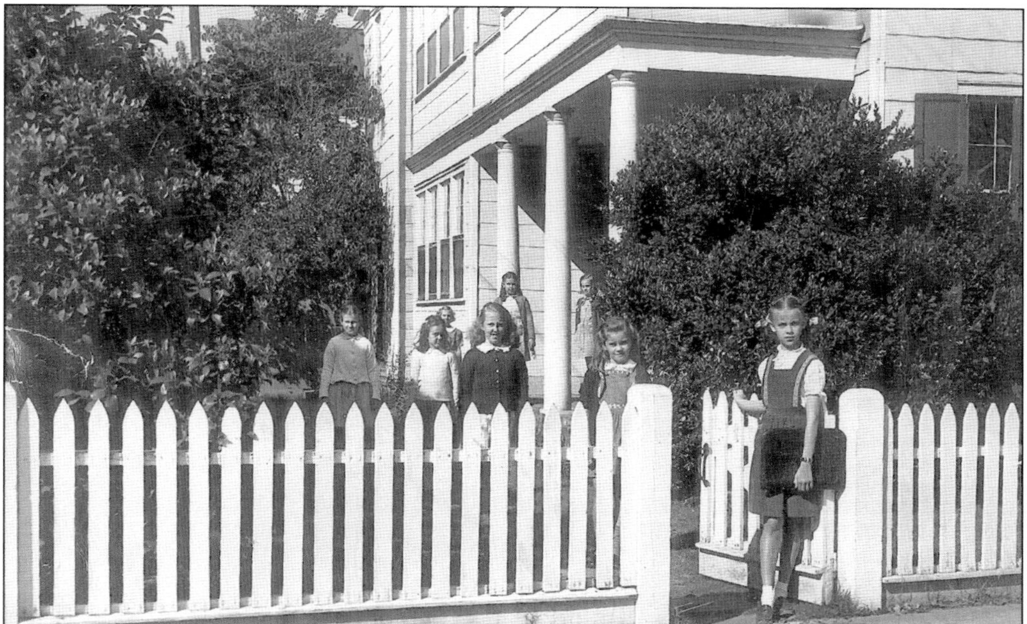

131 Smith Street, 1930s. Here is a photograph of one of the buildings that was converted into a lower school building. The lower school included first through seventh grade at the time of this photograph. The sixth and seventh grades were departmentalized, in order to prepare the girls for the transition into the upper school. An early Ashley Hall brochure states that "the rooms are well-lighted and ventilated. Each one is provided with two exits. The first two grades are furnished with tables and chairs; the other classes have movable desks." (Photo courtesy of the Ashley Hall Archives.)

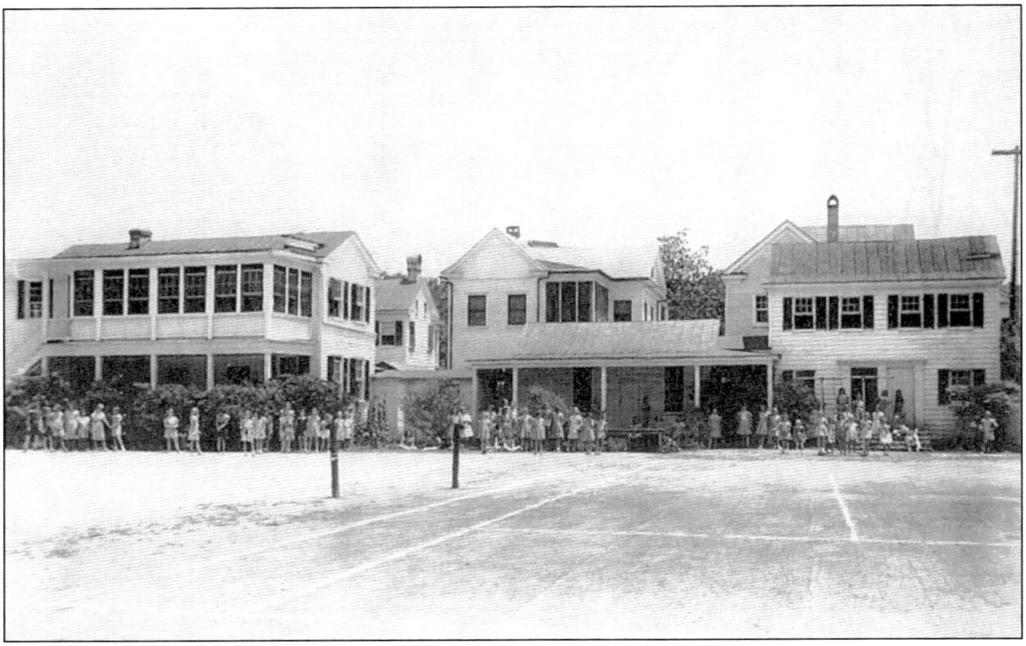

Lower School Campus, 1930s. This photograph shows what the lower school campus looked like before the 1960s. Today these buildings no longer exist and have instead been replaced by Pardue Hall. There were eight classrooms, a music room, and a library in the lower school. The school auditorium, playgrounds, and swimming pool were also used by the younger students. (Photo courtesy of the Ashley Hall Archives.)

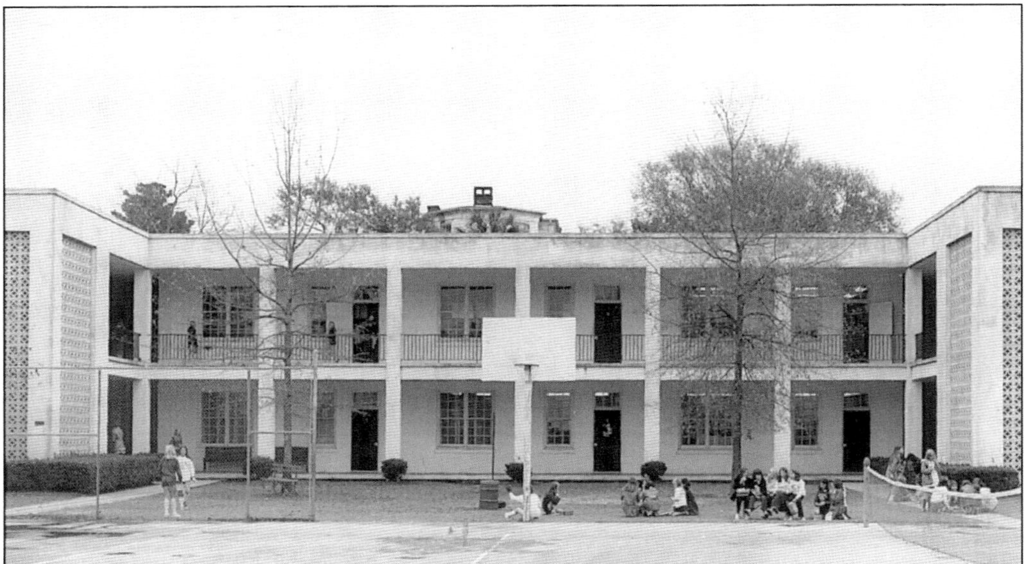

Pardue Hall, 1965. The lower school, built in 1964, was named for the Headmistress at the time, Caroline Pardue. Classes for first through eighth grades were held here. A library in this building, furnished by the Alumnae Association, is named "The Paret Room" in memory of Polly Paret, Miss McBee's long-time secretary and right-hand woman. Miss Paret, a graduate of the school, even gave her time to the Alumnae Association after her retirement. (Photo courtesy of the Ashley Hall Archives.)

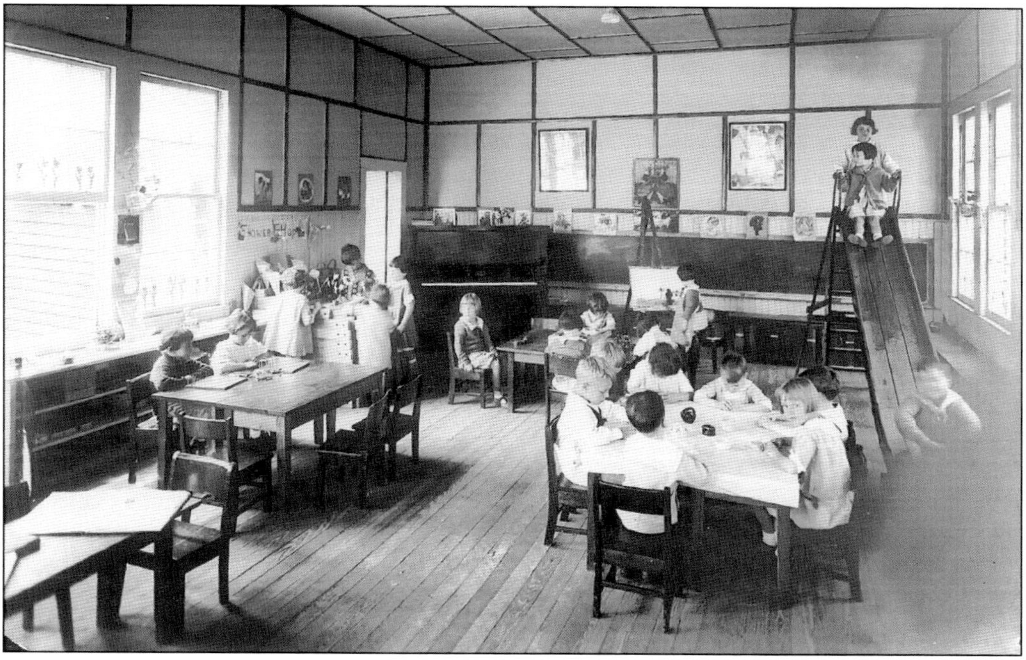

KINDERGARTEN ROOM, 1920s. Mrs. Elizabeth Cole, who attended Ashley Hall lower school in the 1920s, remembers the kindergarten as being a small room surrounded entirely by windows. The head of the kindergarten at the time was a Swedish woman with a firm belief in progressive education who always kept the windows open so the girls would have fresh air. Her motto was "a healthy body comes before a healthy mind." Notice the slide in the right corner of the room. (Photo courtesy of the Ashley Hall Archives.)

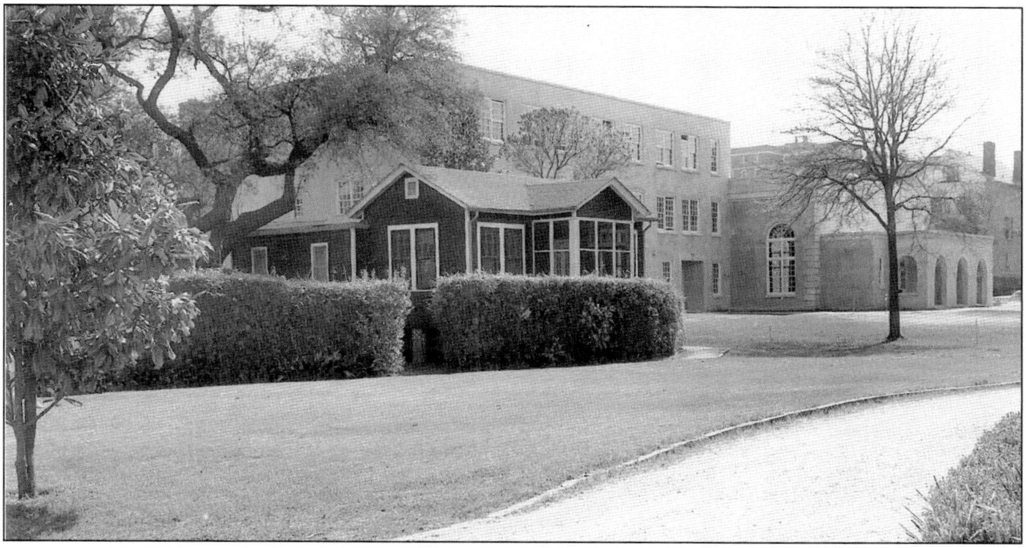

UPPER SCHOOL CAMPUS, 1965. This photo of the upper school campus shows a building that is no longer on the grounds. The senior lawn and Jenkins Hall are visible landmarks and the other building shown is believed to be the music room. Mademoiselle Rugger taught piano and music for many years during the 1930s and 1940s. It seems practical that a separate building would house the noisy beginners of piano and voice. (Photo courtesy of the Ashley Hall Archives.)

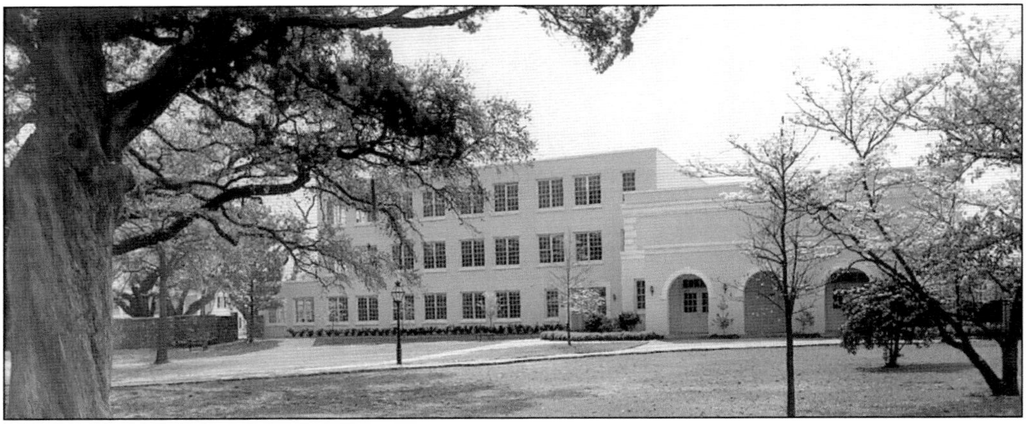

Davies Auditorium and Jenkins Hall, 1966. This photograph shows the current upper school building and Davies Auditorium. Jenkins Hall, completed in 1966, was named in honor of Mr. C. Bissell Jenkins Jr., who was the organizer of the Ashley Hall Foundation and first president of the Board of Trustees. The building is three stories tall and contains about 14 classrooms and up-to-date technology in the computer and science laboratories. Davies Auditorium was named in honor of Mr. Carlton Davies "in appreciation of his untiring efforts in the building program of the school." This auditorium is still used daily for morning announcements, chapel services, plays, and all-school events. (Photo courtesy of the Ashley Hall Archives.)

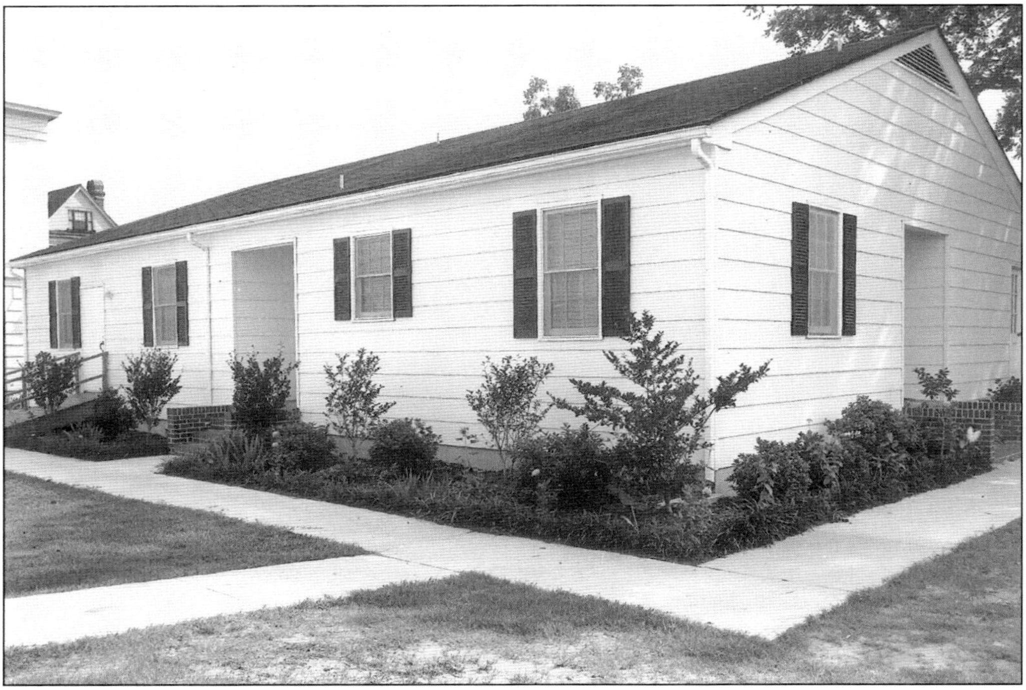

Infirmary, 1967. This "new infirmary" was completed in 1967 and replaced two small buildings that had been "temporary" since World War I. A school brochure boasts of the presence of an on-campus nurse during the entire school day due to the "prime importance of the physical welfare of every child." Still existing today on the Smith Street side of campus behind Burges Auditorium, the building was used as a kindergarten and now as maintenance storage. (Photo courtesy of the Ashley Hall Archives.)

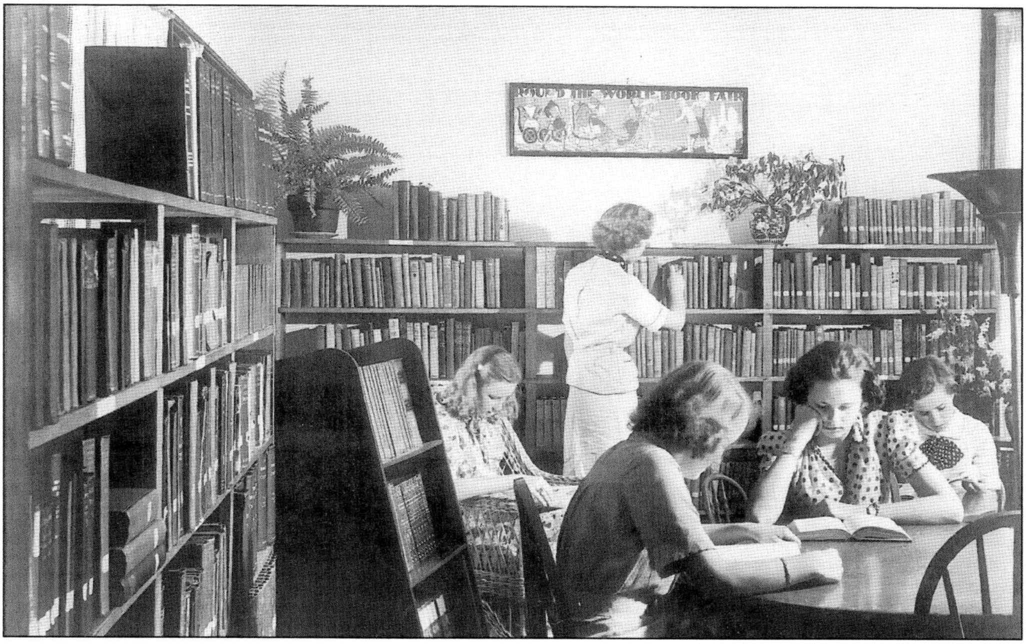

LIBRARY, 1930s. Always an important room on campus, the school library had many locations, from McBee House, to smaller buildings on campus, to the current location below Lane Hall. This photo shows the library when it existed in a building extension added on to the right side of the McBee House. A joke from the 1931 *Cerberus* reads: "Mrs. Rogers: 'Margaret have you done your outside reading yet?' Margaret C.: 'No, Mrs. Rogers, it's too cold to read outside.'" (Photo courtesy of the Ashley Hall Archives.)

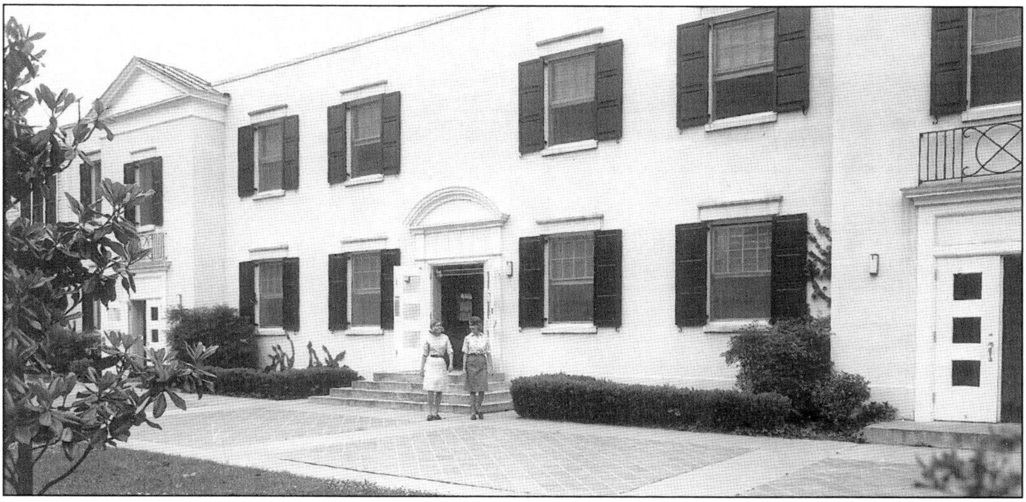

LANE HALL AND RIVERS LIBRARY, 1959. The first step in the Ashley Hall building program, Lane Hall was constructed and named in honor of Mr. Hugh C. Lane, a member of the Board of Trustees, "in appreciation of his kindness and generosity to the school." The building, completed in 1959, contained two study halls, a library, and office space on the first floor and ten bedrooms for seniors and a housemother's suite on the second floor. Today, the first floor still contains the library, and the second floor is now classrooms for the middle school, which includes sixth through eighth grades. (Photo courtesy of the Ashley Hall Archives.)

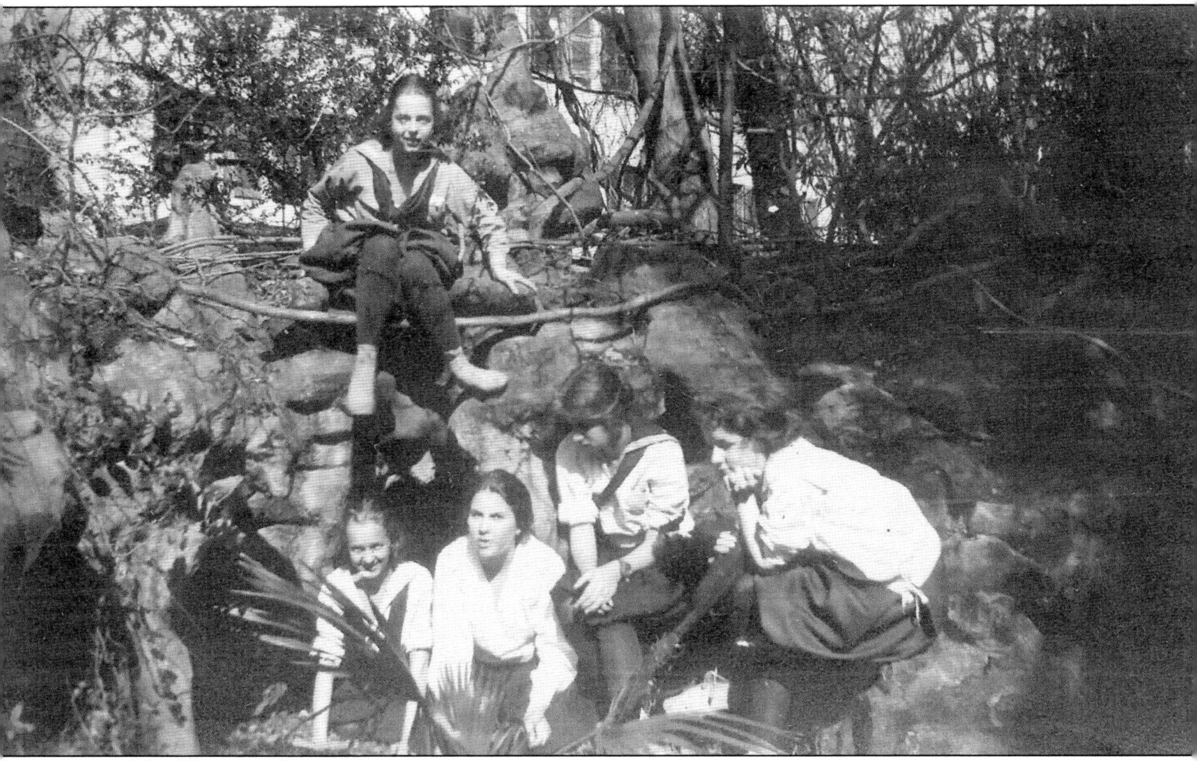

The Bear Cave, 1910s. Some of the first students to attend Ashley Hall pose around the still popular Bear Cave. These caves, added to the property by Mr. Witte, are made of phosphate rock, which was used as ballast on the early sailing ships that passed through the port of Charleston. Witte had a pet bear that was housed in this cave during his ownership of the property; his daughter Laura Witte Waring writes in her book *The Way It Was in Charleston*, "The bear, bought when a cub, was kept until it became too large. When it was small it would stand up on its hind legs and hold a bottle of soda water in its paws and drink it." This cave still exists and the patio in front of it, also known as the grotto, is a popular lunch spot for girls.

Josephine Pinckney sums up the popularity of the spot in her pamphlet *Call Back Yesterday: The First 25 Years of Ashley Hall*: "Nothing could be more acceptable to schoolgirls of the prankish kind then this legacy of caves and small buildings." (Photo courtesy of the Ashley Hall Archives.)

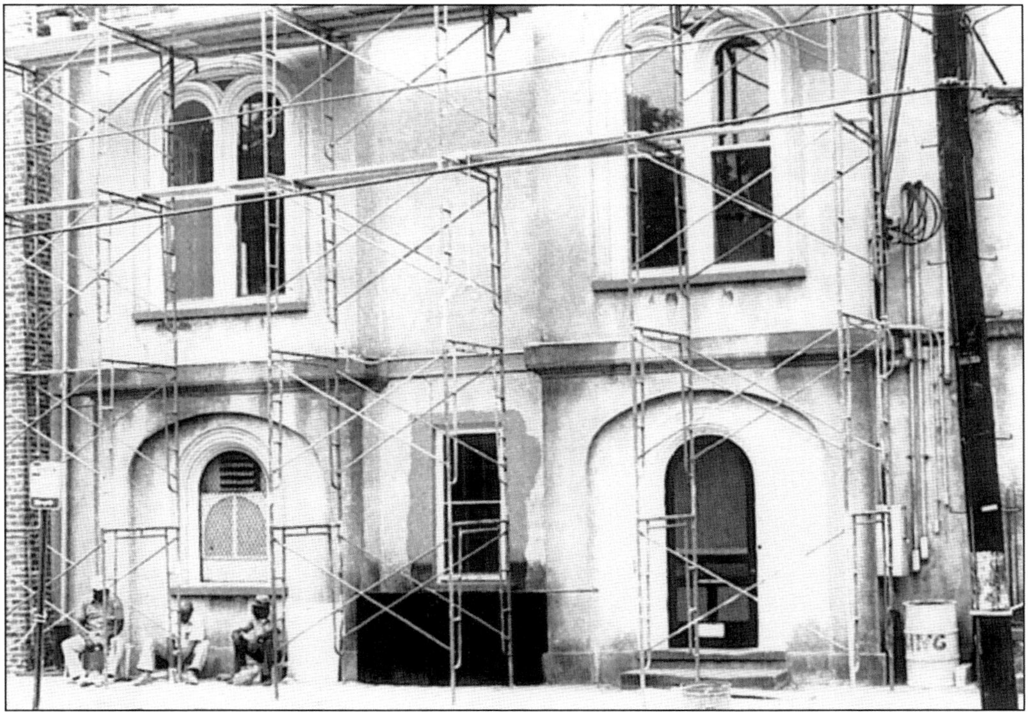

Renovation of McBee House, 1978. The first true effort to renovate the McBee House was in June of 1978. There was a big push to put the house in good condition so it could be registered with the National Registry of Historical Homes. The McBee House and grounds were restored again in recent years and completed in 2002. (Photo courtesy of the Ashley Hall Archives.)

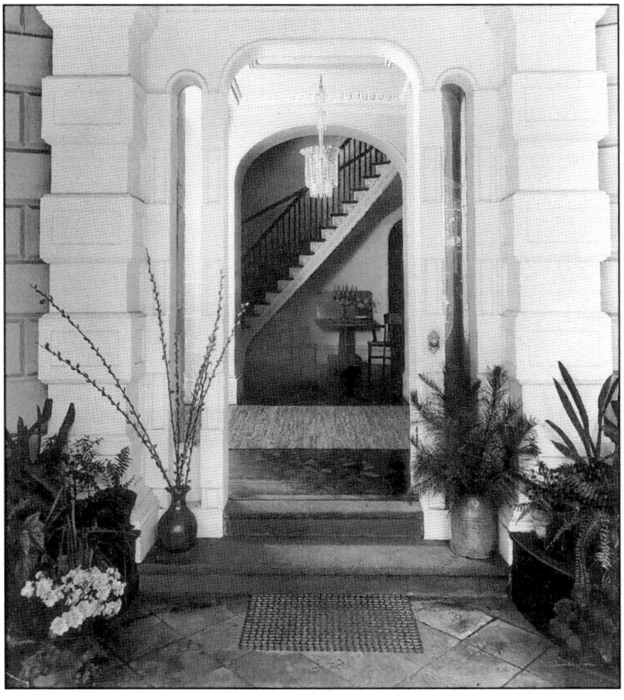

McBee House Entrance, 1931. McBee House is entered through a basement portico, which was enclosed with glass to form a conservatory. Alumnae remember the portico being very warm and therefore a suitable environment for the many rare plants that filled the space. Although it is no longer filled with plants, nothing has been changed besides the furniture of the room and it still makes a perfect entrance to a grand house. (Photo courtesy of the Ashley Hall Archives.)

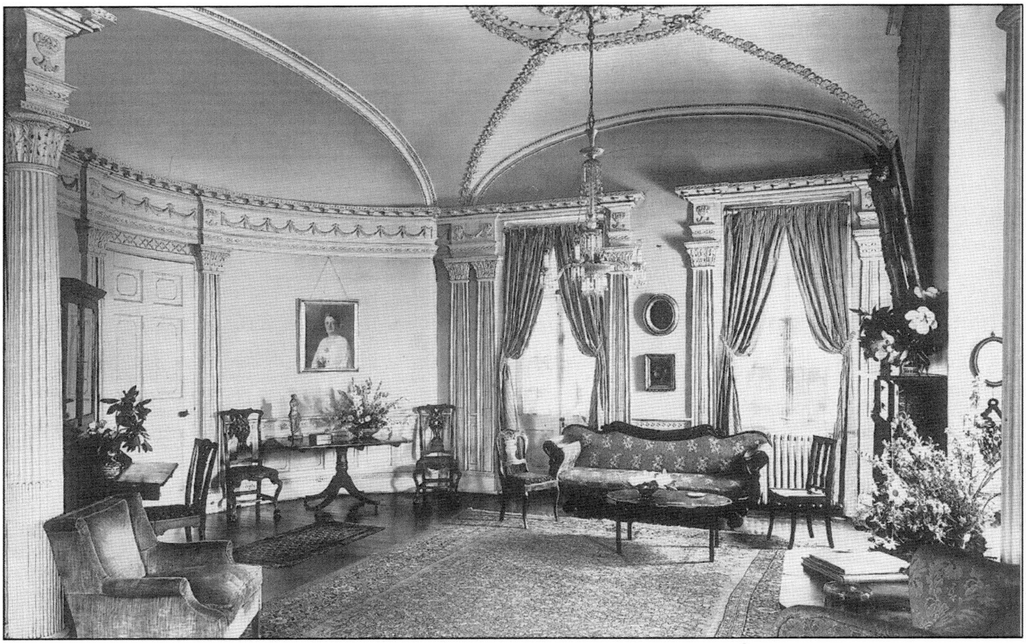

McBee House Drawing Room, 1940s. The most striking aspect of the drawing room is the curves and arches that shape the atmosphere of the room. Most of the original mantels and architecture are unchanged, but it is speculated that the heavy moldings and decorations, representative of the Victorian era, were added during the time the Trenholm family occupied the house. It is no surprise that the New York Metropolitan Museum of Art once offered to buy this exquisite drawing room. (Photo courtesy of the Ashley Hall Archives.)

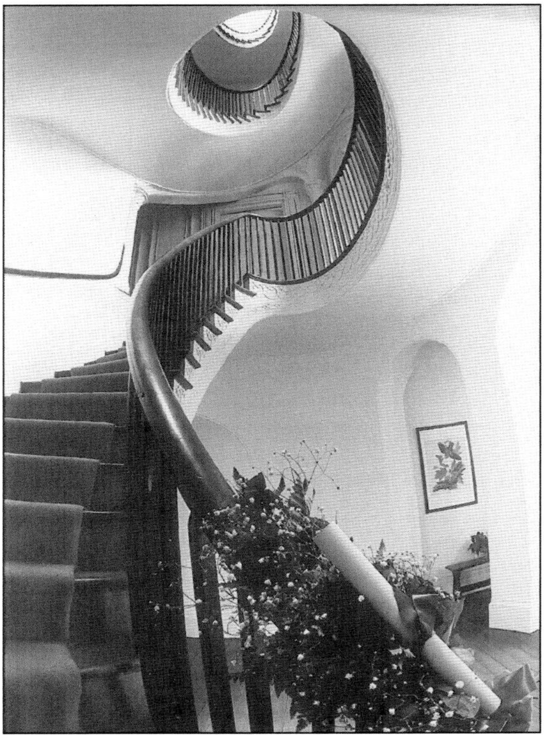

Spiral Staircase, 1970s. Also unchanged since the building of the house is the spiraling staircase, another recognizable Ashley Hall symbol. The curves and arches of the entrance immediately draw the admirer to the staircase with elliptical curves that rise all the way to the fourth floor. The roses on the mahogany banister represent the procession of the graduating seniors out of the McBee House ballroom and to the grotto for the commencement ceremony. (Photo courtesy of the Ashley Hall Archives.)

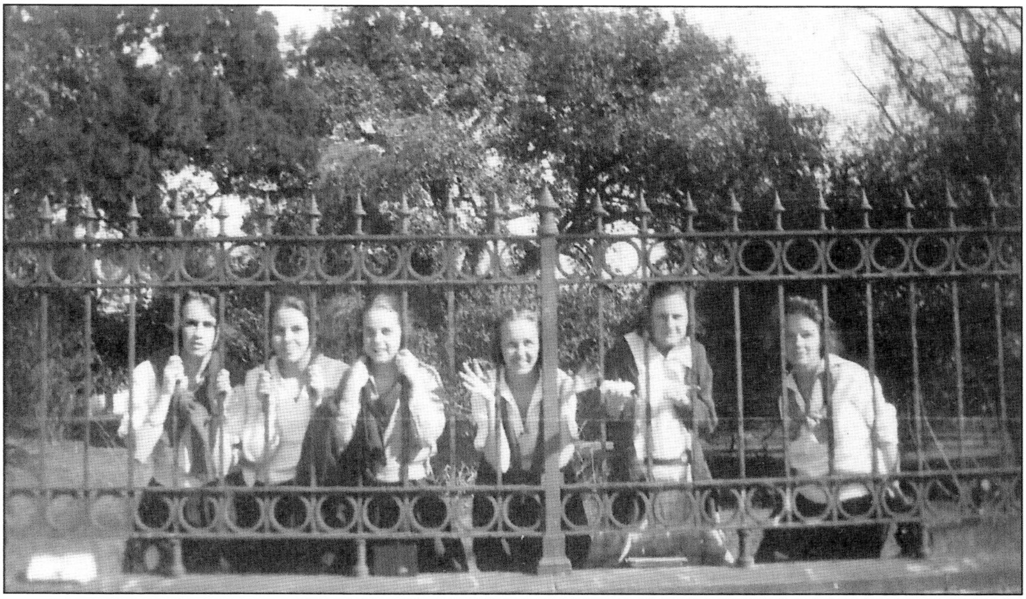

Rutledge Avenue Fence, 1910s. The wrought-iron fence, which encloses part of the school, is still located today on the Rutledge Avenue side of the campus. These young girls pose by the fence when the school was first opened. The hand-hammered iron coverings on the cement show the expense and effort that went into designing and making the fence. (Photo courtesy of the Ashley Hall Archives.)

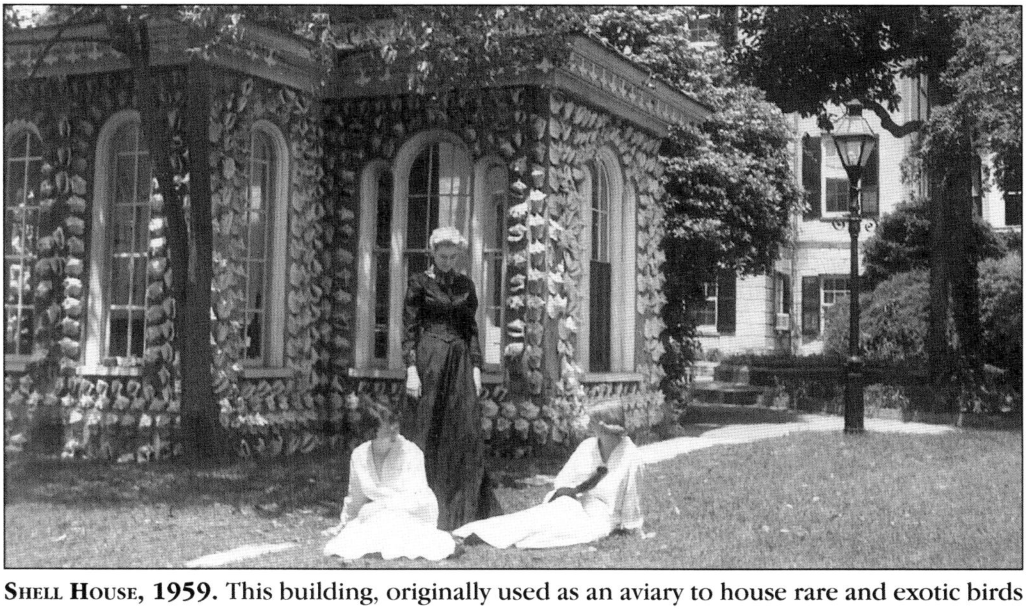

Shell House, 1959. This building, originally used as an aviary to house rare and exotic birds by the Witte family, later became the chemistry lab and then a smoking lounge. It is now the most coveted building of every student at Ashley Hall. Known as the Shell House, this small building has become a lounge for seniors only. It is surrounded by a lawn on which only seniors and faculty members are allowed to walk. If anyone other than a senior is seen on the lawn or in the Shell House without an invitation, she is forced to bake cookies for the seniors and give a sincere apology to the senior class during chapel in front of half of the school. (Photo courtesy of the Ashley Hall Archives.)

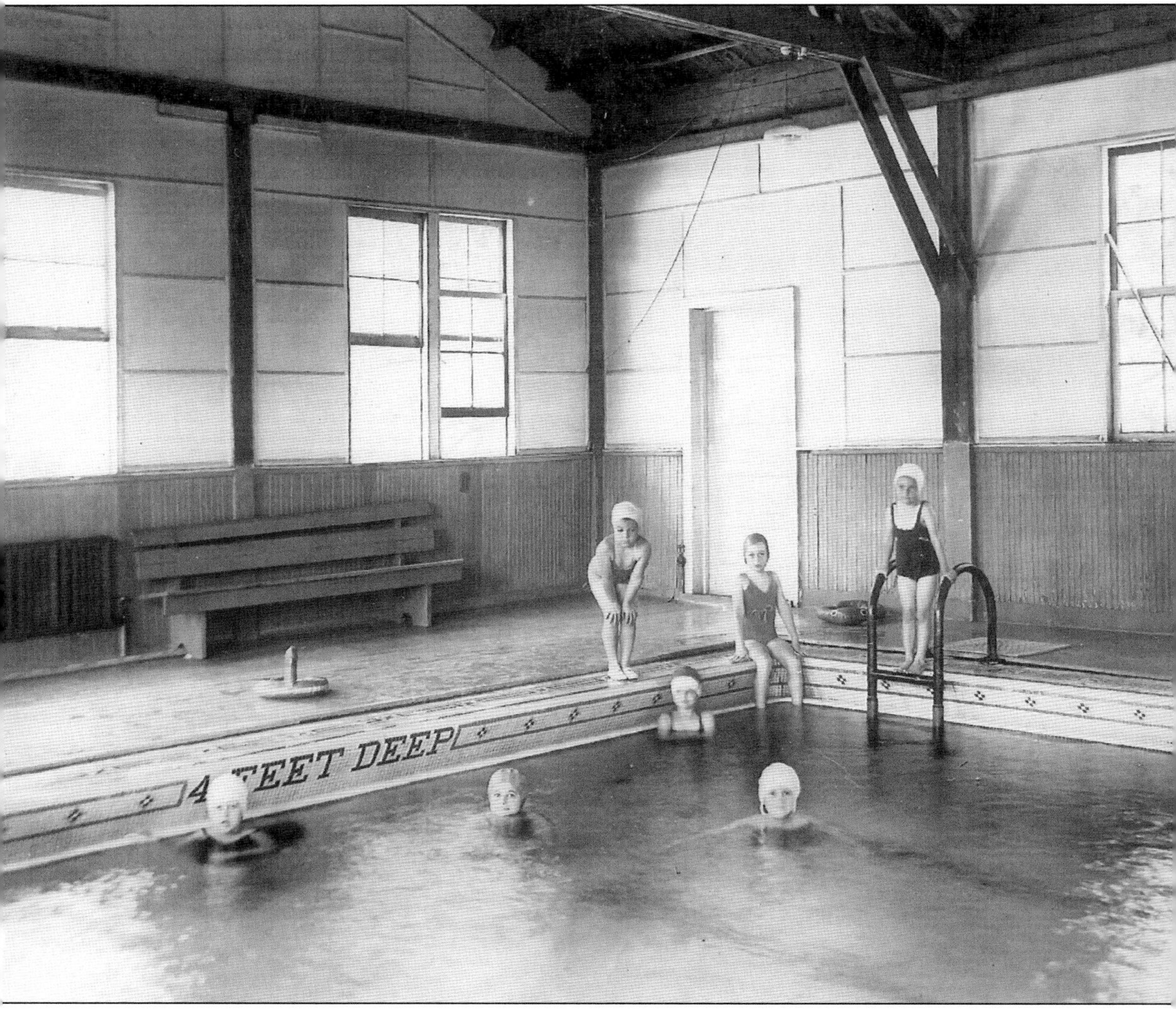

Pool, 1930s. Built in 1918, the Madren Pool was the first school pool to be built in North or South Carolina. The story goes that the Alumnae Association asked Mr. George Williams of Carolina Savings Bank for a loan of $6,000 to build the pool. After much thought he agreed to the loan, and the Alumnae Association raised the money to pay back the bank with house tours, kettledrums, card parties, and dances. (Photo courtesy of the Ashley Hall Archives.)

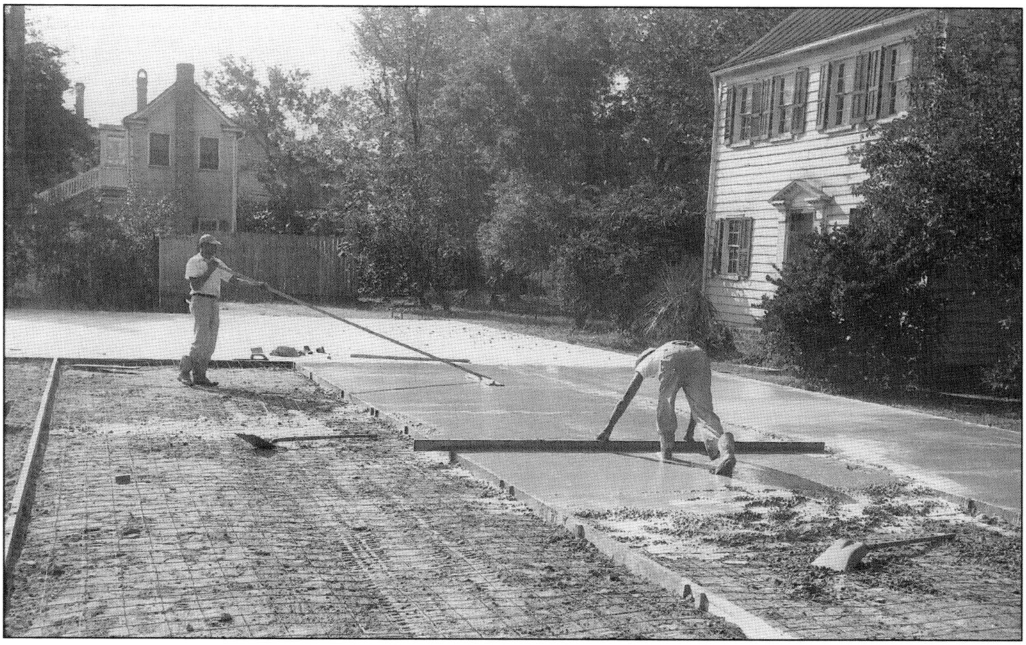

PAVING THE TENNIS COURTS, 1951. Lawn tennis was a sport that was considered suitable for women in 1909 and tennis courts were added to the campus in that year. In 1951, Miss Pardue had the courts paved to keep a consistent surface. (Photo courtesy of the Ashley Hall Archives.)

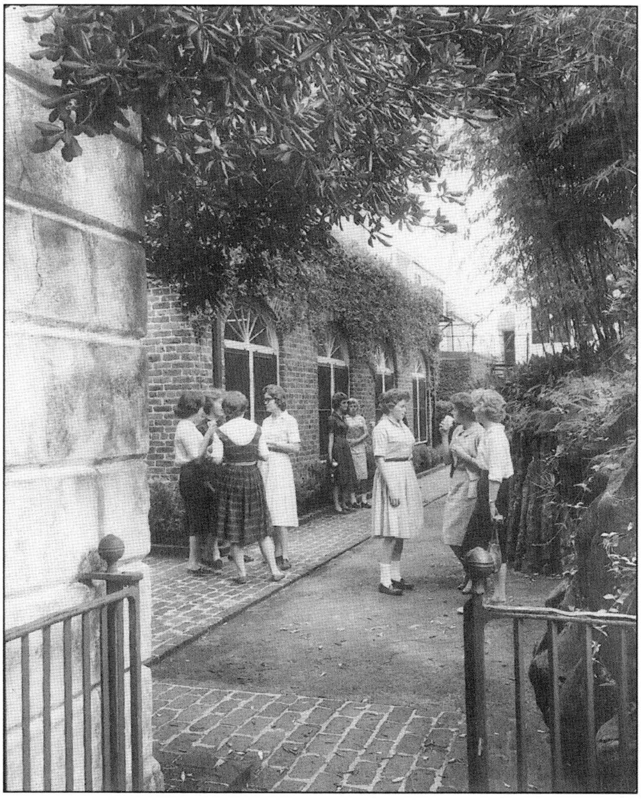

DINING HALL, LATE 1950s. Below the Hubbard room was an area used as an early dining room for the school. In the 1940s, a dining hall was built onto the McBee House with more modern cooking appliances and enough tables to accommodate the growth in the enrolled students. Walk-in refrigerators were added to the kitchen during the years Mr. Piper was headmaster. A joke in the 1931 *Cerberus* reads: "1/c: What kind of soup have we tonight? 4/c: Windmill soup, sir. 1/c: Windmill soup? 4/c: I'll get some if it goes around." (Photo courtesy of the Ashley Hall Archives.)

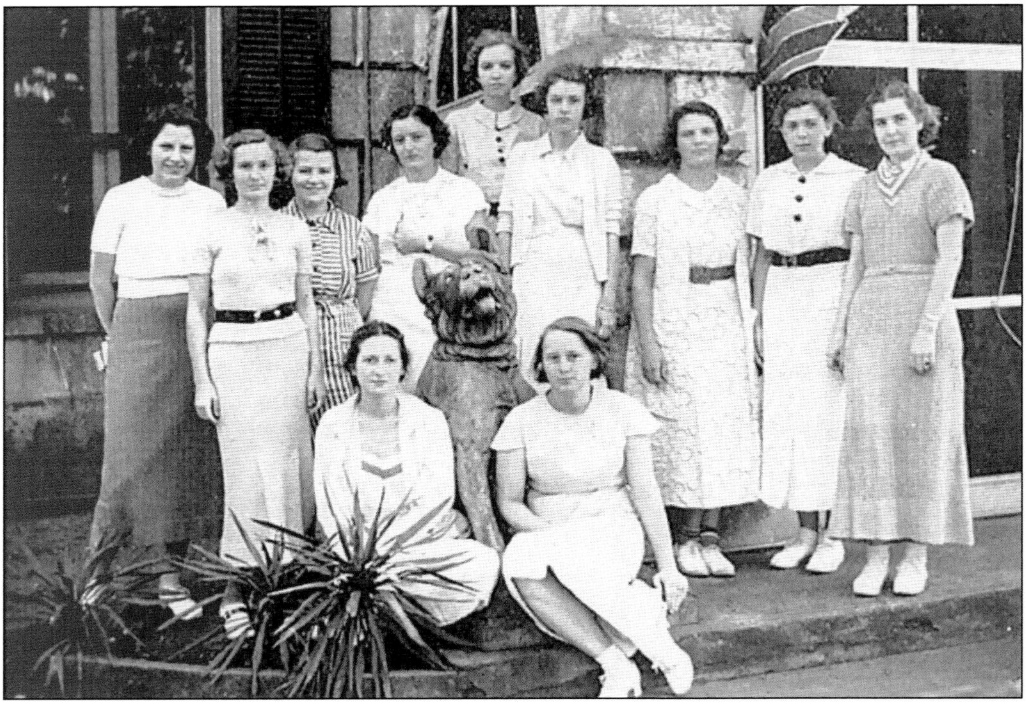

SYMBOL OF *CERBERUS*, 1935. The *Cerberus* Staff poses with one of the bronze Vatican dogs, which used to guard the doors of the McBee House. Sold off at an auction at some point, the dogs are now gone, but the symbolism of these dogs is reminiscent of the Latin and *Cerberus* clubs. Laura Witte Waring writes in her book *The Way It Was in Charleston*, "here and there in the garden were benches, carved seats, an occasional iron table, a painted Indian warrior, a large iron deer, and various smaller bronze and iron animals characteristic of Victorian gardens." (Photo courtesy of the Ashley Hall Archives.)

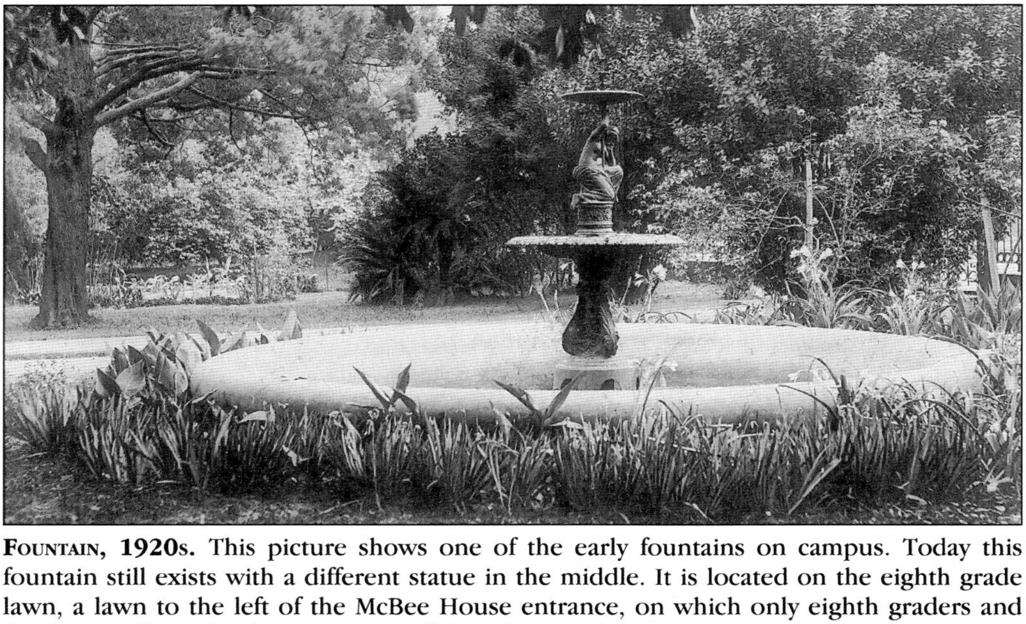

FOUNTAIN, 1920s. This picture shows one of the early fountains on campus. Today this fountain still exists with a different statue in the middle. It is located on the eighth grade lawn, a lawn to the left of the McBee House entrance, on which only eighth graders and faculty are allowed. (Photo courtesy of the Ashley Hall Archives.)

Hirsch Statue, 1950s. This statue, sculpted by well-known Charleston artist Willard Hirsch (1905–1990) was a gift to the school during the days of Miss Pardue and still sits today on the edge of the senior lawn. Every year at Christmas Miss Pardue would add a red ribbon to the statue. The Headmistress award, given annually by the Headmistress to one girl from each class, is a charm of this dancing girl.

Hirsch was the son of a Charleston rabbi. In the 1960s and 1970s Hirsch did a small terra-cotta bust of nearly every child in Charleston. Hundreds of these are still to be found in local houses. (Photo courtesy of the Ashley Hall Archives.)

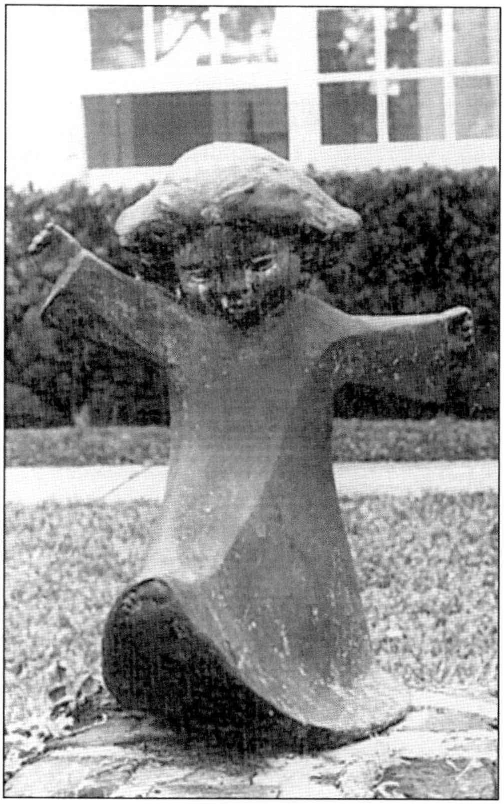

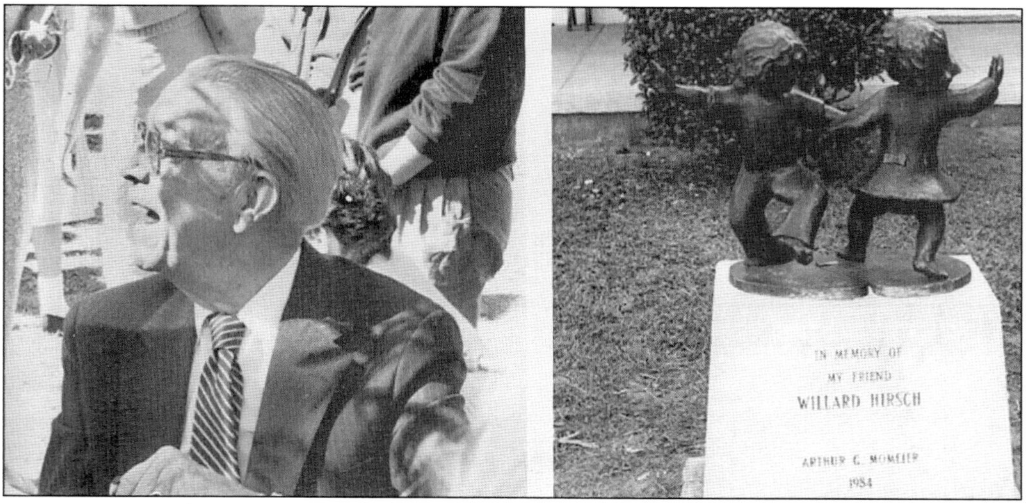

Do Si Do, 1984. Mr. Momeier (pictured above, left) donated the Willard Hirsch statue, above right, called "Do Si Do" in 1984. Both Hirsch's wife, Mordenai Hirsch (née Mordenai Raisin, class of 1934) and daughter, Jane E. Hirsch (class of 1973), attended Ashley Hall. Prominently displayed in the lower school yard, it is a perfect representation of the care-free dancing and playing of younger children. (Photo courtesy of the Ashley Hall Archives.)

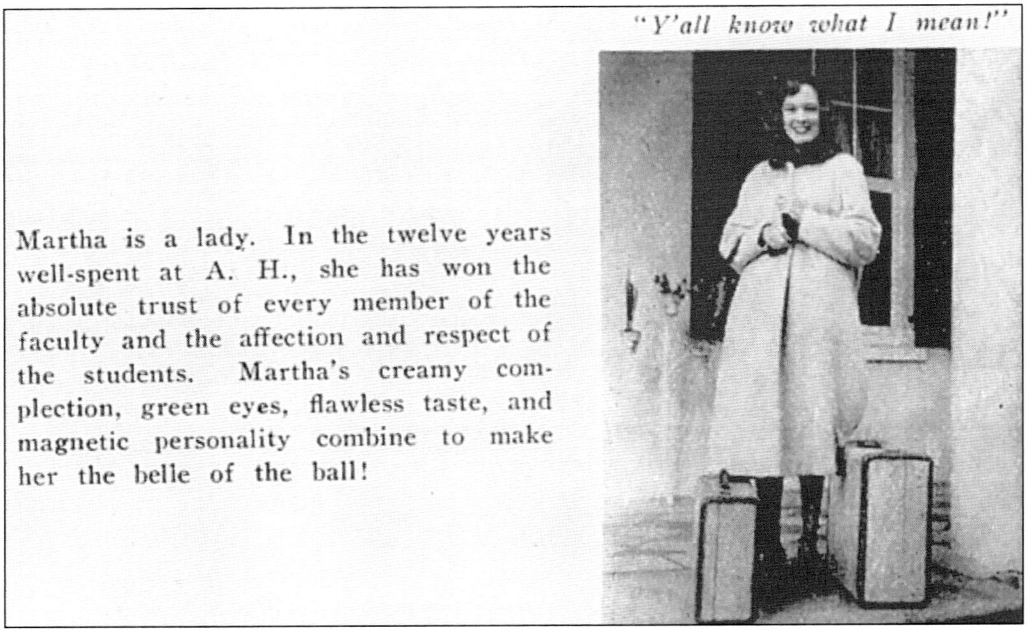
"Y'all know what I mean!"

Martha is a lady. In the twelve years well-spent at A. H., she has won the absolute trust of every member of the faculty and the affection and respect of the students. Martha's creamy complection, green eyes, flawless taste, and magnetic personality combine to make her the belle of the ball!

Martha Rivers Ingram, class of 1953. Attending Ashley Hall from 1941 to 1953, Martha Rivers Ingram is known as a "12-year-girl." She participated actively on campus as a member of the swan club, riding club, and *Le Verre d'Eau*. She went on to become one of the top business women in America. As an active supporter of Ashley Hall, she thought there needed to be a place on campus specifically for the arts. (Photo courtesy of the Ashley Hall Archives.)

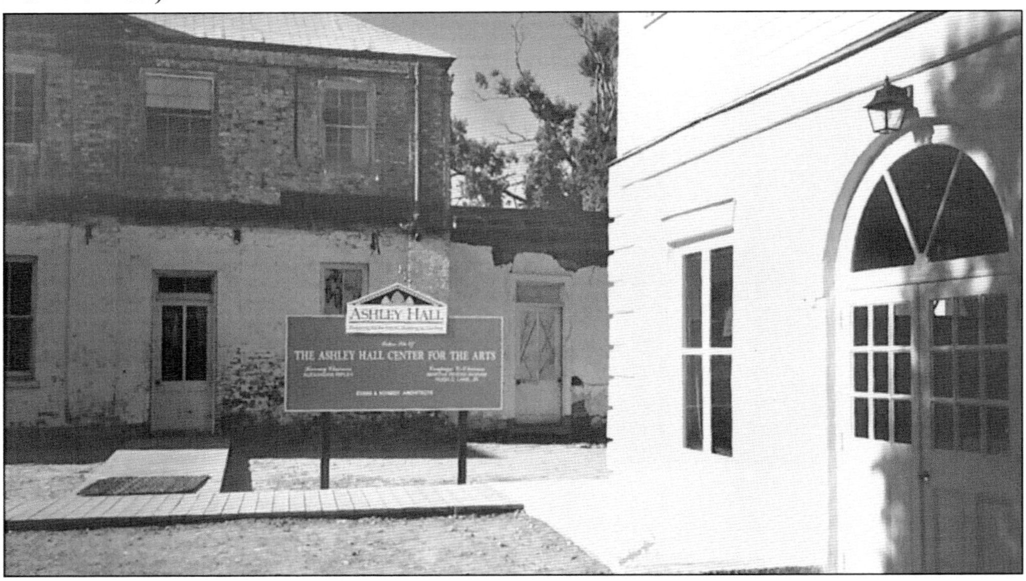

Construction of the Art Center, 1991. The Martha Rivers Ingram Center for the Arts was designed and built specifically for teaching arts for all levels, kindergarten through 12th grade. Through the Capital Campaign, started after Hurricane Hugo in 1990, Martha Ingram and Hugh Lane Jr. co-chaired in raising the funds to build this center. In 1993 it opened with spaces designed for drawing, painting, instrumental and choral instruction, dance, ceramics, and photography. (Photo courtesy of the Ashley Hall Archives.)

Four

Clubs and Organizations

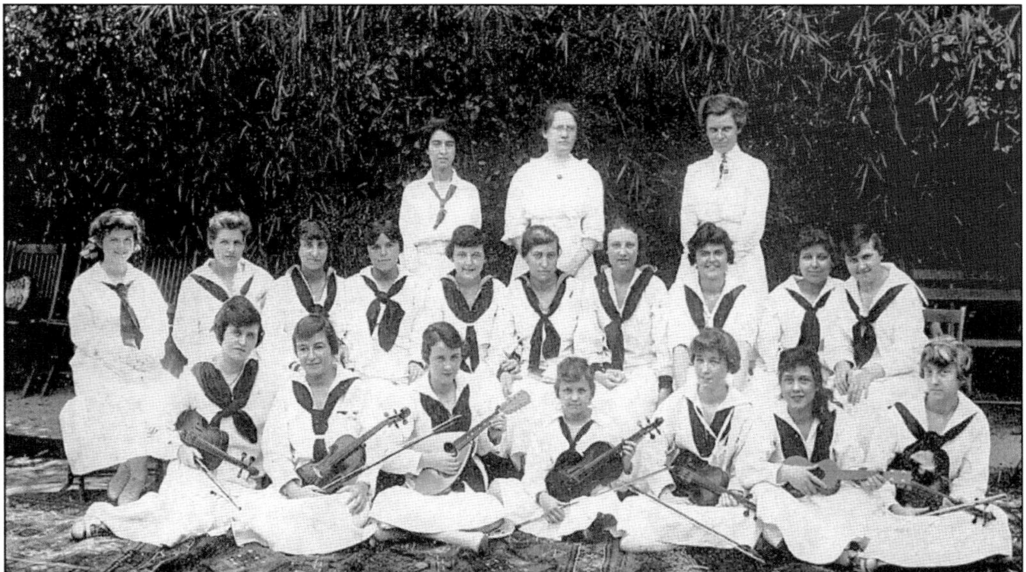

Glee Club Performance of 1916. One of the first official clubs at Ashley Hall, the glee club made its debut performance in 1916 in the old gym (now Burges Auditorium). The girls dressed in Hawaiian costumes and played ukuleles, an instrument that was all the rage. After the program there was dancing for an hour. The small admission price was donated to a free local dental clinic.

"I Ain't Got Nobody" and "La Cucaracha" were popular songs that year. (Photo courtesy of the Ashley Hall Archives.)

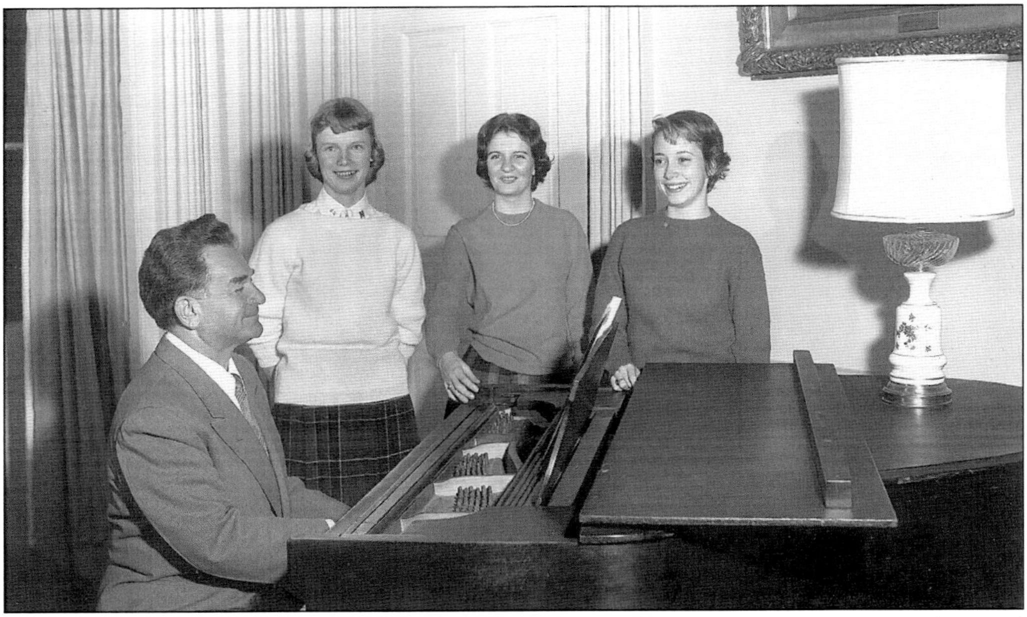

GLEE CLUB OFFICERS, 1959. Sally Barsh, Susanne Riley, and Abigail Booraem are featured here with the choir director, Mr. Fracht. Originally the glee club was a large group of girls who performed an annual spring concert in which they sang fun favorites from musicals. Abigail Van Alyn (née Abigail Booraem, class of 1959) went on to sing in many other choirs including a performance in Carnegie Hall with the Brooklyn College Choral.

The Sound of Music was first produced on Broadway in 1959. *Gigi*, *Irma La Douce*, and the *Flower Drum Song* were huge hits. (Photo courtesy of the Ashley Hall Archives.)

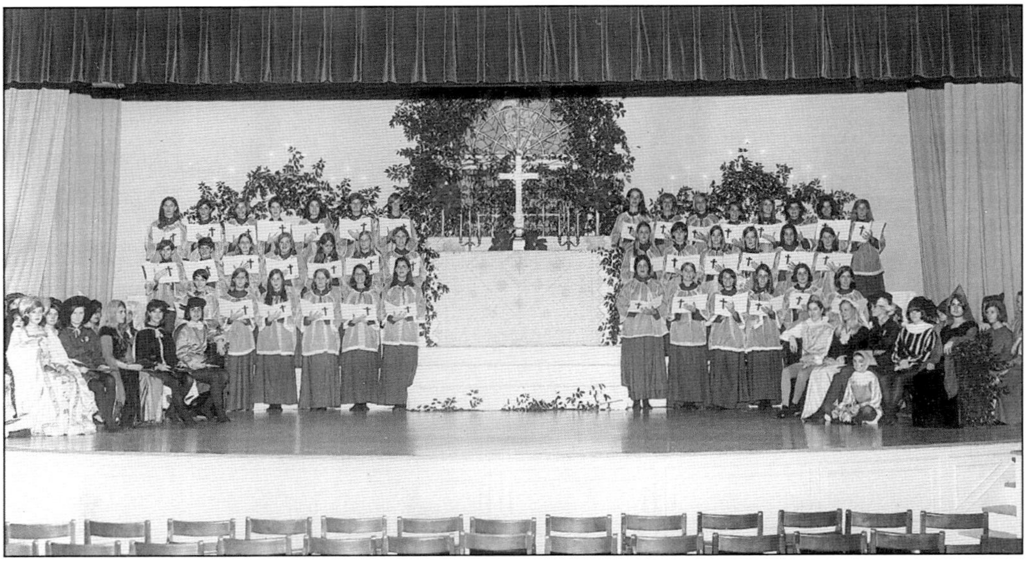

RED CHOIR, 1967. The Red Choir was originally chosen from the glee club to sing in the annual Christmas play. Adorned in red robes and white, waist-length surplices called cottas, the girls stand in the background as singing angels for the entire play. In this photo they are featured performing for the Christmas play in Davies Auditorium. Besides the Christmas play, the choir also gives performances around the world. An annual performance with the Citadel Choral has become another tradition. (Photo courtesy of the Ashley Hall Archives.)

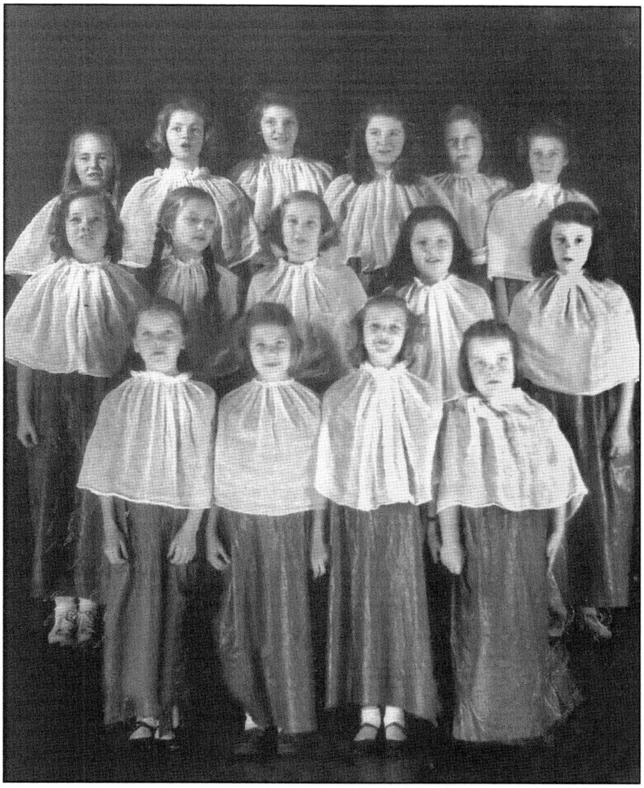

Lower School Choir, 1940s. One can plainly tell that these young girls are not of proper age to be members of the Red Choir; however, they are still dressed in the same fashion with red robes and white cottas. Although they do not dress like this anymore, there are lower and middle school choirs today that give school performances and participate in the Christmas play. A school brochure of that time states that grades five through eight had a glee club that practiced once a week. (Photo courtesy of the Ashley Hall Archives.)

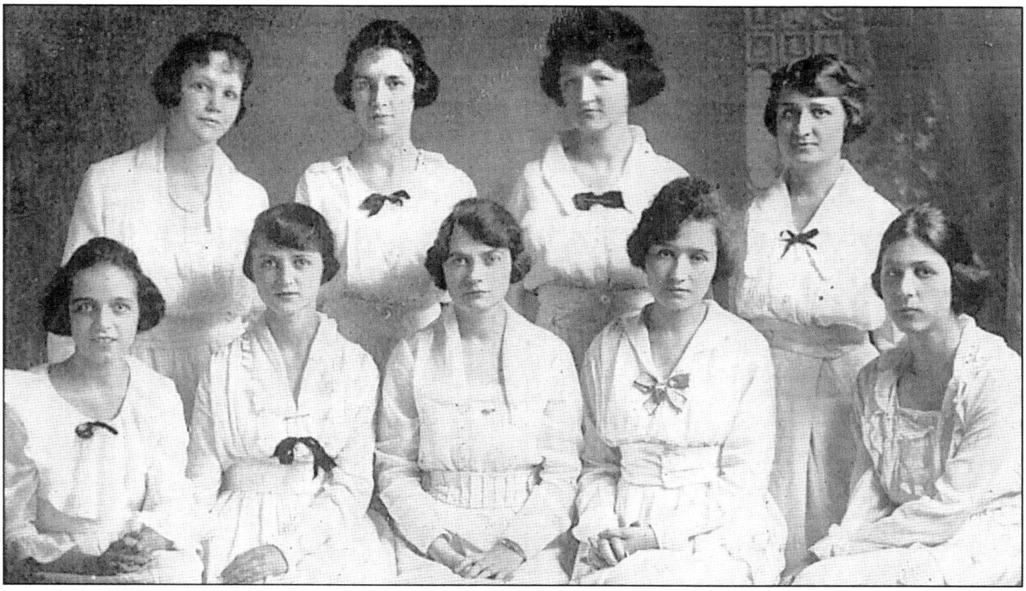

Magazine Staff, 1919. The magazine name *Cerberus* was derived from "a small brown bunting dog with shoe button eyes and an engaging expression brought to school by some now forgotten boarder . . . it is an esteem in which this bit of bunting was held that the magazine was named for it," (Josephine Pinckney, *Call Back Yesterday*). Miss Augusta Dunbar, a teacher in the lower school, also acted as the advisor to the club and was one of the most beloved mentors of the older girls. (Photo courtesy of the Ashley Hall Archives.)

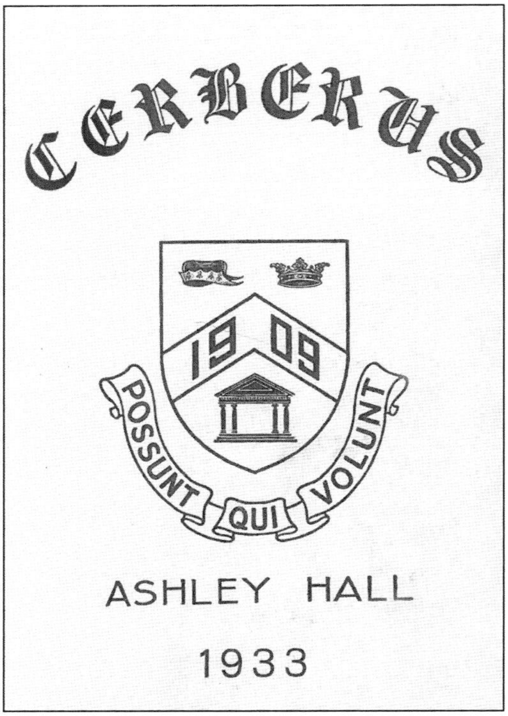

CERBERUS, **1933.** Founded in 1912 by Anne Guerry, Elsa Woolsey, and Josephine Pinckney, *Cerberus* is one of the school's oldest organizations. The girls were nervous about the first issue, but Josephine Pinckney writes in *Call Back Yesterday*, "when Herbert Ravenel Sass gave it a serious and not unfavorable review in the *News and Courier*, the skeptics were impressed, and from then on it grew in prestige." The publication served as a record of the year's events and also as an annual to the girls when technology made printing pictures easy. The publication is packed with short stories, poems, and songs written by budding young writers of the school. The school seal is featured on this particular cover with the school motto on the bottom, "*possunt qui volunt*," meaning, those who want to can. (Photo courtesy of the Ashley Hall Archives.)

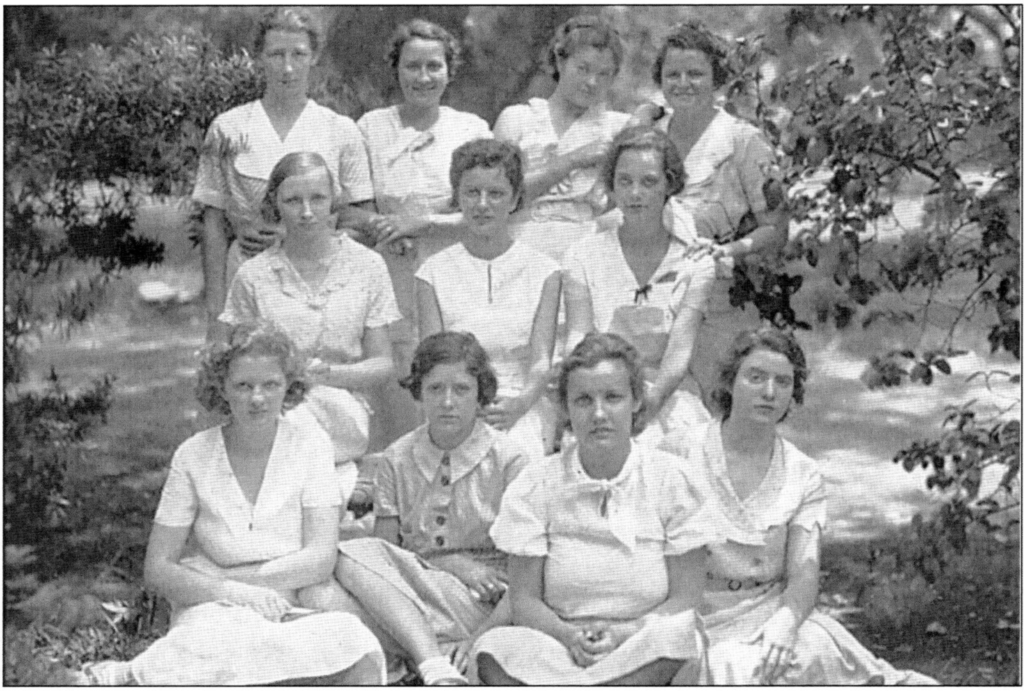

CERBERUS STAFF, **1933.** *Cerberus* of 1933 was edited by Elinor Rittenburg. While at Ashley Hall, she was written up in the *Post and Courier* for winning an essay contest in which the first place prize was a trip to the Bahamas Islands. She went on to gain recognition as the first female editor of the College of Charleston's annual, the *Comet*. (Photo courtesy of the Ashley Hall Archives.)

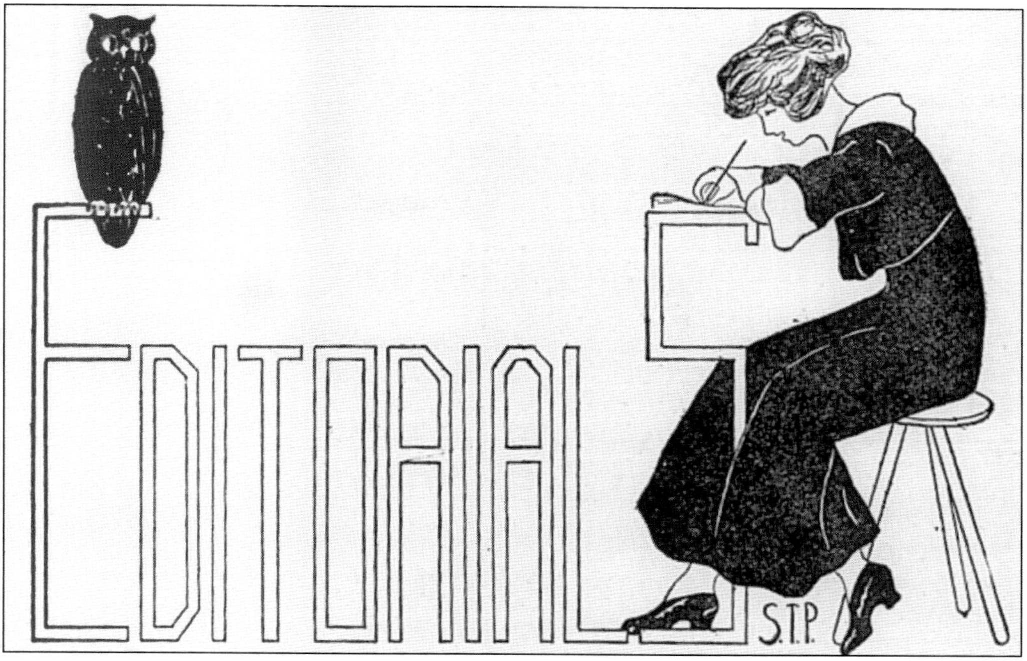

***Cerberus*, 1913.** This issue of *Cerberus* is filled with descriptions of a ball with a Dutch theme held at the school and essays debating both sides of women's suffrage. A letter from the editor states, "We are particularly glad to announce the addition of the lower school department, and want to thank the smaller girls who have shown great interest in making it possible." It goes on to say, "And now girls *remember*, first—that the magazine belongs to the whole school; second—that it can not exist without your co-operation; and third—that you must all get to work and write for it—poems, stories, articles, legends—surely you can manage one of these four." (Photo courtesy of the Ashley Hall Archive.)

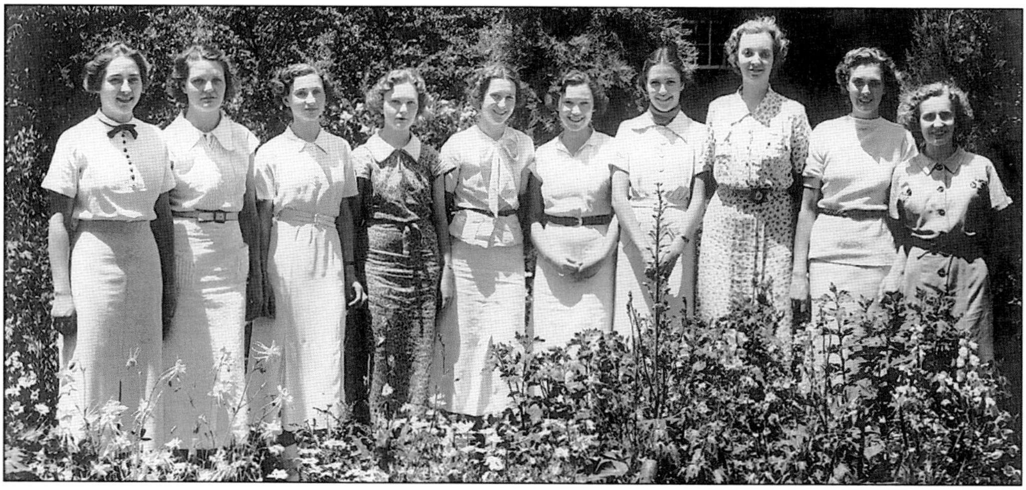

***Cerberus* Staff, 1936.** Any girls' school can be expected to produce writers, and Ashley Hall has a pantheon. Madeleine L. Camp is the tall girl third, from the right. Under the pen name Madeleine L'Engle she published the never-out-of-print novel *A Wrinkle in Time*. Other distinguished authors to graduate from the school are Josephine Pinckney (*Three O'clock Dinner*), Alexandra Ripley (*Scarlett*), and Josephine Humphreys (*Rich in Love*). (Photo courtesy of the Ashley Hall Archives.)

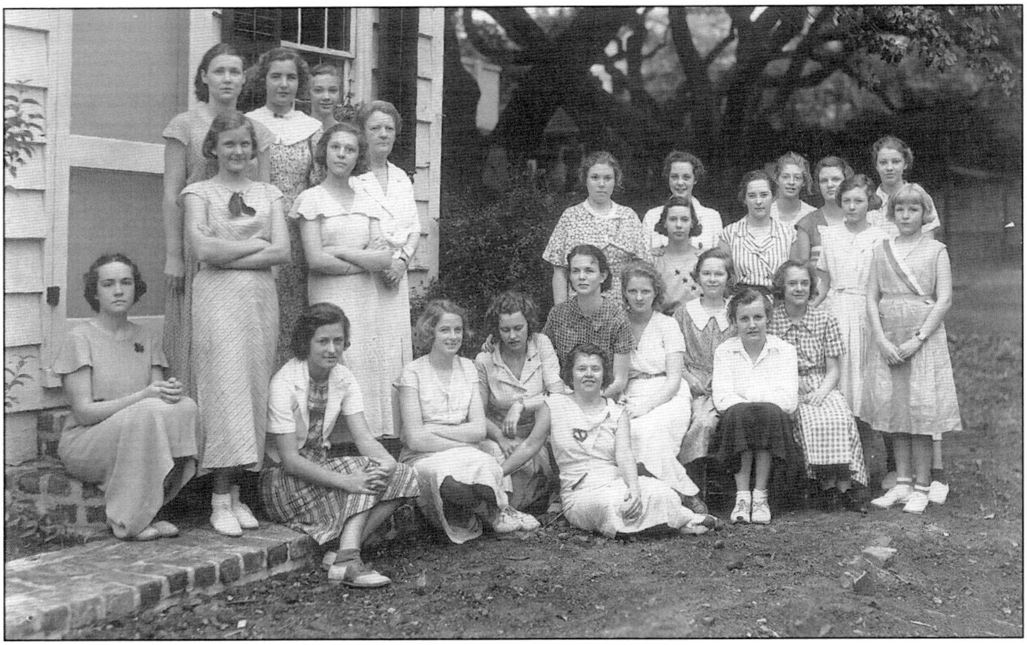

Dramatic Club, 1934. Also another one of the major clubs on campus, the drama club kept very busy with the many plays put on throughout the year. Here the club (note Miss McBee on right side of stairs) is pictured in front of their clubhouse, which is no longer in existence. The girls would store costumes and sets in here, as well as read and rehearse lines for performances. (Photo courtesy of the Ashley Hall Archives.)

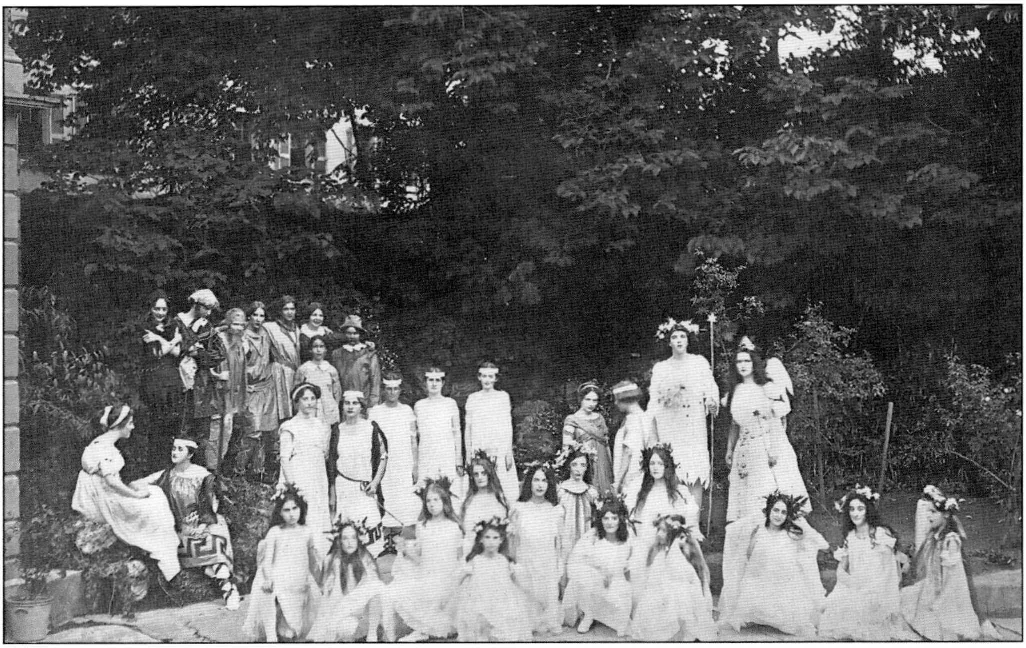

***A Midsummer Night's Dream*, 1910.** This was the first play ever staged at Ashley Hall that would follow with a long tradition of Shakespearean performances. Given at the end of the first year of school, *A Midsummer Night's Dream* was a school-wide performance in which everyone participated. (Photo courtesy of the Ashley Hall Archives.)

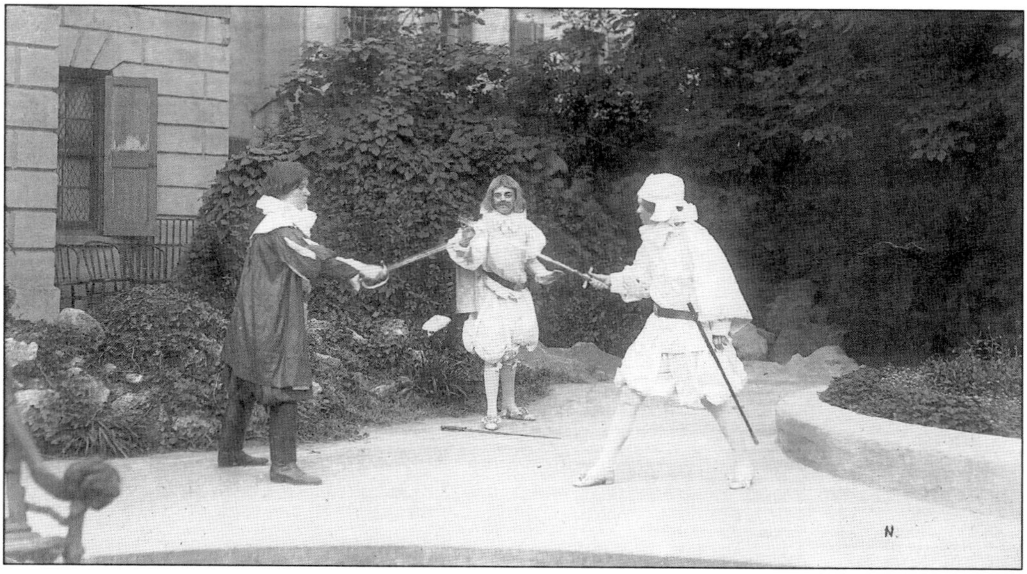

Shakespeare, 1910s. "The Shakespearean plays were important to everyone even if you were not an actor," explains Josephine Hutcheson (née Josephine Humphreys, class of 1963). Girls helped out behind the scenes making sets, costumes, and sound effects. Sometimes the choir sang and there was always a girl willing to take over if someone was sick. "I was always a stage hand, but I think my one speaking part was when a girl got sick and could not perform," Hutcheson recalls, laughing. (Photo courtesy of the Ashley Hall Archives.)

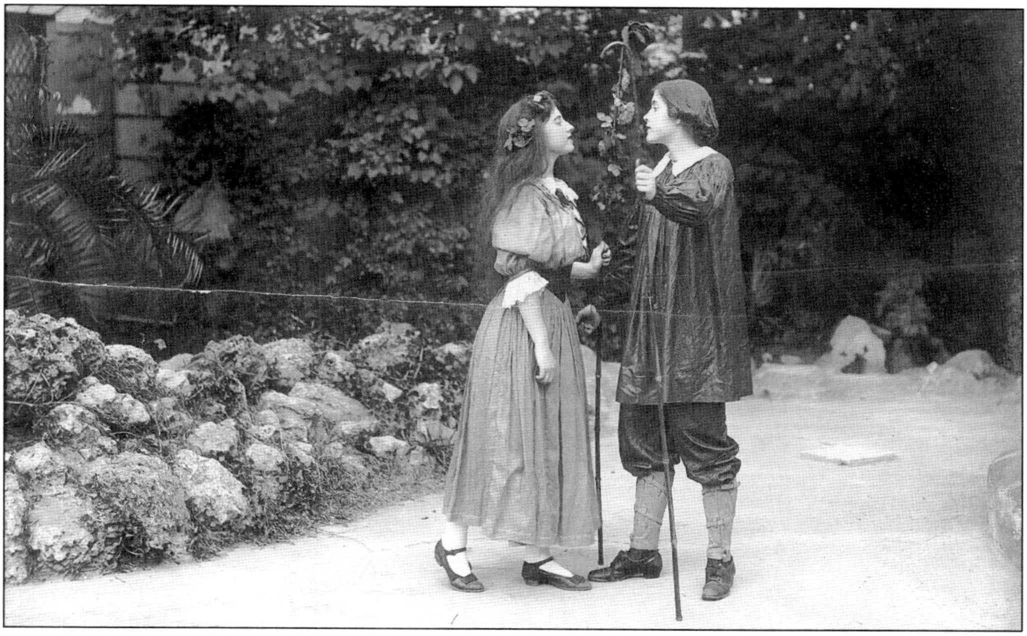

***Romeo and Juliet*, 1920s.** A timeless classic, *Romeo and Juliet* is shown here performed to the right side of the McBee House where graduation exercises were originally held. Plays were performed in this spot until the audiences grew and the location was changed to the grotto. When Davies Auditorium was built, the girls took advantage of the lighting and sound equipment by performing there. (Photo courtesy of the Ashley Hall Archives.)

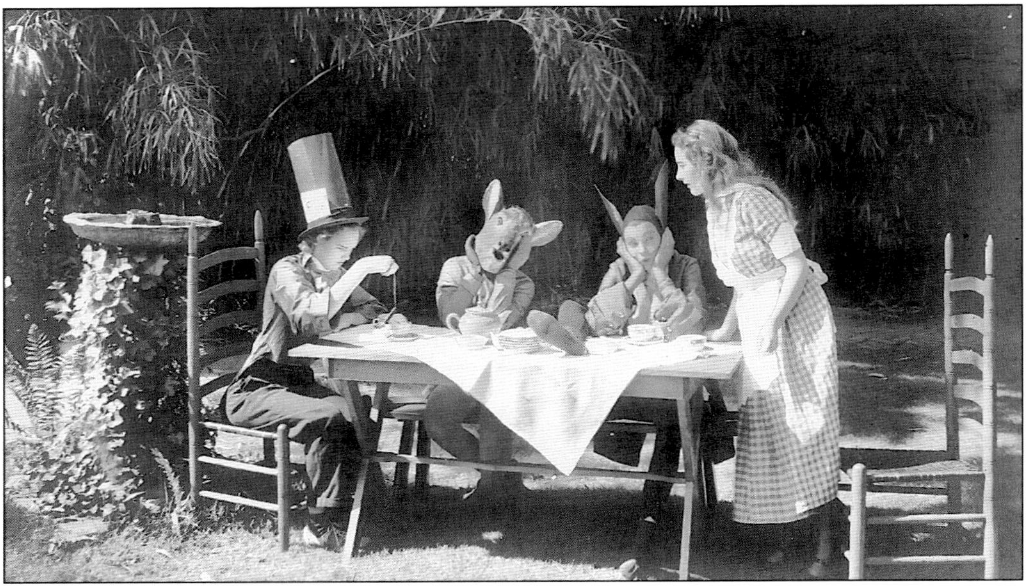

***Alice in Wonderland*, 1930s.** Ann Meredith (née Ann Stakely, class of 1949) remembers the drama club with fond enthusiasm: "As members of the club we were also given the opportunity to volunteer at the Dockstreet Theater, helping to make the sets and other odds and ends." When Mr. Piper was the Headmaster of the school, Ashley Hall collaborated with the staff of Dockstreet Theater to improve the dramatic program. Ashley Hall girls could attend classes twice a week, as an elective for juniors and seniors, to obtain an introduction into drama, as well as experience in stagecraft. Stage techniques and acting were just some of the "many services that the theater hopes to render to community activities this year," said George Hamlin, the managing director of Dockstreet Theater, Inc. during the late 1940s. (Photo courtesy of the Ashley Hall Archives.)

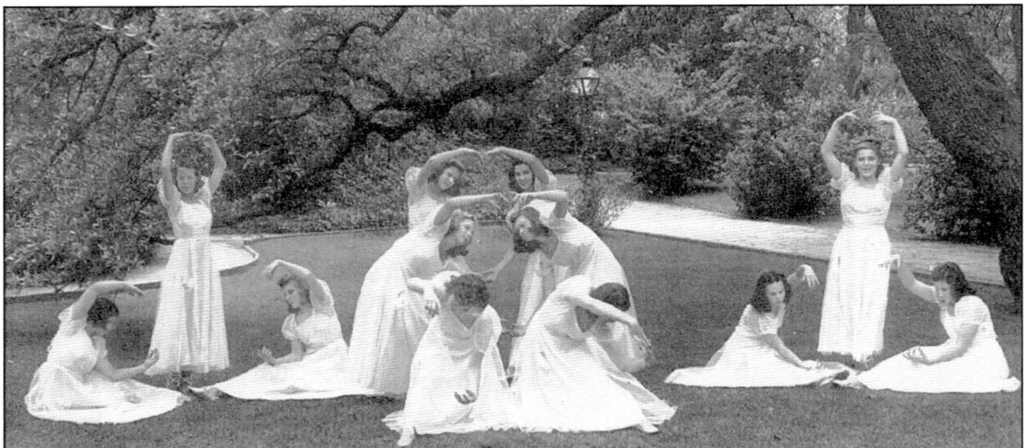

Dance Group, 1939. Girls and dance have always gone hand in hand, so it seems only fitting that there would be a dance group on campus. Mary-Louise Rhodes (née Mary-Louise Strong, class of 1941), shown in the photo above, was the chairman of the dance group from 1939 to 1941. She explains they had performances of ballet and interpretive modern dance in front of the school a few times a year. Today a dance team was recently started again where the girls practice and perform more modern dances for the school at the end of the year. (Photo courtesy of the Ashley Hall Archives.)

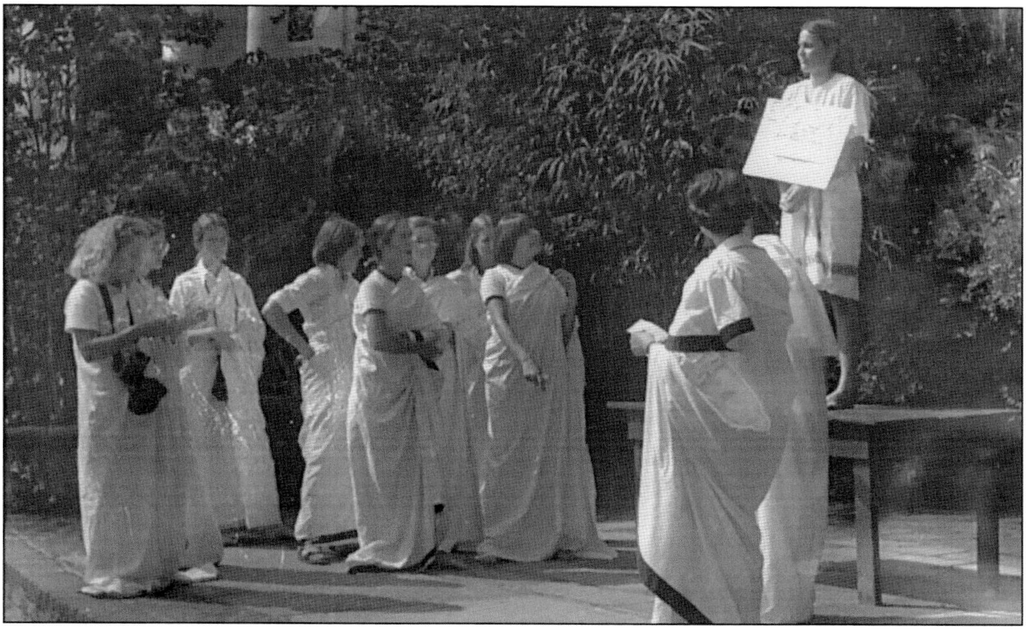

SLAVE AUCTION, 1970s. Proud to be the second oldest club founded, the Latin club, known as SPQR, is still one of the most popular. Second year Latin students who were continuing on for a third year were allowed to become members if they went through the proper initiation rituals. Featured in this photo is the annual slave auction, in which the underclass candidates act as slaves to the members of the club for one week. The entire school goes to watch as the younger girls are auctioned off and then made to push eggs with their noses and step on grapes. (Photo courtesy of the Ashley Hall Archives.)

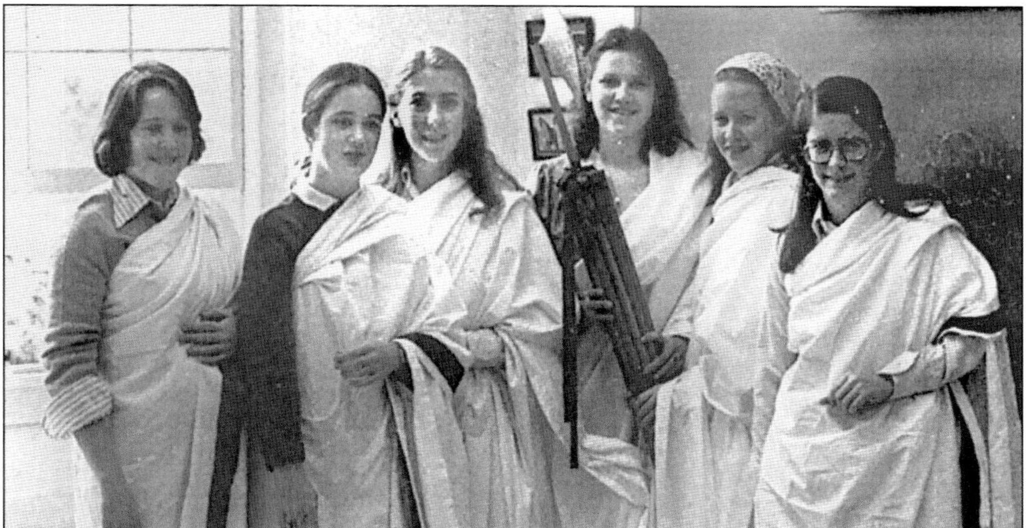

SPQR (SENATUS POPULUSQUE ROMANUS—THE SENATE AND THE ROMAN PEOPLE), 1978. The auctioning and initiation is all done in jest, and the initiates are rewarded with a banquet in the spring. Ann Burger (née Anne Mitchell, class of 1980), a well-known local columnist for the *Post and Courier* recalls the banquet as being authentically Roman. They went to the old auditorium (Burges) where they lounged on floor cushions as they feasted and relaxed after an exhausting initiation week. (Photo courtesy of the Ashley Hall Archives.)

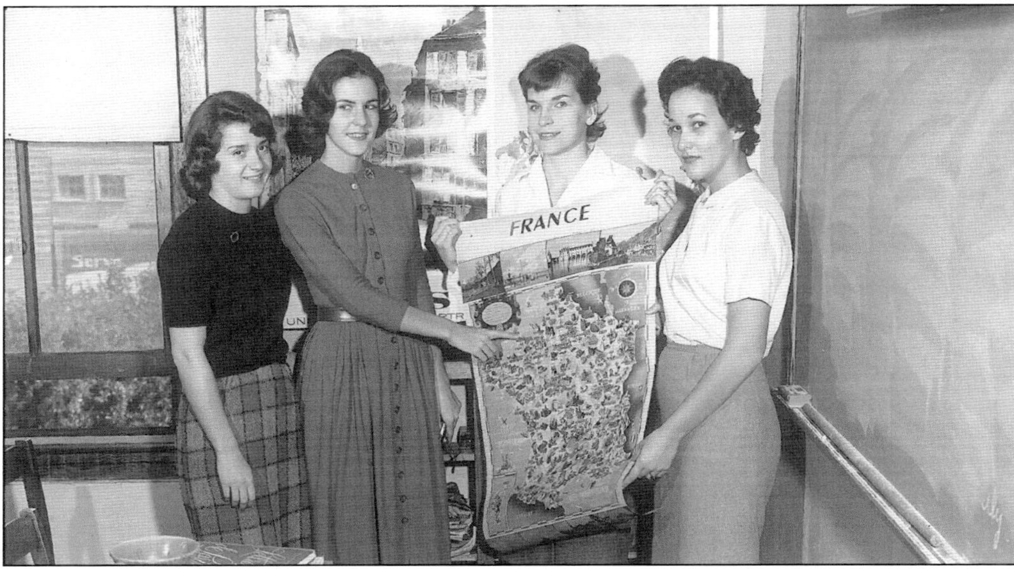

French Club Officers, 1960. Although it does not have as many old traditions and secret events, another popular club still in existence on campus is the French club. It meets weekly and has discussions in French, giving the girls a chance to hone their skills. Also, to exist as a club, they must participate in a philanthropic event. Every night at supper, Miss McBee would have the girls say the Lord's Prayer in French. Girls taking French had to sit at a French table and could only speak that language during the meal. (Photo courtesy of the Ashley Hall Archives.)

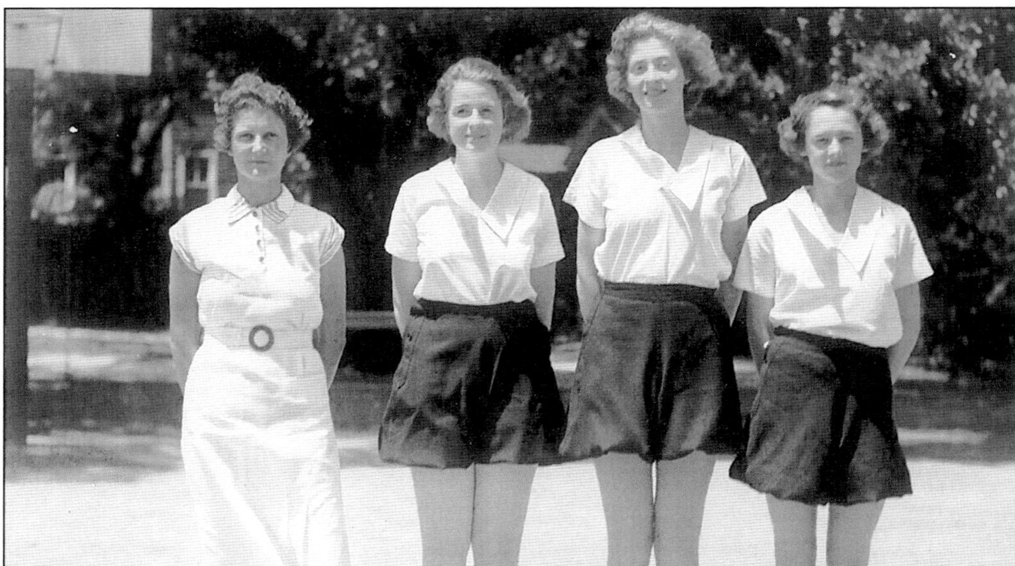

Athletic Association Officers, 1936. The AA (Athletic Association) Board is made up of the athletes of the school. Their job is to promote school spirit for all events, academic and athletic. The AA Board consists of officers as well as team captains and co-captains of the Purple and White teams. The 1933 *Cerberus* talks about a walking club, life-saving course, and ping-pong tournament, all events encouraged and supported by the Athletic Association. (Photo courtesy of the Ashley Hall Archives.)

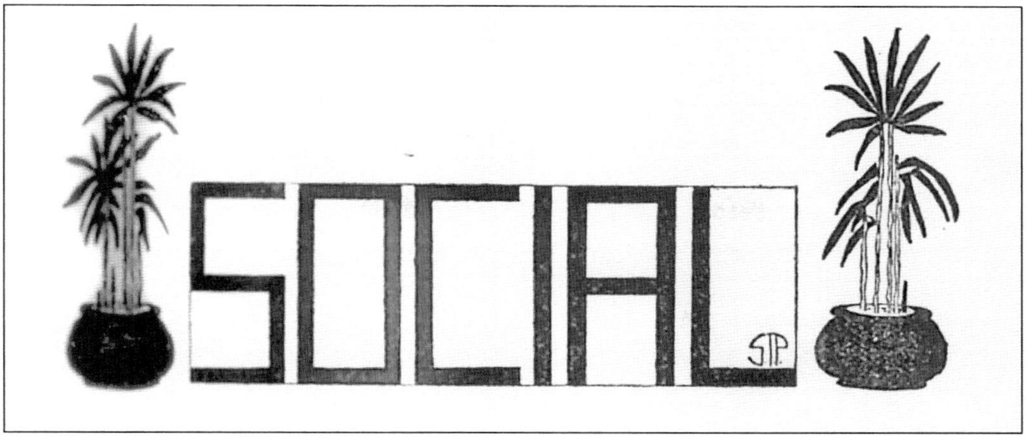

Cerberus, **1916.** One of the most important clubs for a girls' campus is the organization that plans the major social events. Angie LeClercq (née Anne Whaley, class of 1960) recalls a story her mother used to tell about her first year at Ashley Hall. Mrs. Emily Whaley (née Emily Fishburne, class of 1928) was only 11 when she became a boarder at Ashley Hall and was too young to attend the dance that year. She recalls sitting on her bed calmly reading, when Miss McBee flung open the door and began to search frantically the closets, drawers, and under beds. A Citadel cadet had left the dance and was loose somewhere in the dormitory. Later Angie's father, a Citadel man, recalls the young cadet had broken his ankle and was in the infirmary because he had jumped off the second floor balcony of the Main Building to escape the wrath of Miss McBee. (Photo courtesy of the Ashley Hall Archives.)

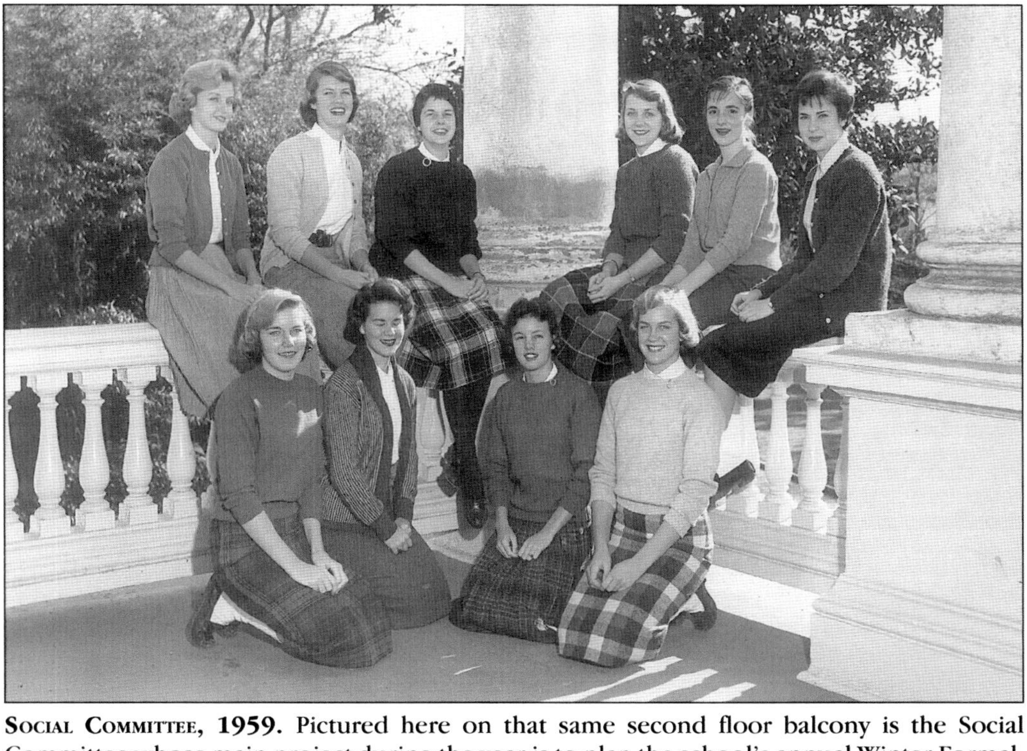

Social Committee, 1959. Pictured here on that same second floor balcony is the Social Committee whose main project during the year is to plan the school's annual Winter Formal. Teen heart-throb Paul Anka had two hit songs that year, "I'm Just a Lonely Boy" and "Put Your Head On My Shoulder." (Photo courtesy of the Ashley Hall Archives.)

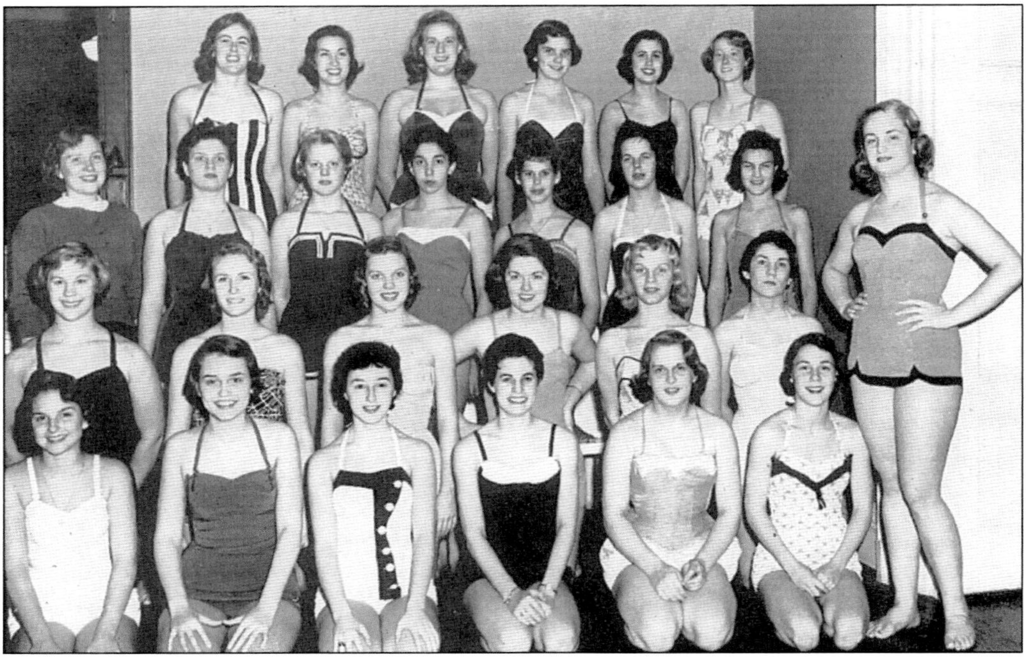

SWAN CLUB, 1956. The girls of Ashley Hall formed a water ballet team, another advantage of having a school pool. Angie LeClercq remembers performing to music with six girls who all made circles, did leg maneuvers on their backs, and other acrobatics simultaneously. Angie says, "We all fancied ourselves to be Esther Williams." (Photo courtesy of the Ashley Hall Archives.)

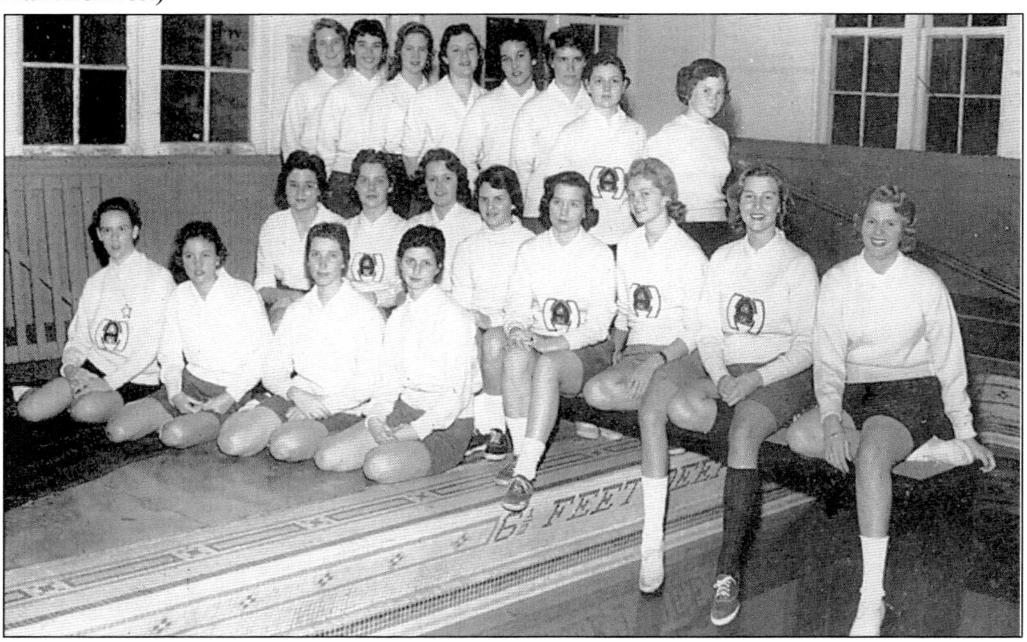

CYGNETS, 1959. The Cygnets or baby swans was a spin-off of the popularity of the Swan club. Younger girls could join the Cygnets and practice hard in hopes of one day being a Swan. As part of the more recent Kettledrum events, the Cygnets and Swans would perform a water ballet for an audience. (Photo courtesy of the Ashley Hall Archives.)

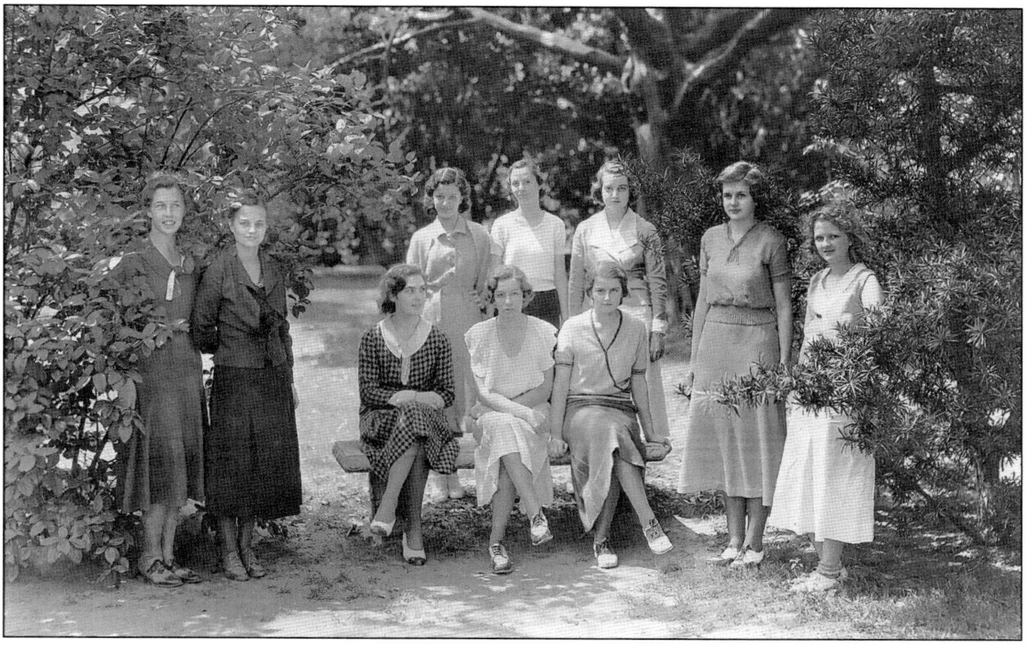

STUDENT GOVERNMENT, 1952. The student government, founded in 1915, has always played a key role in keeping good relations among the students and faculty. As Ashley Hall grew in size, it became necessary for the girls to feel their ideas and opinions were being presented to the faculty and administration. Understanding democracy has always been a key component of the curriculum. (Photo courtesy of the Ashley Hall Archives.)

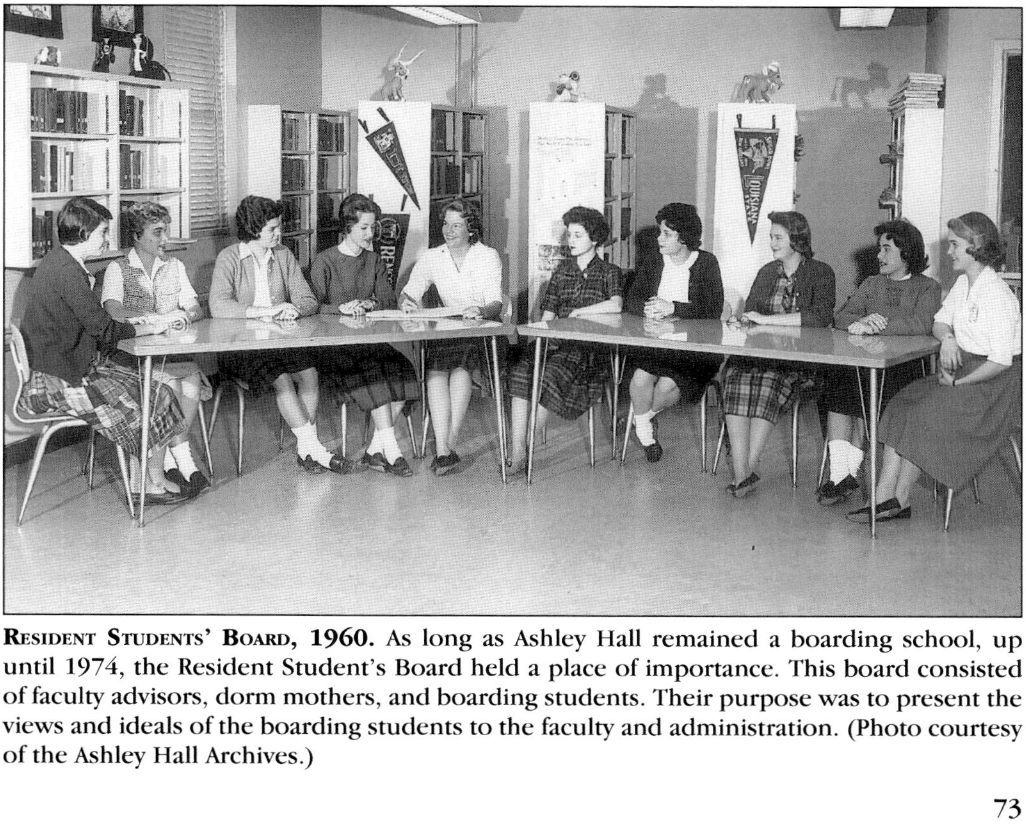

RESIDENT STUDENTS' BOARD, 1960. As long as Ashley Hall remained a boarding school, up until 1974, the Resident Student's Board held a place of importance. This board consisted of faculty advisors, dorm mothers, and boarding students. Their purpose was to present the views and ideals of the boarding students to the faculty and administration. (Photo courtesy of the Ashley Hall Archives.)

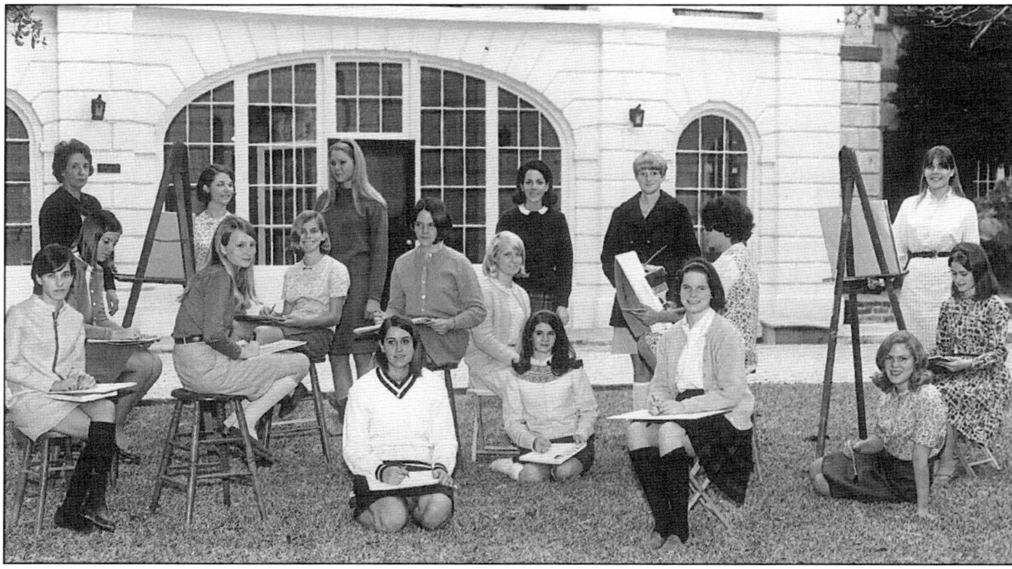

Art Club, 1968. Art has always been a strong program at Ashley Hall and the art club was formed for the many girls who shared that love. Standing in the background to the right is Edith May Smith, affectionately known as E. de May Smith, a long time art teacher and mentor to many of the girls pursuing art careers. (Photo courtesy of the Ashley Hall Archives.)

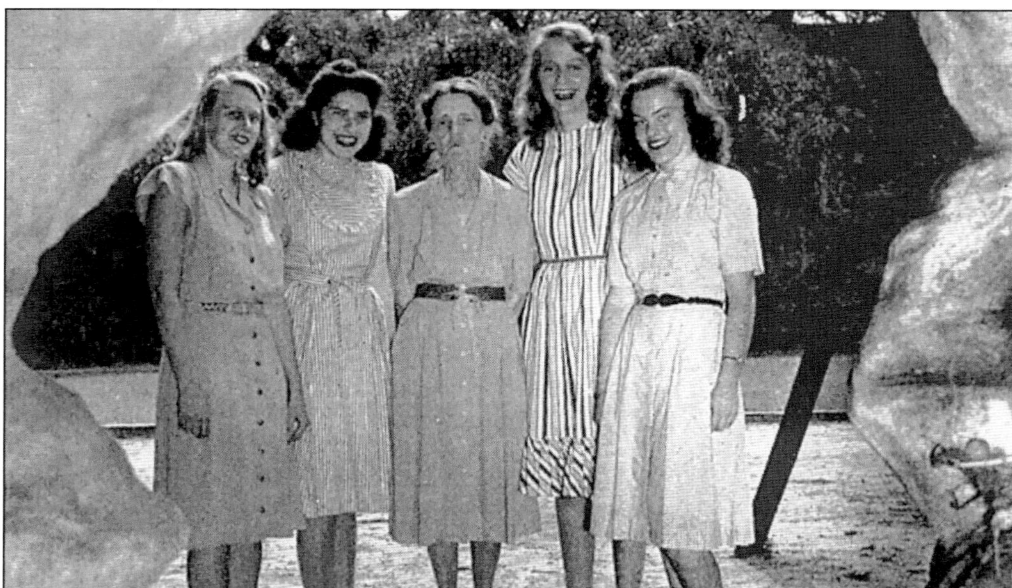

***Le Verre d'Eau*, 1946.** Founded in 1912 by Anne Guerry, *Le Verre D'Eau* was a purely philanthropic organization that quickly became popular. Their first cause was to dress dolls for under-privileged children for Miss McBee's Christmas tree. Other charitable causes included supporting an Assyrian orphan, building a Free Kindergarten on Upper King Street that was later given to the city, and starting the first dental clinic in Charleston that the girls equipped with supplies for several years. While Miss Baker was the advisor, the girls organized a small library in the children's ward of Roper Hospital and made clothes for the Red Cross and Star Gospel Mission. (Photo courtesy of the Ashley Hall Archives.)

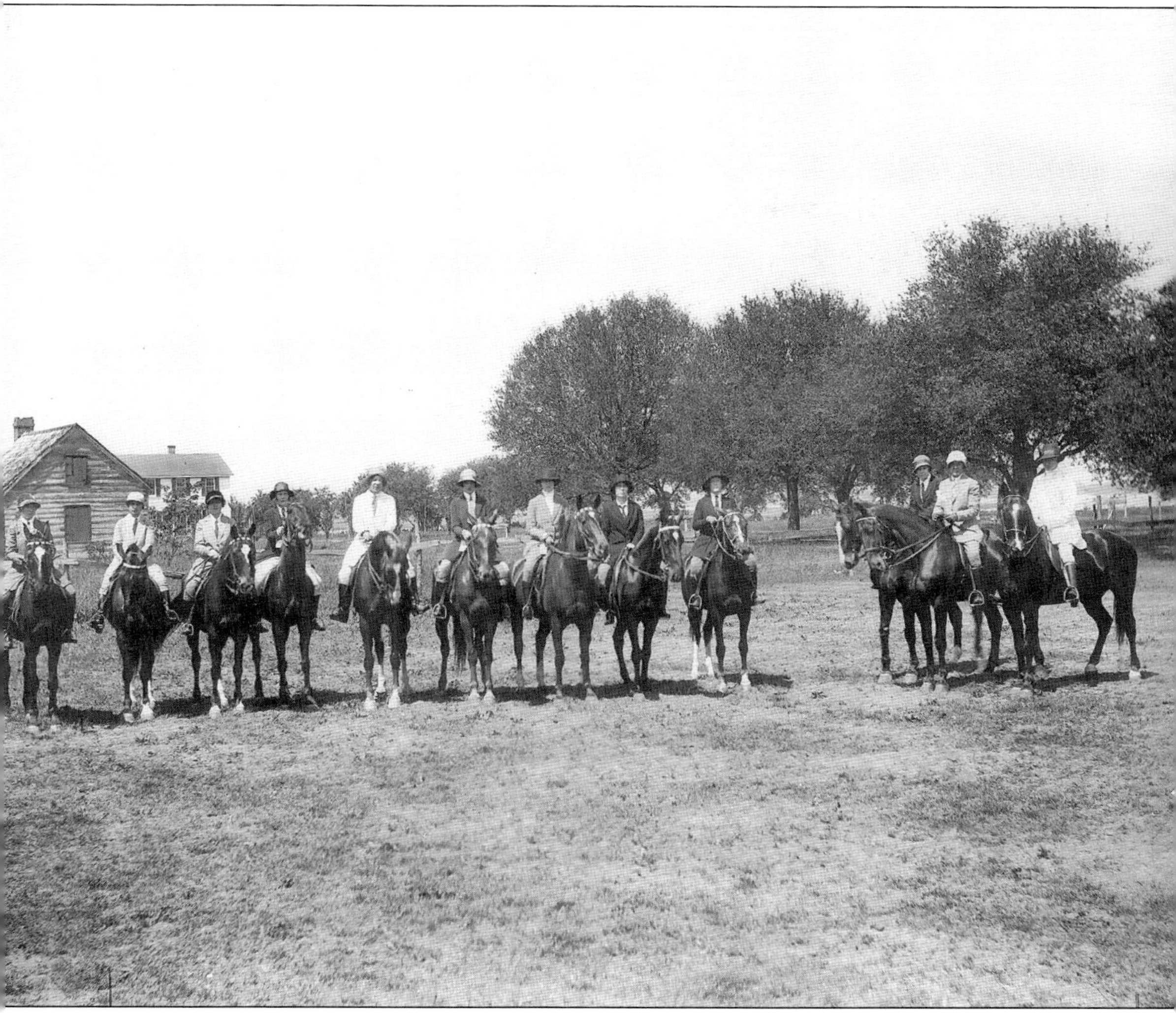

Saddle Up, 1920s. This photo taken in Miss McBee's time shows the early popularity of the riding club, which continues today with the tradition of the annual horse show. Each year girls of all ages compete for the cup in dressage, jumping, and other horse show events. At the time of this photo, the rivers were still lined with the great plantations providing a wonderful rural landscape. Moonlight rides and cookouts also made the club popular. The 1933 *Cerberus* reports that the riding club hosted a weenie roast for the boarding students and also rode in a fox hunt on which "much to the relief of many, no fox was captured." (Photo courtesy of the Ashley Hall Archives.

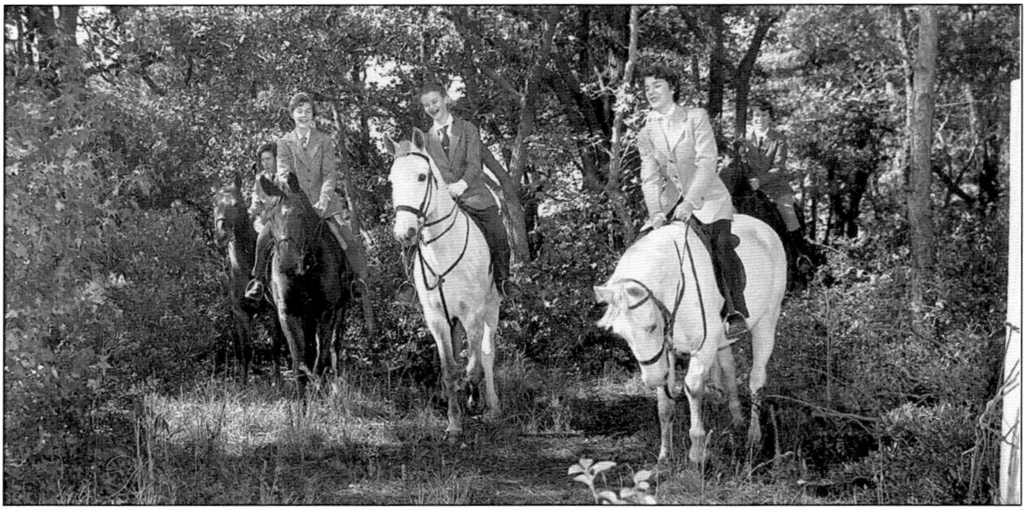

Afternoon Ride, 1957. Rosalie Smithy and Ann Gibbes are pictured here on an afternoon trail ride at one of the local Charleston farms. The first subdivisions were being built, but the rural landscape was still quite close and the sea islands were entirely agricultural. Many Ashley Hall girls kept their own horses at the local stables. A 1933 *Cerberus* joke follows:
Crew coach: 'Say, mister, have you ever rowed before?'
Plebe: 'You mean ridden, don't you sir?' (Photo courtesy of the Ashley Hall Archives.)

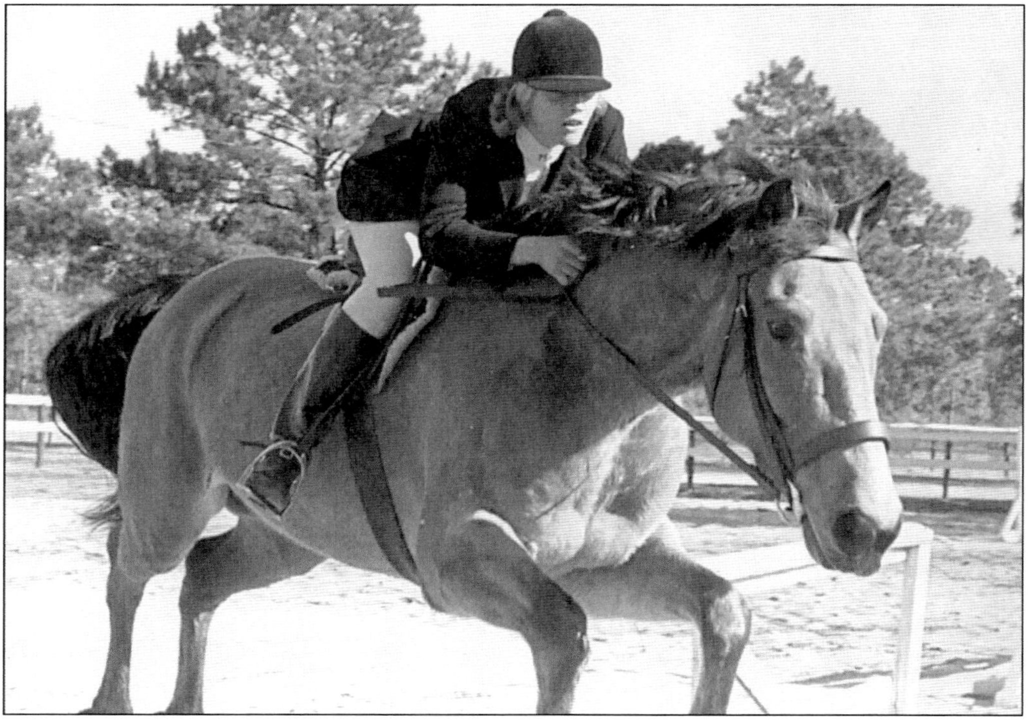

Jumping, 1971. Barbara Blount takes a leap with her horse. Mrs. Ruus was the first riding club instructor and she would take the girls to the St. Andrews Riding Academy to participate in fox-hunting and cross-country riding. Besides the Ashley Hall Horse Show, first hosted in 1927, the girls could compete in the Charleston and Summerville Horse Shows. (Photo courtesy of the Ashley Hall Archives.)

Five

Faculty, Staff, and Curriculum

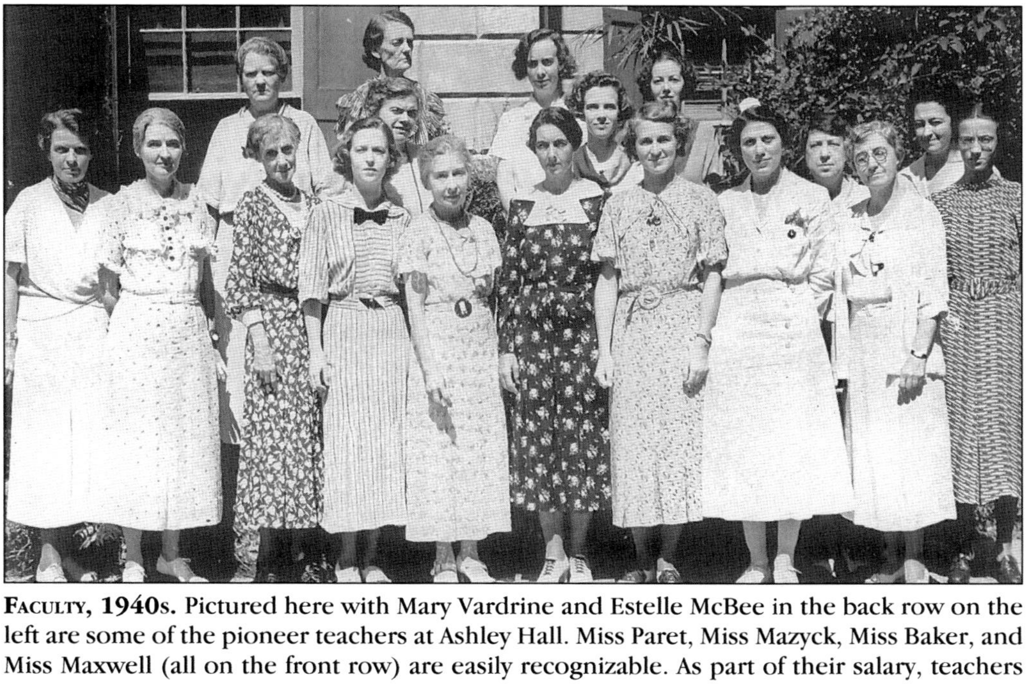

Faculty, 1940s. Pictured here with Mary Vardrine and Estelle McBee in the back row on the left are some of the pioneer teachers at Ashley Hall. Miss Paret, Miss Mazyck, Miss Baker, and Miss Maxwell (all on the front row) are easily recognizable. As part of their salary, teachers were given housing. Many of the smaller houses located very close to campus were owned or rented by the school. If a teacher had to stay late in the evening to proctor a study hall for boarding students, Bob Johnson, the maintenance and all-around handyman for the school, would walk them home through the unsafe neighborhood.

"The teachers really were inspiring; they were absolutely incredible the way they made it fun, but also taught us the value of education," recalls Josephine Hutcheson. (Photo courtesy of the Ashley Hall Archives.)

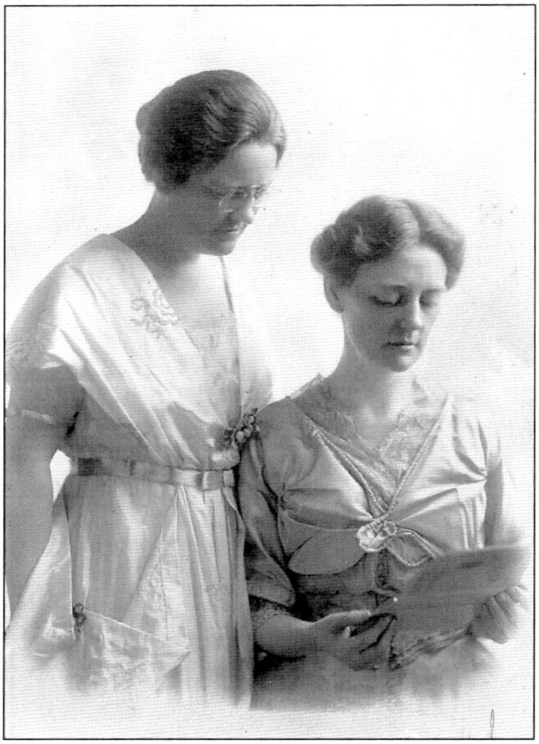

Sisters, Early 1900s. Always very close, Vardrine and Estelle McBee shared the ups and downs of the beginning days of the school. Acting not only as Headmistress, Vardrine needed the help of her sister in taking care of meals and teaching lower school classes. The 1949 *Spiral* says of Miss Estelle, "as unofficial mother, advisor, dietitian, nurse, and helper and teacher, she has relieved some day in the life of every student. She is endowed with limitless energy, warmth and imagination, and her activities in school as well as out have made her a dearly beloved member of the community." (Photo courtesy of the Ashley Hall Archives.)

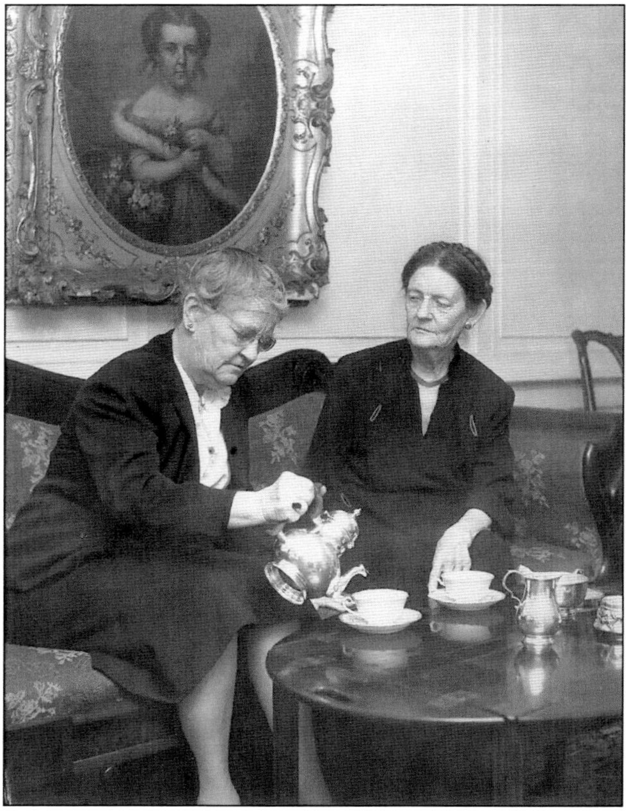

Afternoon Tea, 1950s. Up until death, the two sisters helped and cared for each other. After retirement, they lived together in a house where Davies Auditorium now stands until Estelle passed away in 1964. Miss Vardrine McBee, the junior, only lived a year after her sister's death. Vereen Coen (née Vereen Huguenin, class of 1951) says, "They [Estelle and Mary Vardrine] were a vital part of our lives, and we had a tremendous regard for them." (Photo courtesy of the Ashley Hall Archives.)

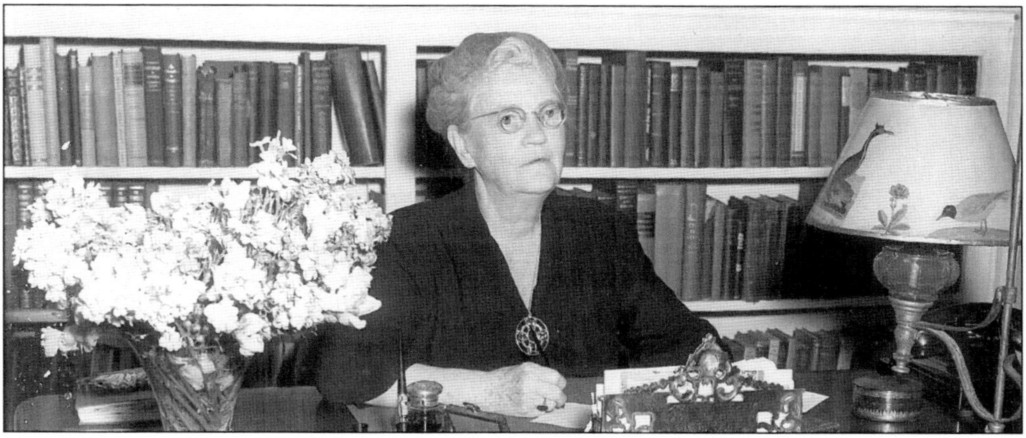

HEADMISTRESS, 1930S. Besides managing a very successful girls' school, Vardrine McBee was extremely involved in the community. She was on the executive committee of Pinehaven (a local tuberculosis hospital), the Free Kindergarten, the Girl Scouts, the InterRacial Relations Committee, the Poetry Society, and the Civic Club. McBee was instrumental in establishing the Free Library and later became the president. She founded and served as president for the American Association of University Women, was a member of the County and State Teacher Associations, and served as first woman commissioner on the Charleston School Board. Also a member of the Chamber of Commerce, the Garden Club, the National Association of School Administrators, and the Southern Association of Private Schools, McBee kept very busy. She was an elected member of the highly prestigious Headmistress Association of the East. (Photo courtesy of the Ashley Hall Archives.)

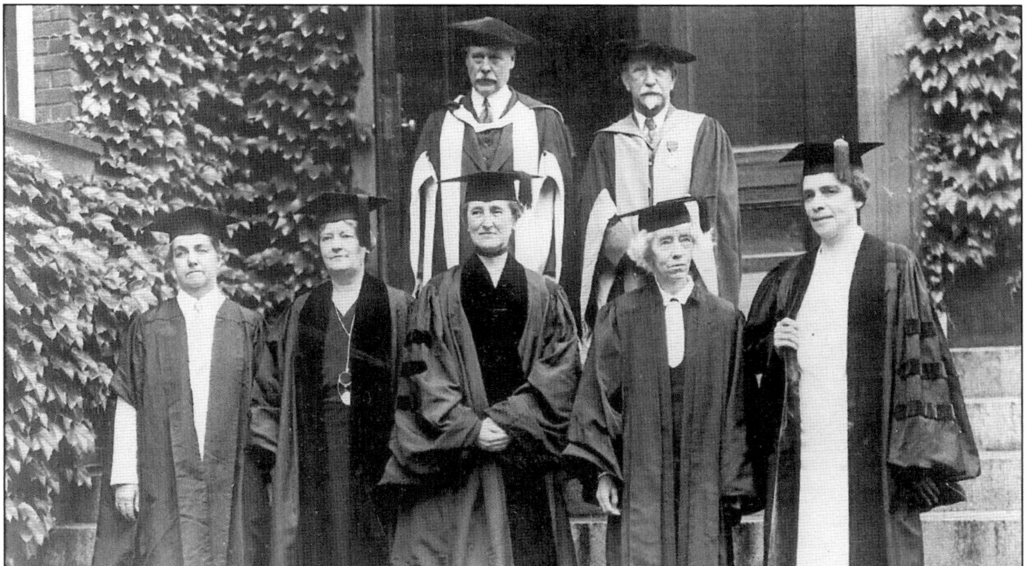

SMITH COLLEGE, 1936. Due to her long list of accomplishments, McBee received honorary degrees of Litt D. from Converse in 1932 and Furman in 1937. She is pictured here receiving an honorary Doctor of Humane Letters from her alma mater, Smith College, in 1936. Despite her time dedicated to volunteering and overseeing the school, Miss McBee made a point to know every student's name and they were all captivated by her; it has always been said that she had a great presence in front of a group. (Photo courtesy of the Ashley Hall Archives.)

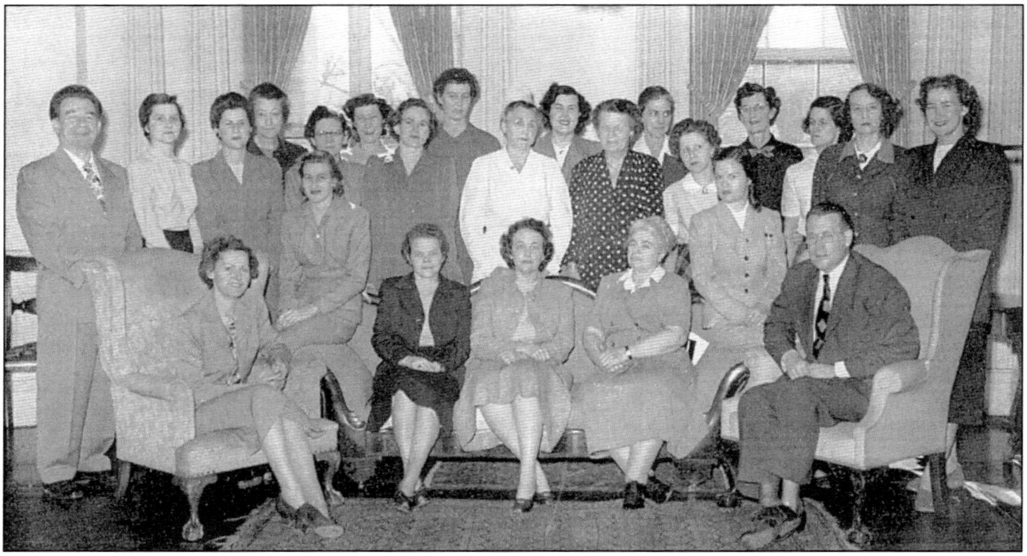

Faculty, 1949. This faculty photo, taken in 1949, shows Mr. William Sanford Piper Jr. (seated in the armchair on the right), chosen by the Board of Trustees to succeed McBee as Headmaster of the school. A graduate of Deerfield Academy and Bowdoin College, Piper was previously a teacher and administrator at the University School in Cleveland where he led a successful fund-raising campaign. He did graduate work at Johns Hopkins and Harvard and received his M.A. in Secondary Education from Western Reserve University. His wife, also a teacher, acted as his assistant and saw that the school made a successful transition from a privately owned institution to a private school under a Board of Trustees. Following in the wake of Miss McBee, Piper had high expectations to meet and only stayed at the school until 1954. (Photo courtesy of the Ashley Hall Archives.)

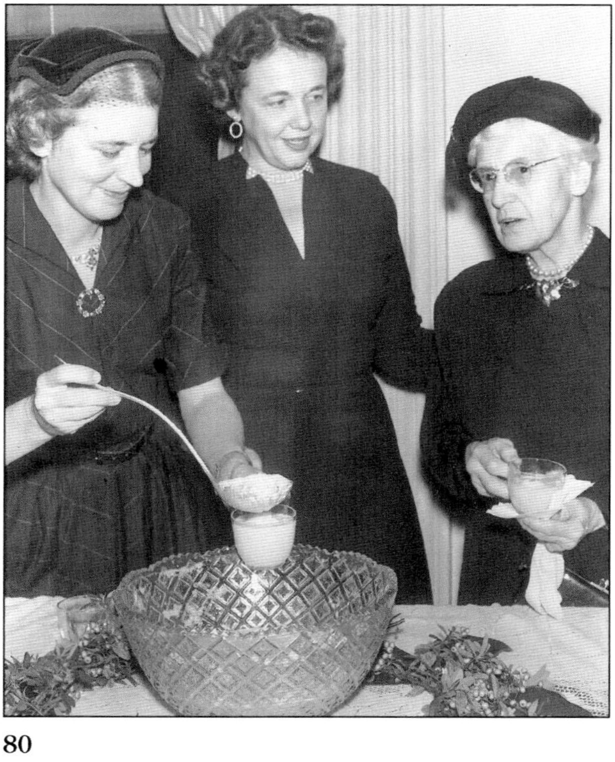

Headmistress Caroline Pardue, 1954. Miss Caroline Pardue (in the middle) became the Headmistress of Ashley Hall in 1954. Responsible for most of the building and expansion of the school, Miss Pardue played an integral role in improving and enlarging the school. She kept a close relationship with Miss McBee and would have tea with her on a regular basis to discuss the changes in the school. Alumna Abigail Van Alyn says of Miss Pardue, "she was the perfect balance of warmth and discipline, making her a perfect example for all of us. She held every girl to a high standard because she knew we were all capable of achieving." (Photo courtesy of the Ashley Hall Archives.)

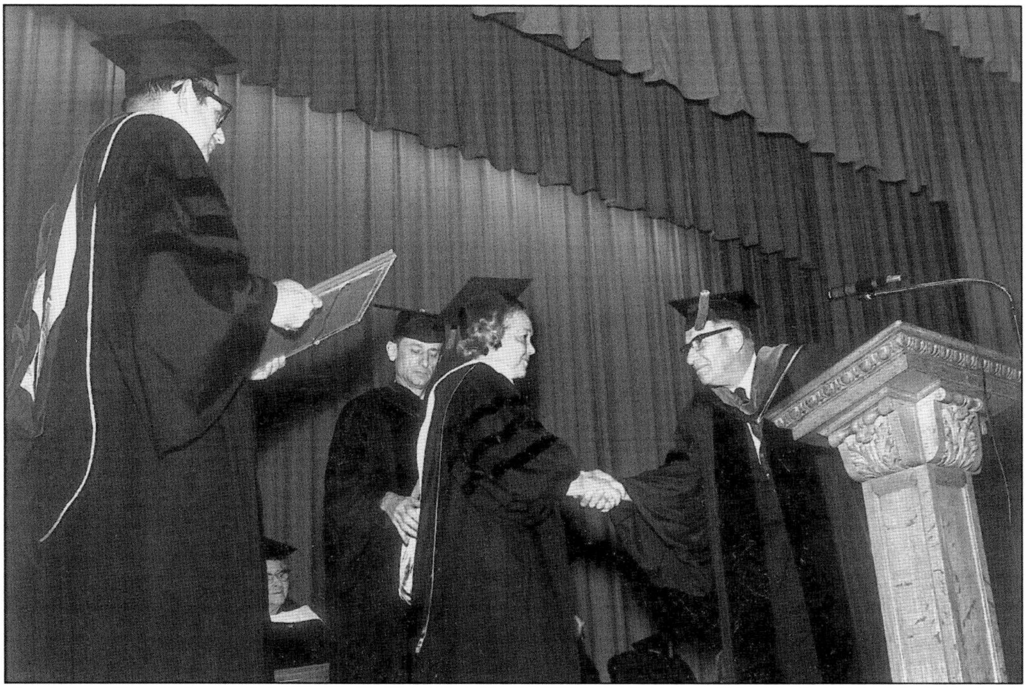

WINTHROP COLLEGE, 1970. "Style and grace were the two adjectives to describe Miss Pardue," says alumna Angie LeClercq. "Being a lady was of utmost importance to her and her students." Pictured here, Miss Pardue receives an honorary Doctor of Humane Letters degree from Winthrop College. Miss Pardue originally received her A.B. from Winthrop and then her M.A. at the University of South Carolina. She also studied at Duke and Middlebury College. An active member of the Charleston community, she was the first female member of the vestry at Grace Episcopal Church. (Photo courtesy of the Ashley Hall Archives.)

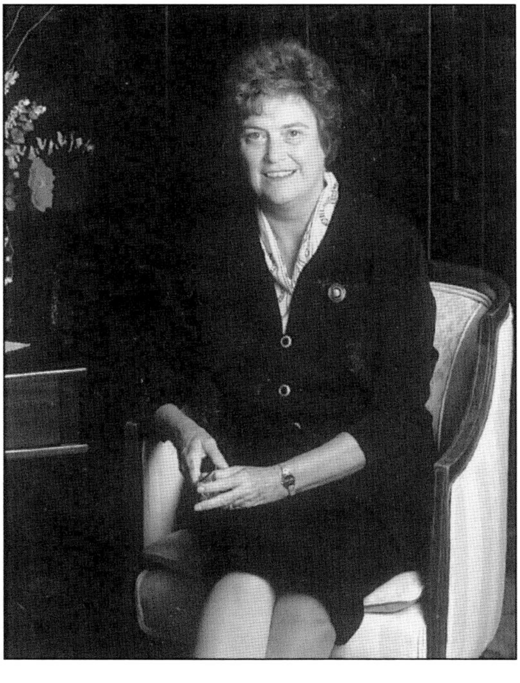

HEADMISTRESS MARGARET MACDONALD, 1999. Appointed Headmistress of Ashley Hall in 1985, Mrs. Margaret MacDonald led the school into the technologically updated 21st century. She began financial aid programs, added arts and admissions departments, opened the Ross Early Education Center, constructed the Ingram Center for the Arts and the John's Island Sports Complex, received the Zucker technology grant, and renovated the Madren Pool and McBee House. Through it all, she kept the old school charm and traditions. (Photo courtesy of the Ashley Hall Archives.)

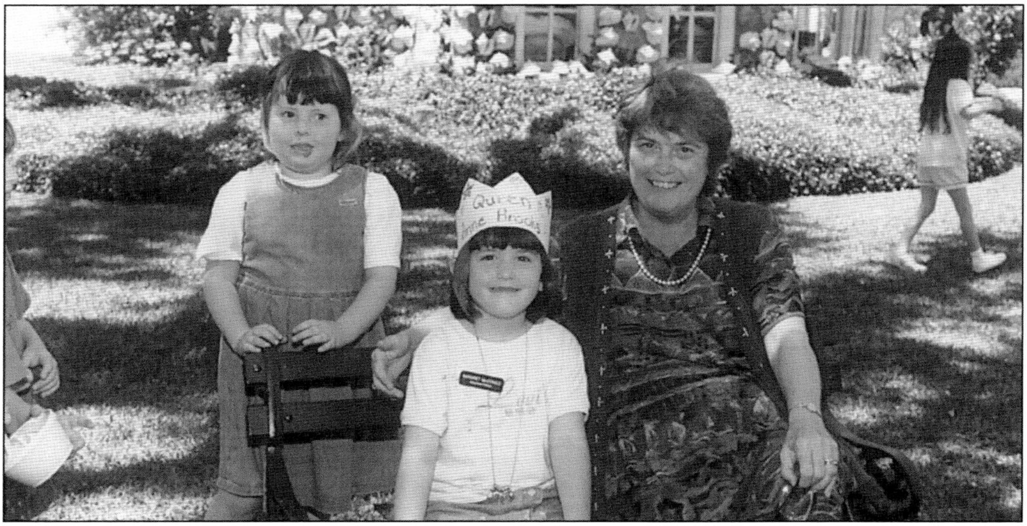

Headmistress for a Day, 2000. Pictured here with Anne Brooks, who is posing as Headmistress for the day, MacDonald shows that the small school charm of Ashley Hall still exists. Although enrollment has increased to approximately 600 students, the faculty, administration, and students still recognize names and faces, creating a loving atmosphere conducive to learning. This all-school event is just one more of the advantages of a smaller school. This was a celebration of Miss McBee's birthday where each upper school student takes her little sister (a student from the lower school) to the senior lawn for ice cream and socializing. (Photo courtesy of the Ashley Hall Archives.)

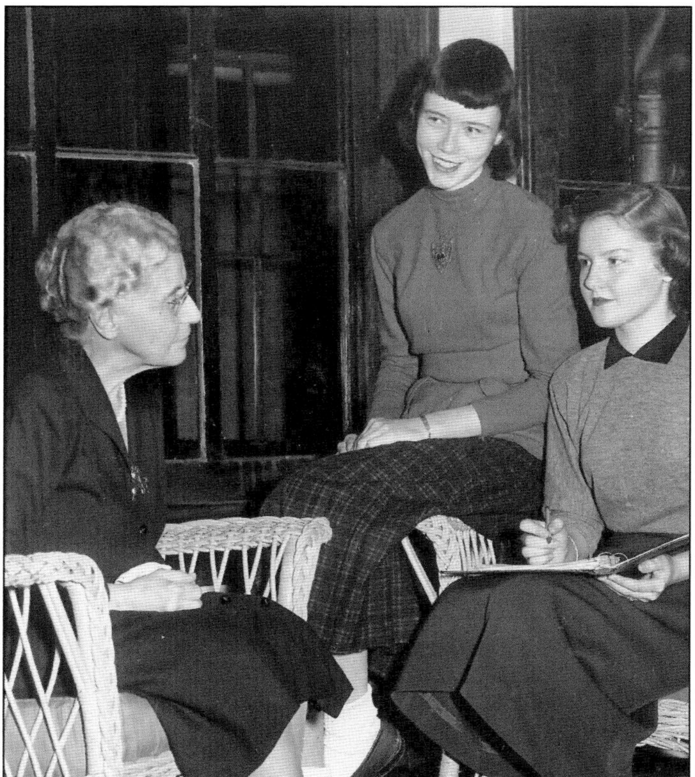

Miss Mazyck, 1951. Miss Mazyck, Head of the Latin Department for almost 30 years and former principle of the Confederate College in Charleston, was a favorite advisor to the students. Caroline Haydock (née Caroline Prioleau, class of 1951), pictured with Miss Mazyck, remembers her as being "a good teacher with a distinguished look who made us really learn the material." Mrs. Haydock recalls that Latin had been a strong part of the curriculum, which she is still grateful for today due to the aid the Latin roots provide when learning new languages. (Photo courtesy of the Ashley Hall Archives.)

"Green-thumb McBee," 1940s. Many of the exotic plants were brought to the Ashley Hall grounds by the third owner, Mr. Otto Witte, and Miss McBee, an avid gardener, kept up and added to the beautiful school landscaping. A 1936 article in the *News and Courier* writes about a flower show sponsored by the Garden Club of Charleston in which ten schools from the Charleston area competed: James Simons, Courtenay, Mitchell, Benett, Ashley Hall, Memminger High School, Crafts School, the Cathedral School, Mrs. Harvey Watts's School, and Miss Sadie Jervey's School. The article says, "Blue, red and yellow ribbons were given for first second and third place, respectively, at the Ashley Hall exhibit." (Photo courtesy of the Ashley Hall Archives.)

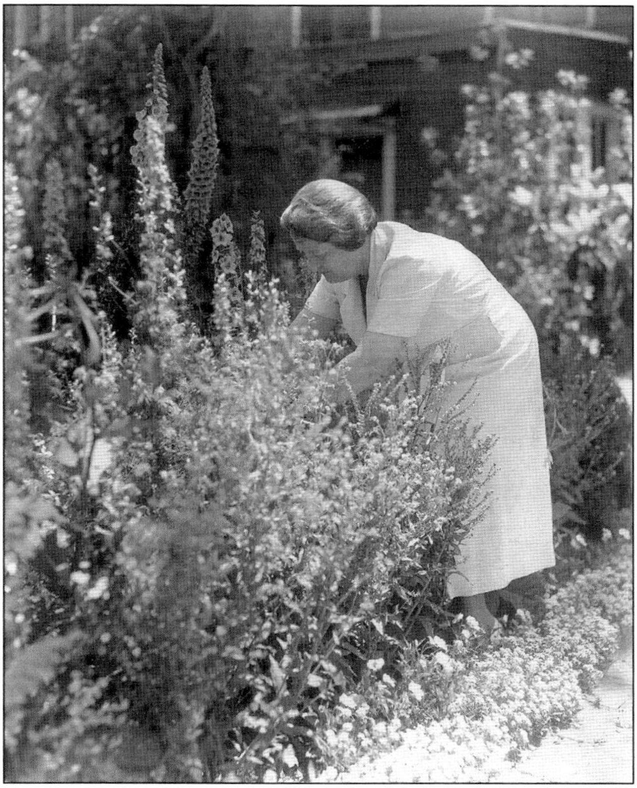

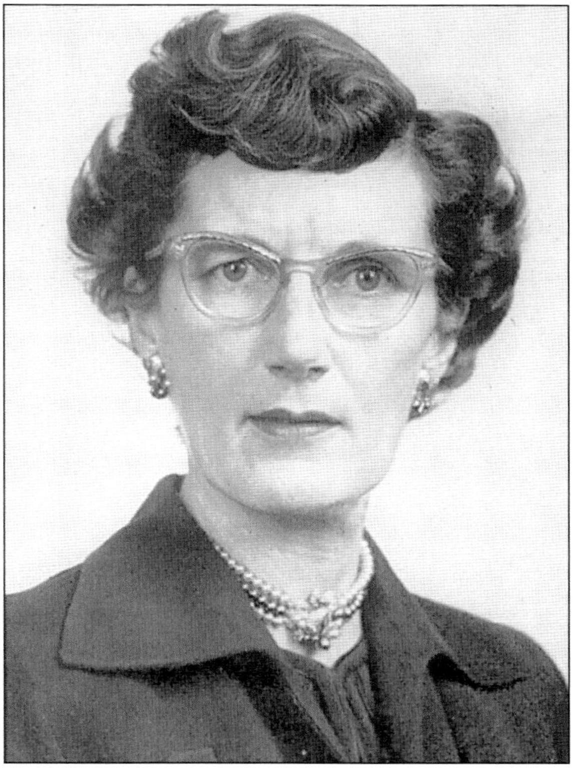

F.J. Jervey, 1953. A Latin teacher for many years at Ashley Hall, Mrs. F.J. Jervey is featured in 1953 when the school yearbook, *The Spiral*, was dedicated to her. The dedication reads, "To Mrs. Jervey whom we shall remember not only as our teacher and friend, but also as one to whom we have always turned and upon whom we have always depended for inspirational guidance and cheerful capability." (Photo courtesy of the Ashley Hall Archives.)

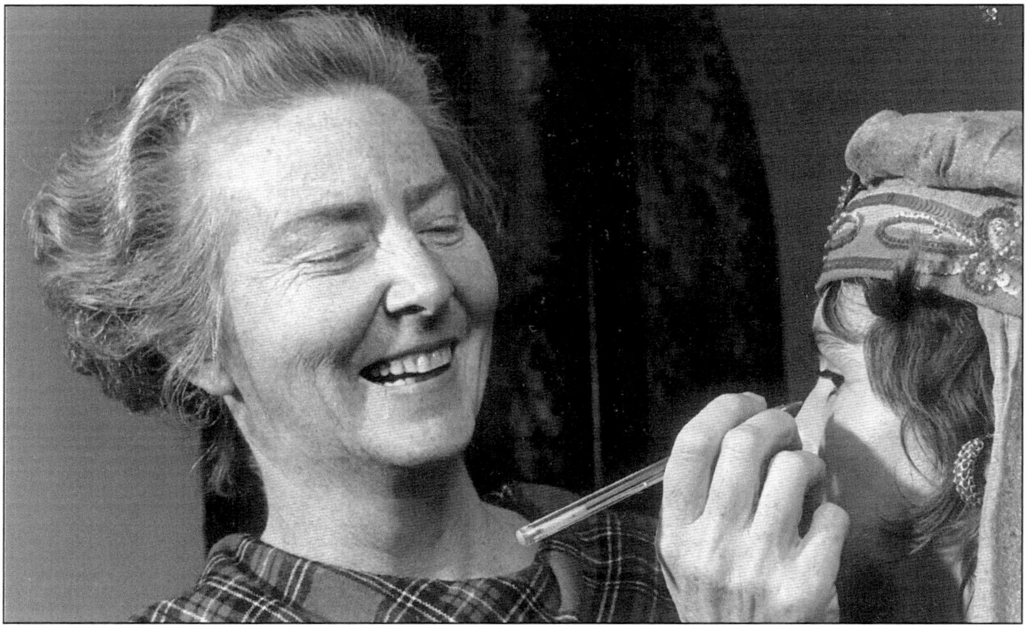

Getting into Costume, 1979. Mrs. Elizabeth Keith, teacher of English and drama for 23 years at Ashley Hall, was known as a great teacher with demanding ideals. Angie LeClercq recalls having to "memorize reams of Shakespeare for Miss Keith. She was a brilliant woman who did not put up with unprepared students."

Here Miss Keith helps apply last minute make-up to a king during the annual school Christmas play. One of the greatest advantages of going to Ashley Hall, Mrs. Cole says, is that "there are not as many students, so the teachers can be more relaxed and act more like themselves." This photo shows the joy a teacher has while watching her students perform a major production for a large audience. (Photo courtesy of the Ashley Hall Archives.)

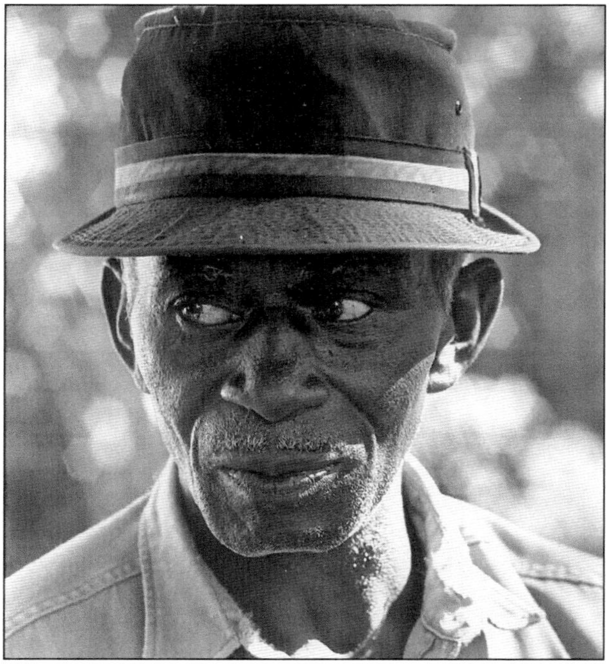

Bob Johnson, 1940s. Pictured here was Ashley Hall's most loyal, hard worker, Bob Johnson, who once had the yearbook dedicated to him. Johnson handled everything around the school from the grounds to buildings and maintenance problems. He would escort teachers home after late night study hours for boarders. He worked even when there was not enough money to pay him; somehow Miss McBee always found something to give him and his family. He was employed by the school until old age forced him into retirement in the 1960s. (Photo courtesy of the Ashley Hall Archives.)

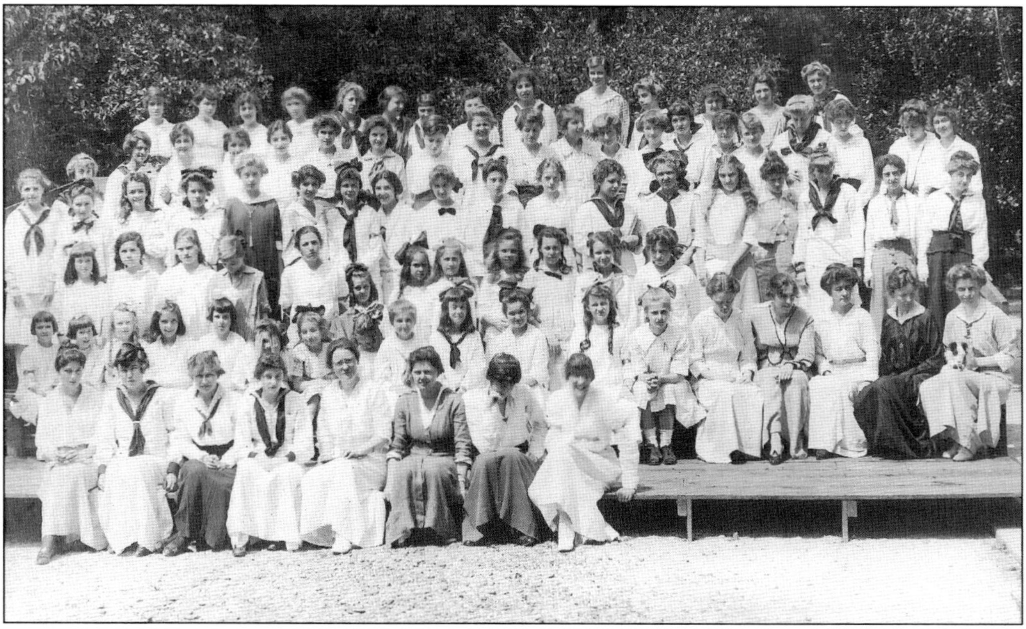

Ashley Hall School, 1920s. A short column titled "Activities at Ashley Hall" in the *News and Courier* reads, "The first open forum meeting of the student government body was very successful. . . . Armistice Day was commemorated at Ashley Hall by a most inspiring speech by Mr. Way, in which he emphasized the solemnity of the day and the importance of heroes of peace rather than heroes of war . . . the first Purple and White basketball game was played Tuesday . . . the Whites won, 25–17." (Photo courtesy of the Ashley Hall Archives.)

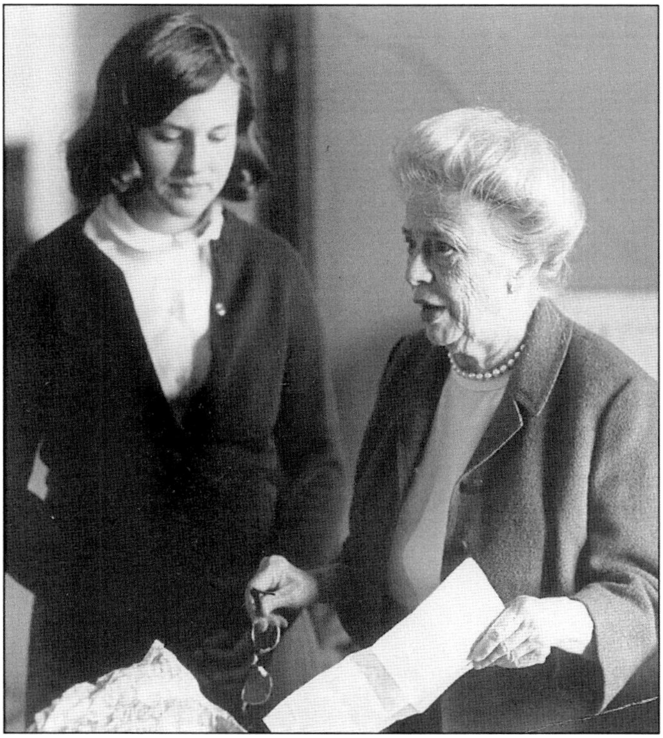

Mary Trott Jervey, 1960s. Mrs. Mary Trott Jervey, a teacher of sewing for 38 years at Ashley Hall, is shown here. "Ashley Hall was where I learned to sew, and it led to an 18 year career in the fabric industry for me," claims alumna Vereen Coen. (Photo courtesy of the Ashley Hall Archives.)

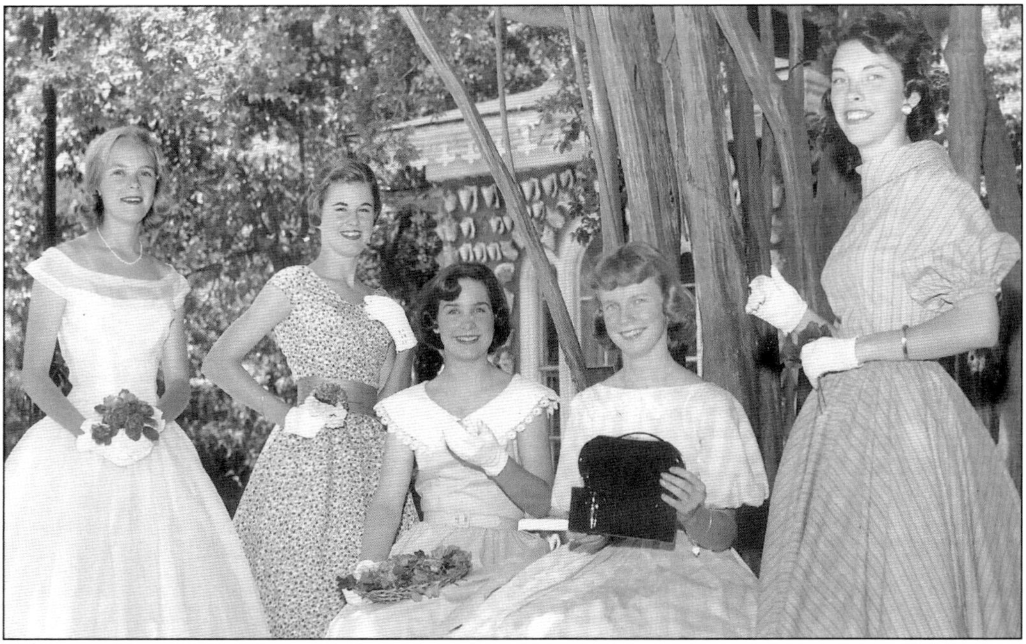

Sewing Class Models, 1950s. Sewing classes were held in the ballroom for many years and some girls did not take the class due to the extra cost. Jane Thornhill went to Ashley Hall during the time of the Great Depression and remembers the poverty and destitution of the city. There was no extra money, so many of the girls just took the core classes and went home after school. (Photo courtesy of the Ashley Hall Archives.)

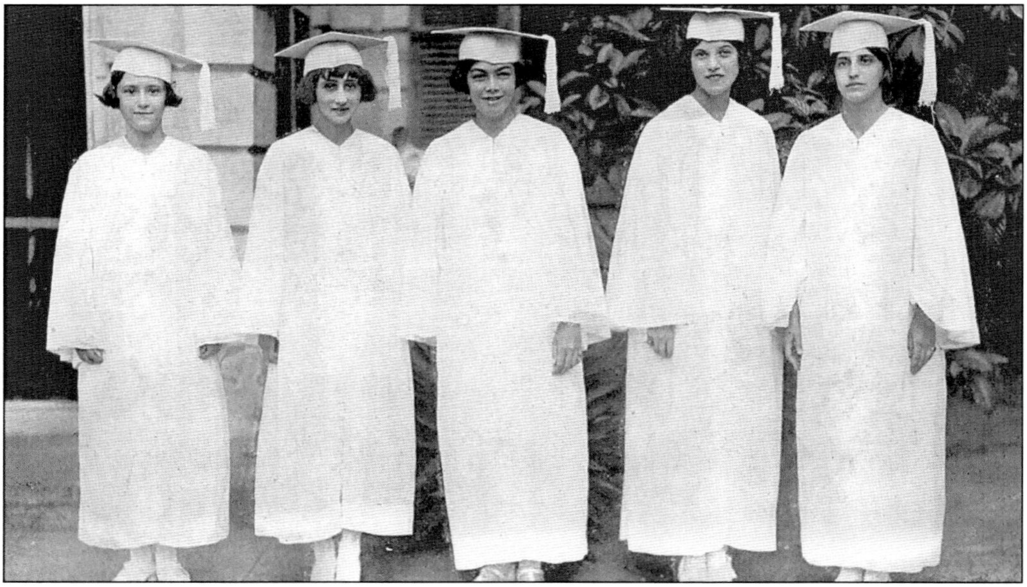

Normal School Graduation, 1925. The Normal School had the ideals of training young women to be capable teachers of little children in the home and in school, to expand and improve their own lives and the lives of others through charity, and to develop the desirable qualities of women. The girls pictured above are graduating with the responsibility to "promote the ideals of the modern progressive education" (*Cerberus* 1931–33). (Photo courtesy of the Ashley Hall Archives.)

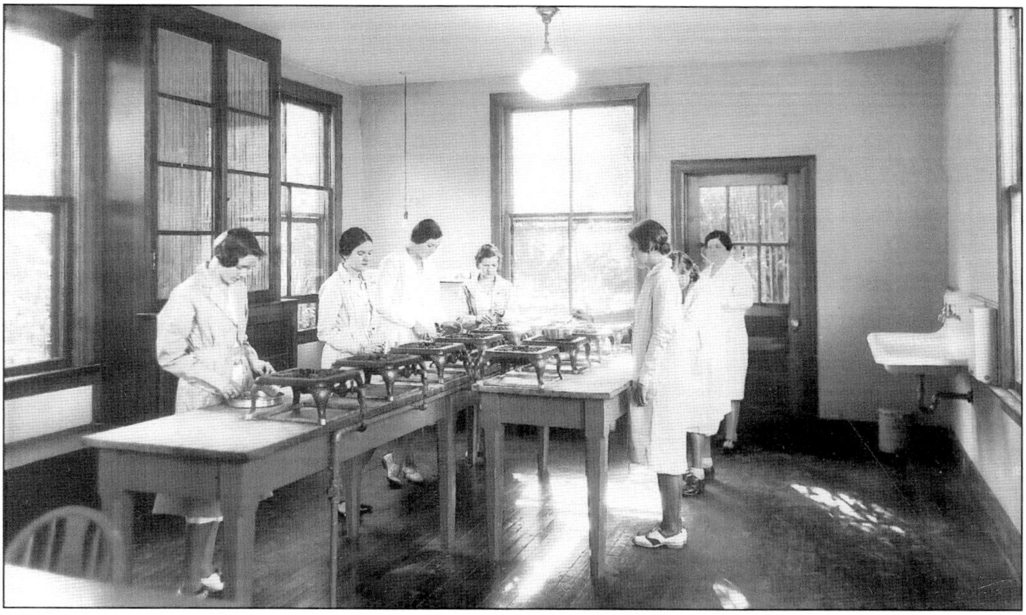

Cooking Up, 1931. Although the origin of this photo is unknown, it recalls the days of mixing chemicals in chemistry classes. After being an aviary, the Shell House became the science lab for the class. Josephine Pinckney explains why in *Call Back Yesterday*: "if in search of some elixir she unwittingly mixed unsympathetic elements and blew herself up only a few classmates would share her doom, and the rest of the school would stand unrocked at a safe distance." (Photo courtesy of the Ashley Hall Archives.)

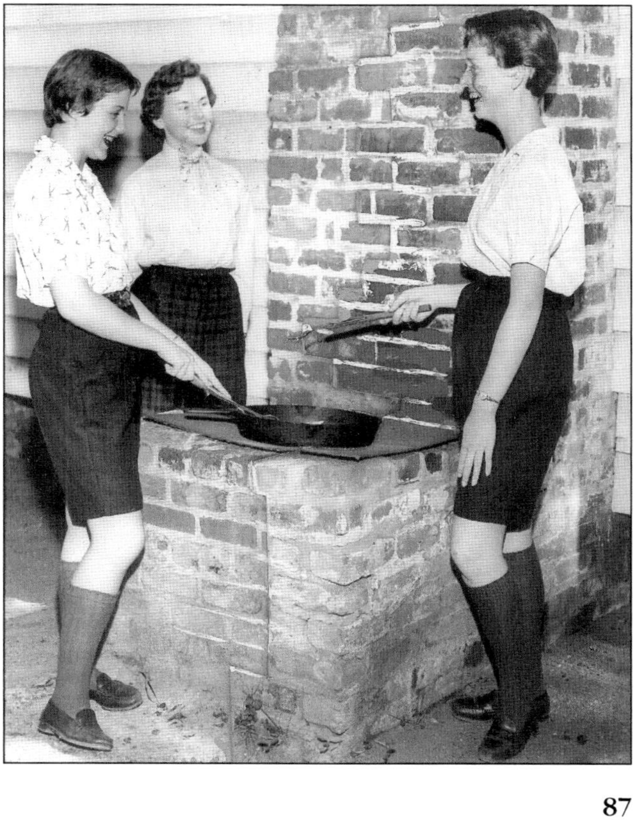

Grilling Out, 1959. Besides teas and dances, cook-outs were fun social atmospheres for the boarders to spend time together and also meet boys. Weekly events with the Citadel and Porter Military Academy were some of the most popular. The 1933 *Cerberus* reminds us: "Never break your bread or roll in your soup. —Etiquette hint in an English paper." (Photo courtesy of the Ashley Hall Archives.)

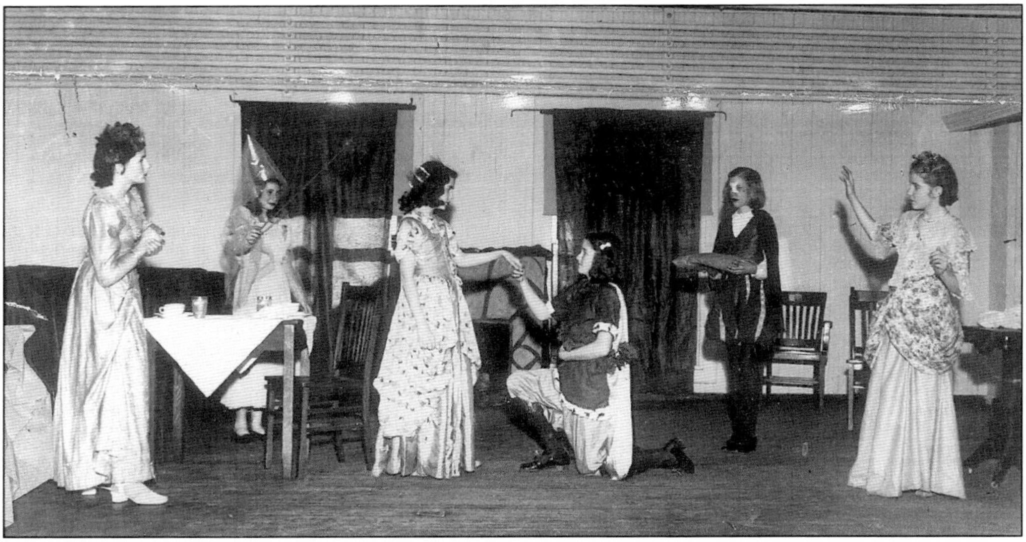

Cinderella, 1930s. Lower school plays were one of the main focuses of their curriculum during the year. Each grade spent most of the year preparing for a play to give during chapel in front of the upper school. *Peter Rabbit* was a popular one, as well as holiday plays, such as Thanksgiving and Easter productions. Shown here, the seventh grade French class performs *Cinderella* in French in the old Burges Auditorium. French was taught very early-on to the lower grades at Ashley Hall, and the importance of learning a foreign language was stressed. (Photo courtesy of the Ashley Hall Archives.)

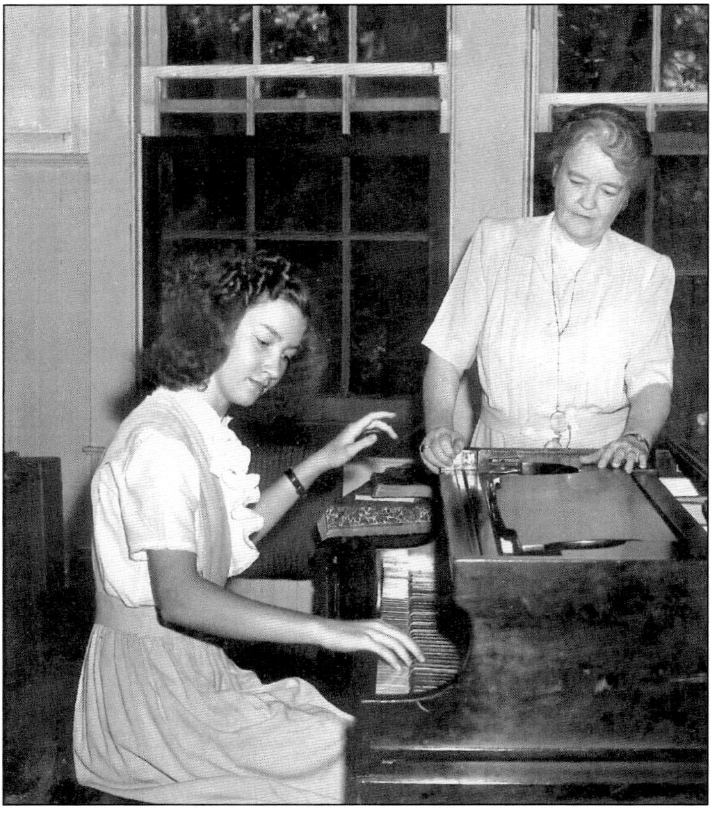

Carolyn Powell, class of 1949. Always a strong believer of a background in music, Miss McBee offered instruction at Ashley Hall for girls who wished to improve their musical talents. Shown here is Carolyn Powell, class of 1949, who won a spot playing with the Charleston Symphony and later went to the University of South Carolina and became a music teacher. (Photo courtesy of the Ashley Hall Archives.)

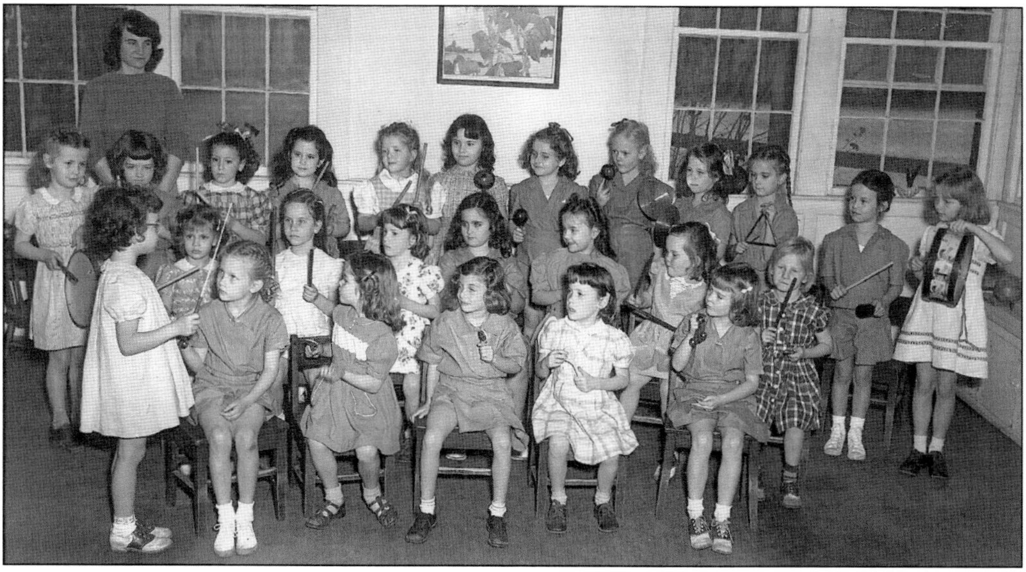

Music Class, 1930s. Part of having a well-rounded education included instruction in music. Starting in the first grade students took a music class once a week under a full-time instructor. An early school brochure reads, "The choral classes strive to develop in every girl her best singing voice and an appreciation and repertoire of worthwhile songs." The music classes also included music theory, rhythmic games and dances, and stories of the lives of masters. (Photo courtesy of the Ashley Hall Archives.)

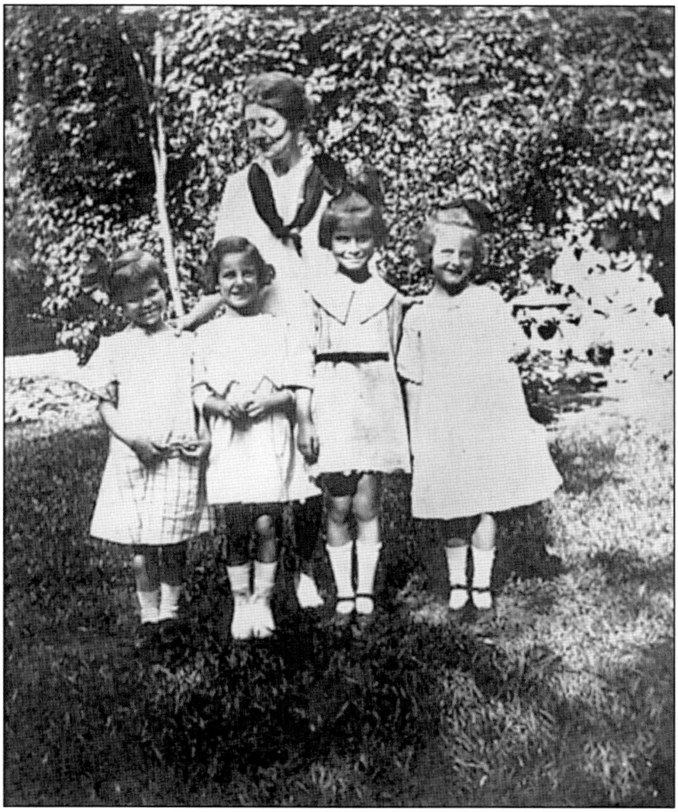

Estelle with Her Students, 1930s. Always known as a kind, little woman to the students, Estelle McBee was also a well-known actress in the town of Charleston. Her students would watch her perform regularly at the Footlight Players Theater. A 1934 *News and Courier* review of *The Late Christopher Bean* states "and what one can now speak of as that 'well-known comedy team' of McBee and Parker (Miss Estelle McBee and Luther W. Parker) pulled down most of the big laughs with their very realistic family squabbles." (Photo courtesy of the Ashley Hall Archives.)

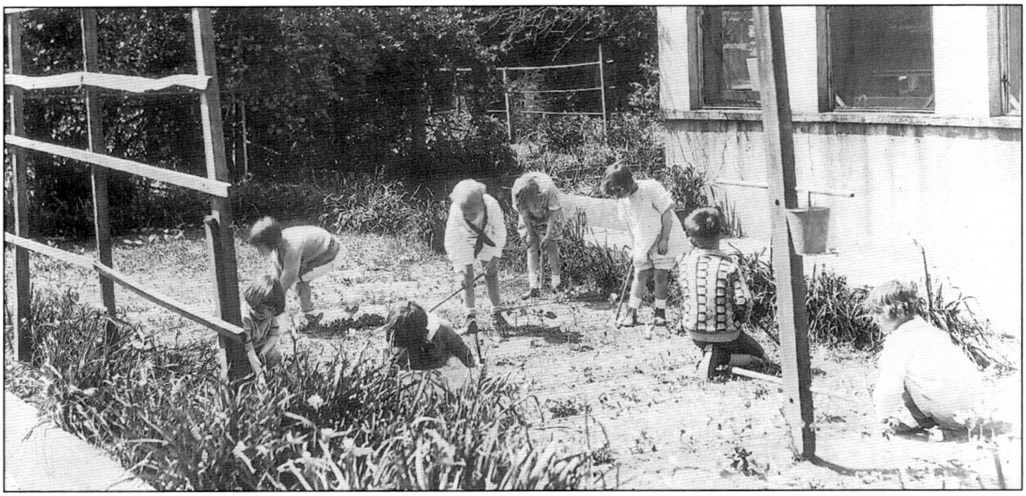

Gardening, 1930s. Here, the members of the lower school are getting fresh air and exercise as well as doing their part to keep up the beautiful gardens on campus originally planted by Otto Witte. Mr. Witte's daughter Laura Witte Waring recalls the gardens in her book *The Way It Was in Charleston*, "The magnificent trees, so long as they live, cannot but be admired. Covering such a large amount of ground, bordering on three streets, the garden lasts over the years in all of its beauty . . . formal beds, where bulbs were cultivated in season . . . hyacinths, tulips, lilies, daffodils, daisies and pansies, heliotrope, anemones, ranunculi, mignonette . . . violets . . . star jasmine grew on trellises, while delicate ladyslippers . . . hibiscus, snapdragons, and pinks had special beds of their own . . . and in the countless masses and varieties were roses . . . hiding the back part of the garden were cane, banana trees, strawberry vines, and banana shrubs . . . behind the gardens were vegetable beds." (Photo courtesy of the Ashley Hall Archives.)

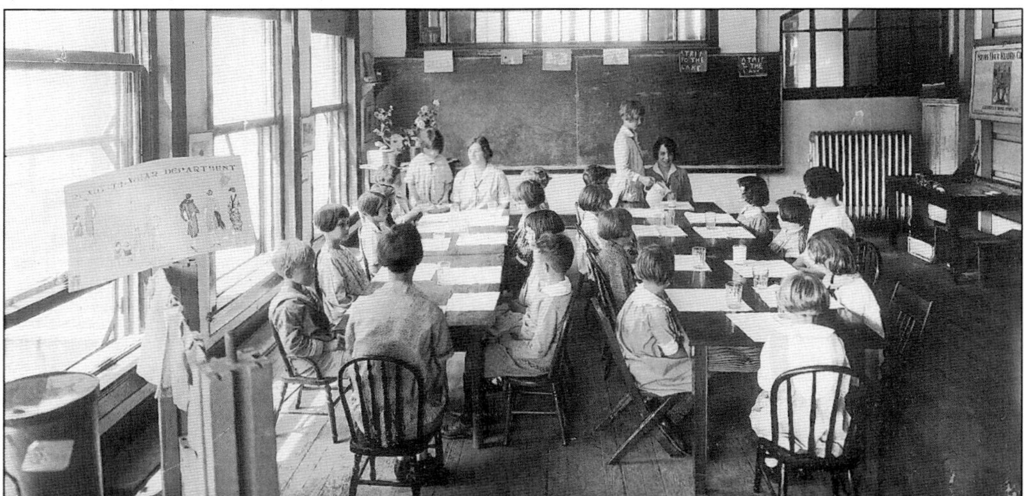

Mid-morning Lunch, 1930s. Because the school day for lower school went from 8:30 a.m. to 1:50 p.m., there was always a mid-morning lunch of milk and crackers served. At the end of the school day, all the girls went home for a big 2 p.m. dinner with their families. The Southern tradition of a large family dinner has now died out, but many alumnae fondly recall the large meals with the entire family of soup, rice and gravy, vegetables, meat or fish, bread, and always dessert. (Photo courtesy of the Ashley Hall Archives.)

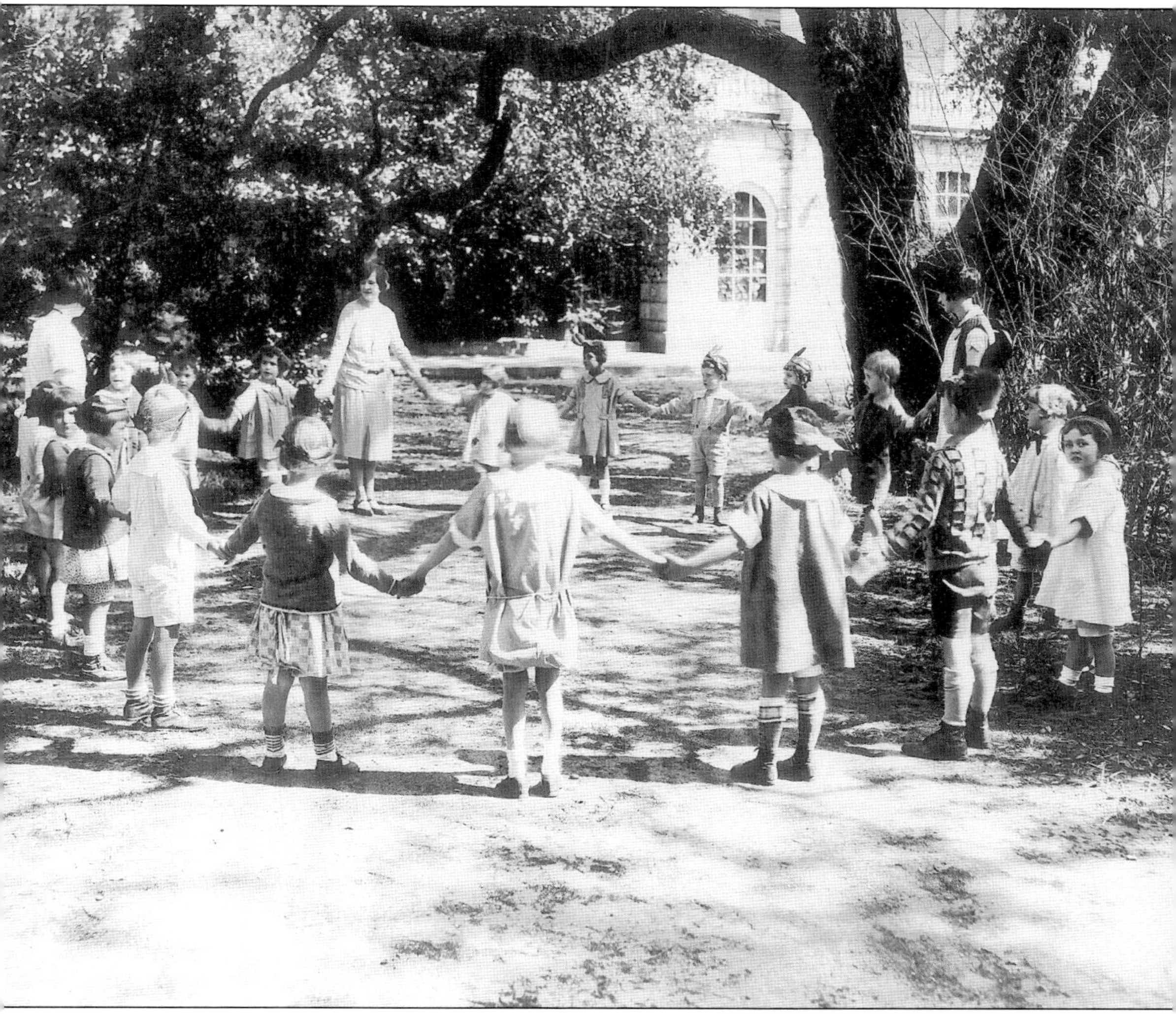

Fun and Games, 1925. These lower school children are playing "drop the handkerchief," in which a player runs around the outside of a circle and drops a handkerchief behind one student and tries to get back to his/her spot in the circle without being caught. Notice the boys in the circle who were allowed to attend Ashley Hall up until first grade. (Photo courtesy of the Ashley Hall Archives.)

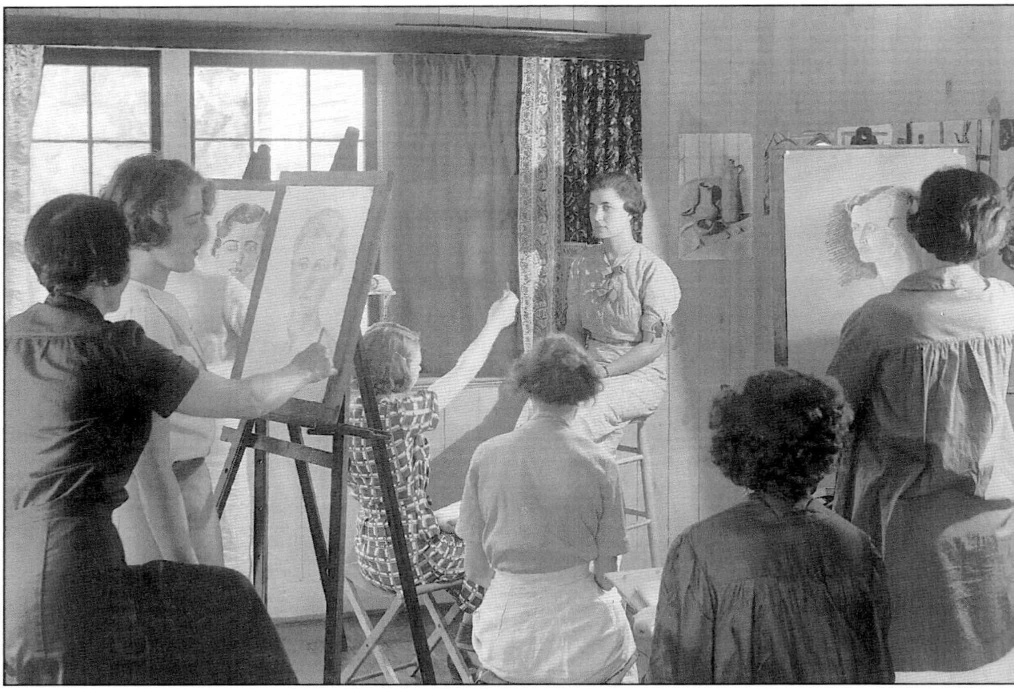

Art Class, 1930s. Extra classes of sewing, art, and music were offered to students who wished to learn or improve a skill. Here these girls may be in an art class or they may be part of the art club. (Photo courtesy of the Ashley Hall Archives.)

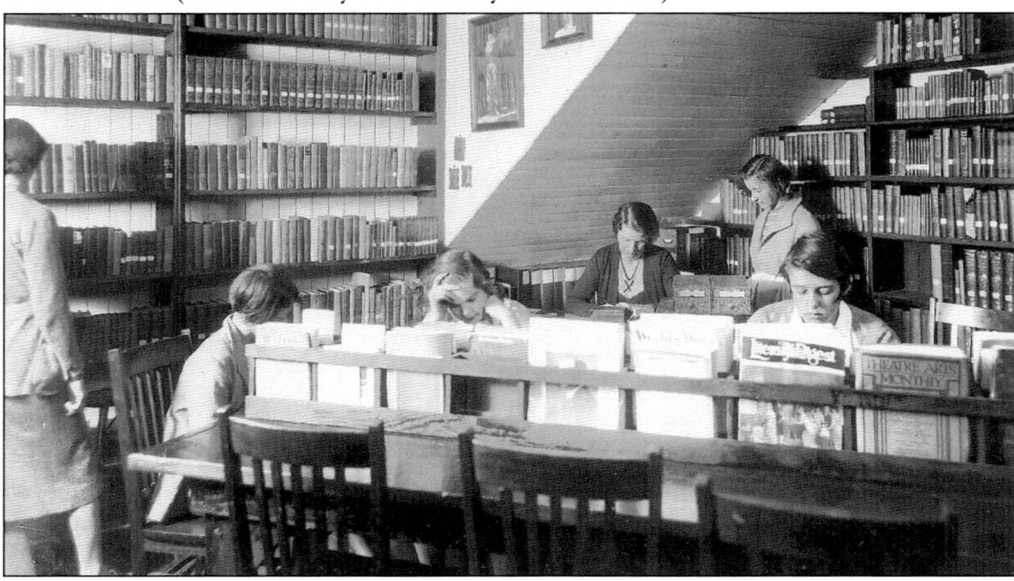

Studious Girls, 1930s. There were daily study hall hours for boarding and day students to give them adequate time to do their homework. "Study Hall was a terrific place," recalls Josephine Hutcheson. "At that time it was located in a building which is now essentially the corner of Radcliffe and Smith. It was a big old creaky room and there was always someone getting in trouble." A joke from *Cerberus*: "1/c: 'You were to write a poem and this paper has nothing on it.' 4/c: 'Oh, that's blank verse entitled 'my thoughts in class.'—*The Log*." (Photo courtesy of the Ashley Hall Archives.)

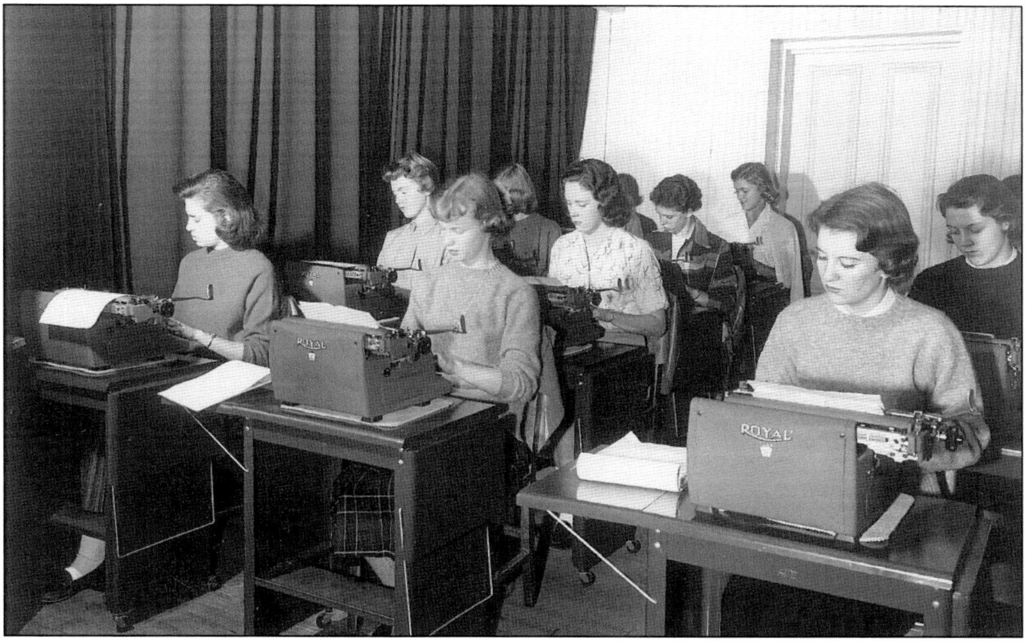

Typing Class, 1950s. Although not a required class, typing was offered for students who wished to take it. Rosemary Hutto, a former teacher at Ashley Hall, claims the class was originally held in a dressing room next to the stage in Burges Auditorium. (Photo courtesy of the Ashley Hall Archives.)

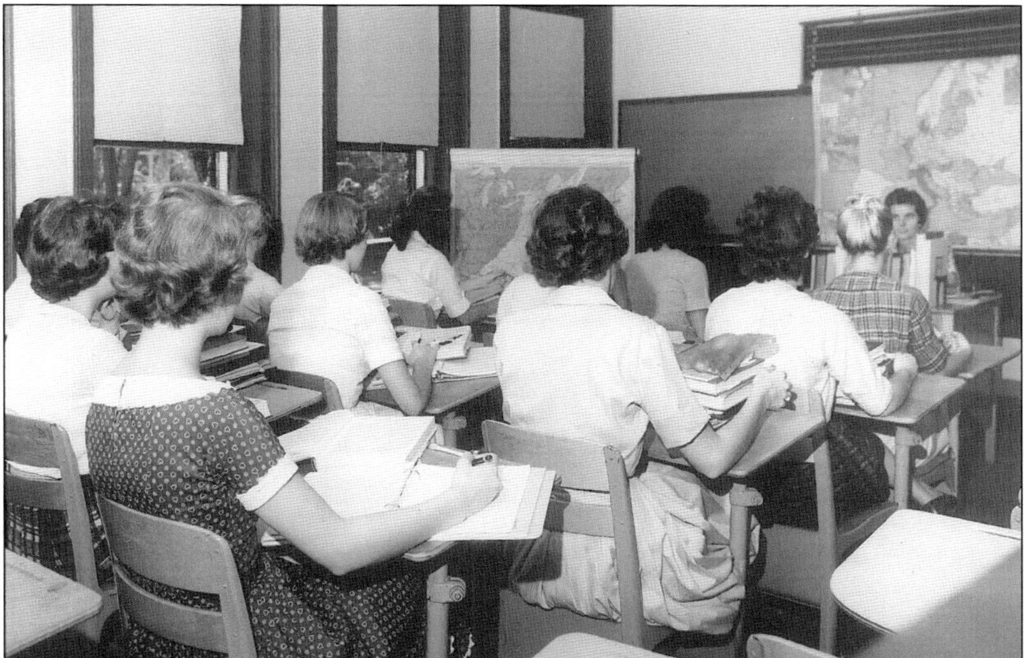

History Class, 1957. When the school first opened, Miss McBee taught history to the upper school girls. A *Cerberus* joke: Miss Sylvia: 'When was the War of 1854?' Polly: '1904?'" (Photo courtesy of the Ashley Hall Archives.)

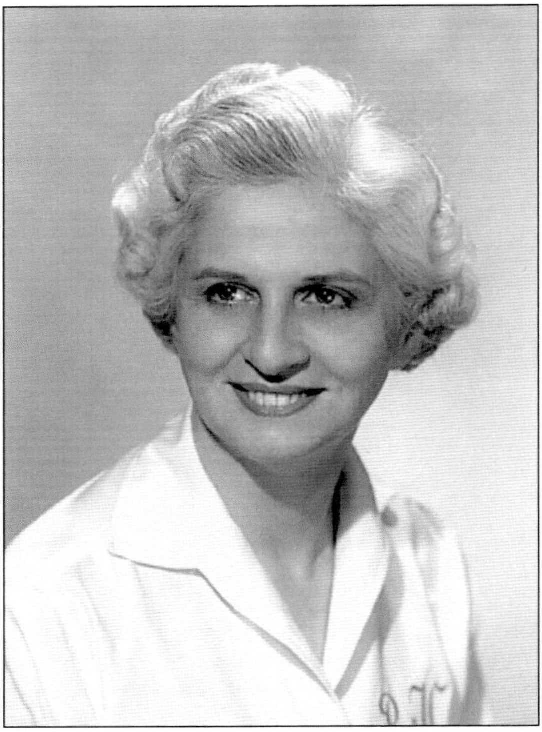

Rosemary Hutto, 1960s. "All you need is a teacher, a student, and a book," claims Rosemary Hutto, a Latin teacher at Ashley Hall for over 25 years. She saw the new buildings added and the closing of the boarding school. "I remember when there was no air conditioner in my classroom. Ashley Hall was nothing physically like it is today with all of the new, updated facilities, but it was a good school, and people sent their daughters there because they knew they would get a good education." (Photo courtesy of the Ashley Hall Archives.)

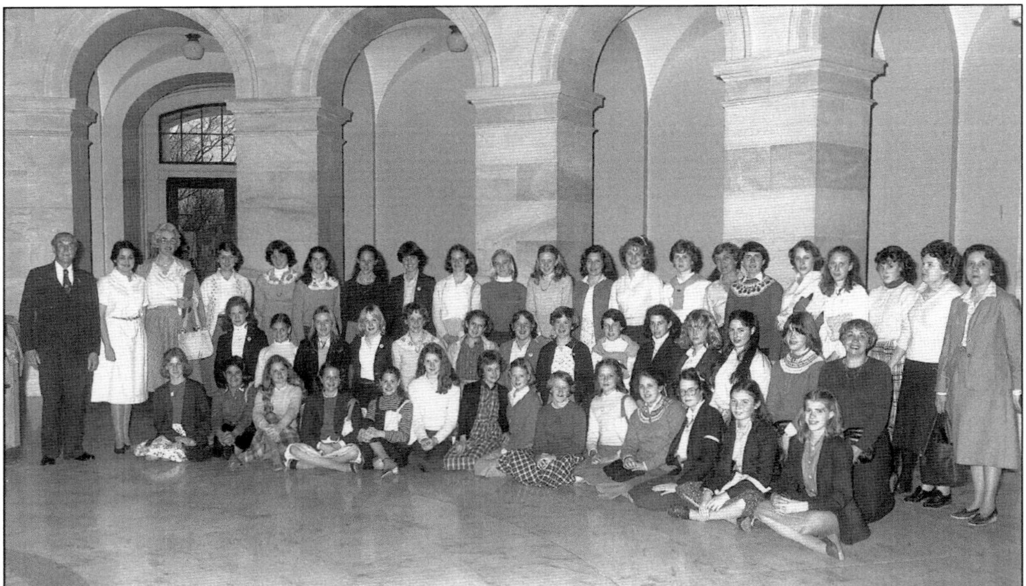

Class Trip to Washington, 1980s. Class field trips have always been an enjoyable part of school. Shown here in the 1980s, the seventh and eighth grade classes went to Washington, D.C. On the far left is South Carolina Senator Strom Thurmond, a well-known South Carolina icon and beloved servant of the state, who would frequently meet with the Ashley Hall girls on their trips to the Capitol. "He always took a photo with the girls and then shook everyone's hand," remembers Daisy Leland (also pictured above), the Head of the middle school from 1974 to 1992. (Photo courtesy of the Ashley Hall Archives.)

Six

Sports

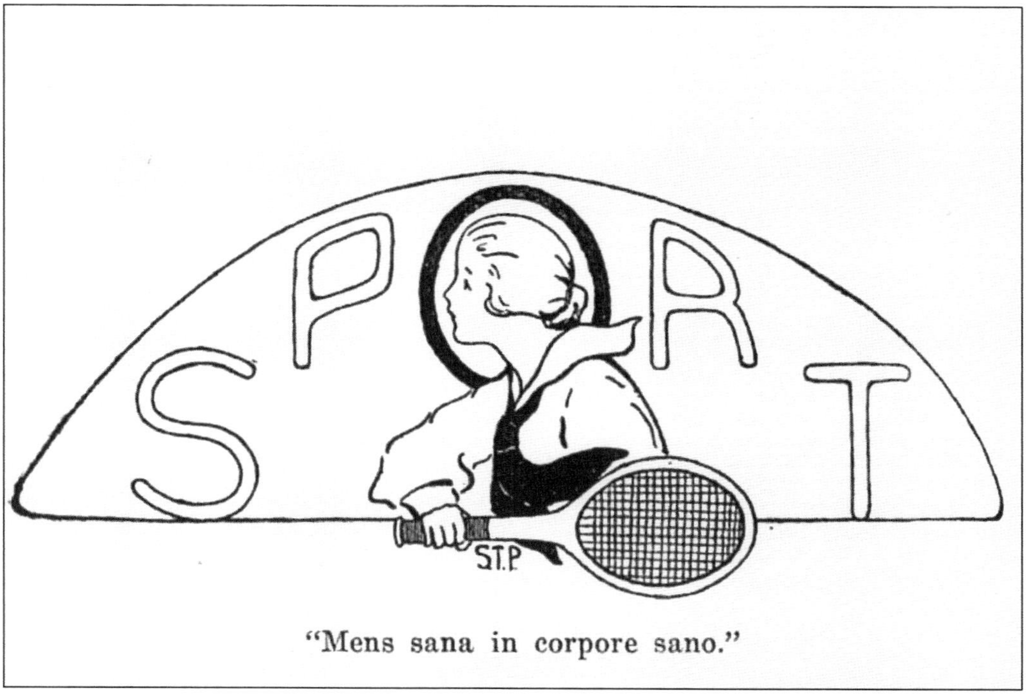

Cerberus, 1916. Sports were always a key part of the education at Ashley Hall. Besides physical education classes, there were many athletic clubs and intramural sports in which the students could participate. Miss McBee was known to play a game of basketball with the girls. (Photo courtesy of the Ashley Hall Archives.)

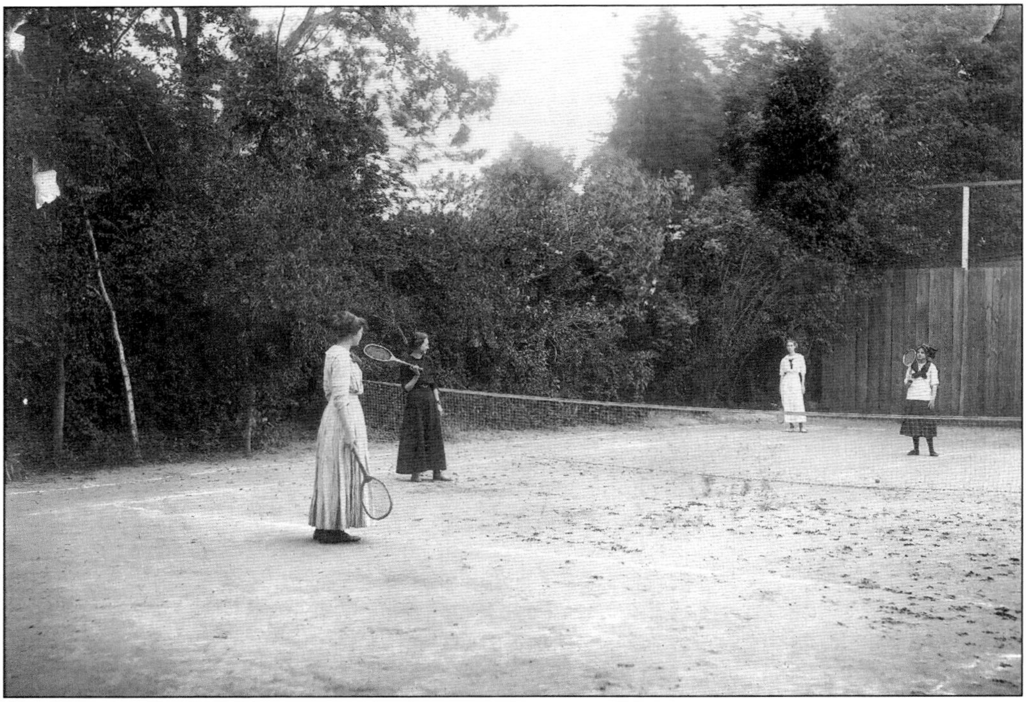

EARLY TENNIS, 1910S. The tennis courts were built in 1909 and a club was started in 1912. Students could compete against each other in upper and lower school tournaments during field days or other sporting events. Notice the long tennis skirts, which have progressively gotten shorter over the years. (Photo courtesy of the Ashley Hall Archives.)

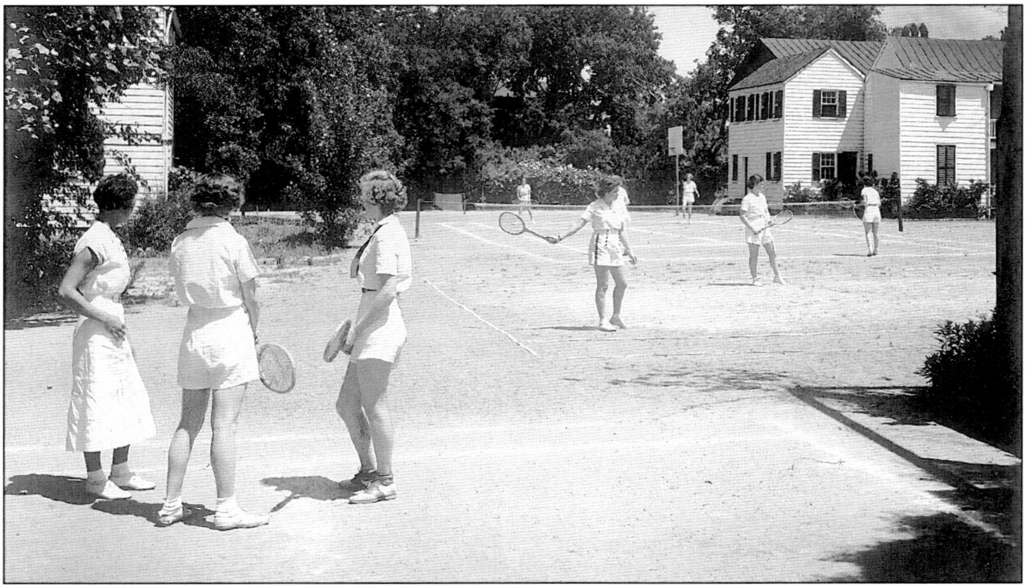

TENNIS, 1936. Tennis was played in the spring. It began in January after volleyball season and the Christmas play. Due to the lack of teams around the city, Ashley Hall girls relied mainly on intramural sports for competition. Besides annual field days and physical education classes, there were also afternoon matches and a tournament held every year during graduation week. (Photo courtesy of the Ashley Hall Archives.)

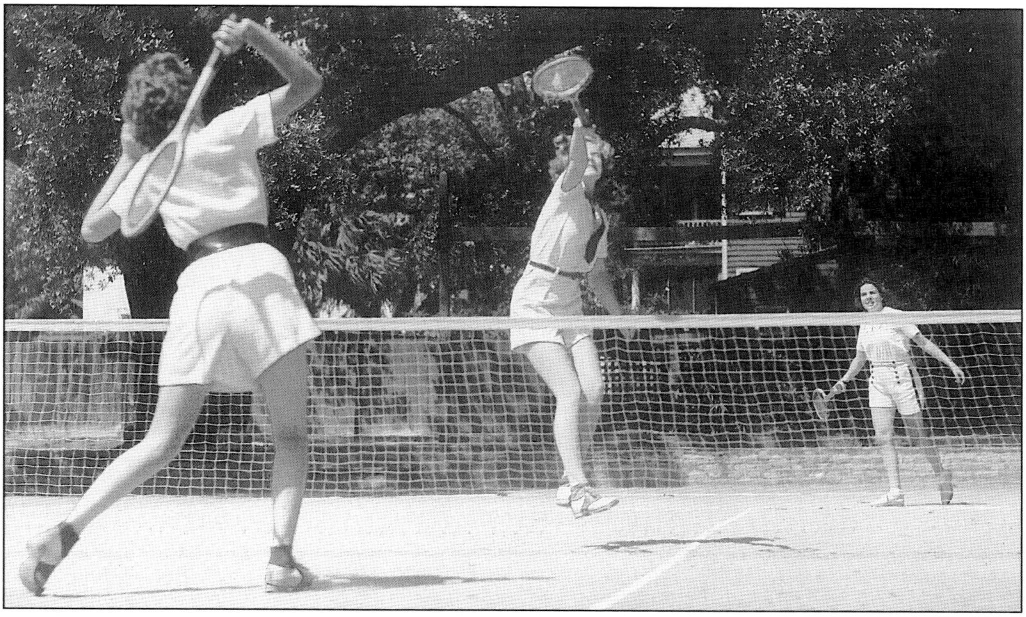

Game of Tennis, 1936. Girls would go home for their 2 p.m. dinner and return to the school for club meetings and sports practices. The 1935 *Cerberus* reports Ashley Hall winning their singles match, but losing the doubles game to Memminger. (Photo courtesy of the Ashley Hall Archives.)

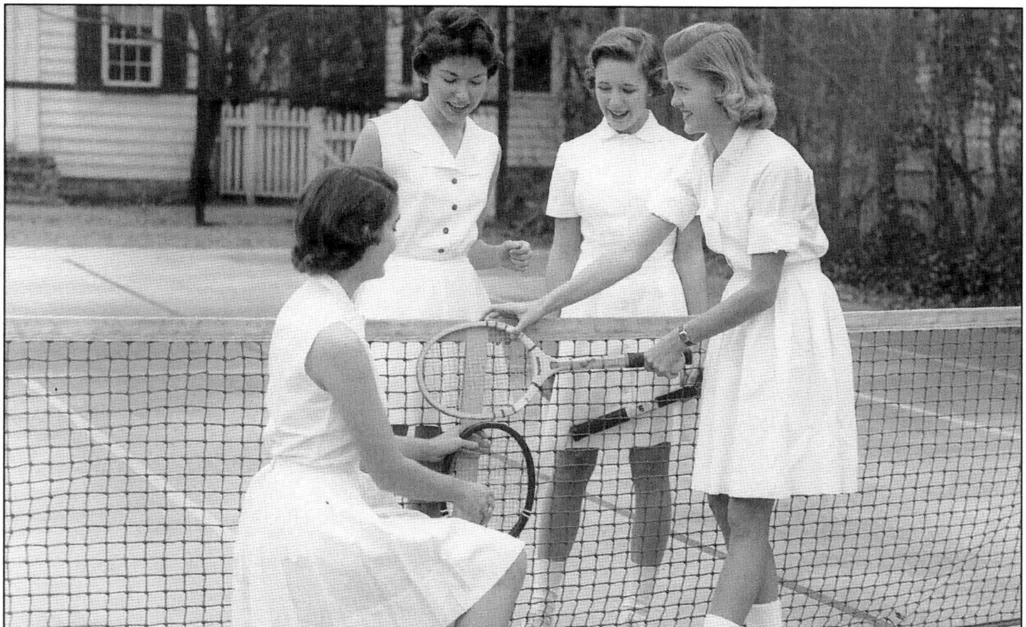

Tennis Team Captains, 1959. Angie LeClercq, pictured above, was the captain of the tennis team for two years. She fondly remembers her mother, Mrs. Emily Whaley, the acting coach of the girls team, driving the girls to Belton in a black Chevrolet. Belton was the number one team in the state, but the tennis champions of Ashley Hall beat them in an unheard of upset. Ashley Hall also played Bishop England and a team in Darlington. (Photo courtesy of the Ashley Hall Archives.)

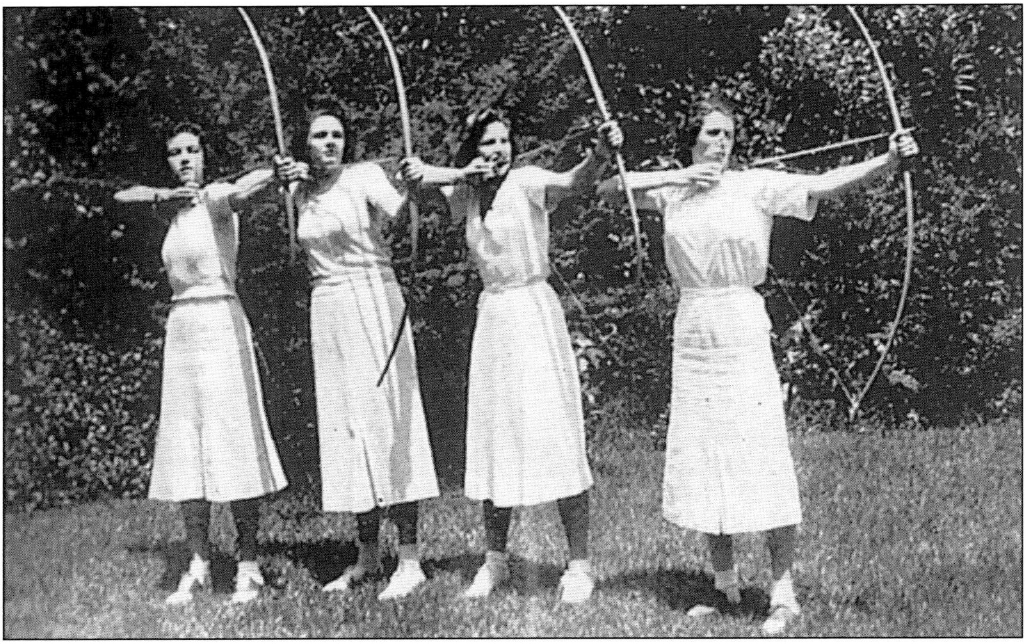

ARCHERY TEAM, 1937. Katherine Orr (née Katherine Wilkinson, class of 1939) pictured above was one of the founding members of the archery team. After teaching archery at Camp Greystone in Tuxedo, North Carolina, for the summer, she decided to start a school team. The girls practiced in the back of the school near the tennis courts and out of the way of any bystanders. Archery at one time was an event at the annual field day. (Photo courtesy of the Ashley Hall Archives.)

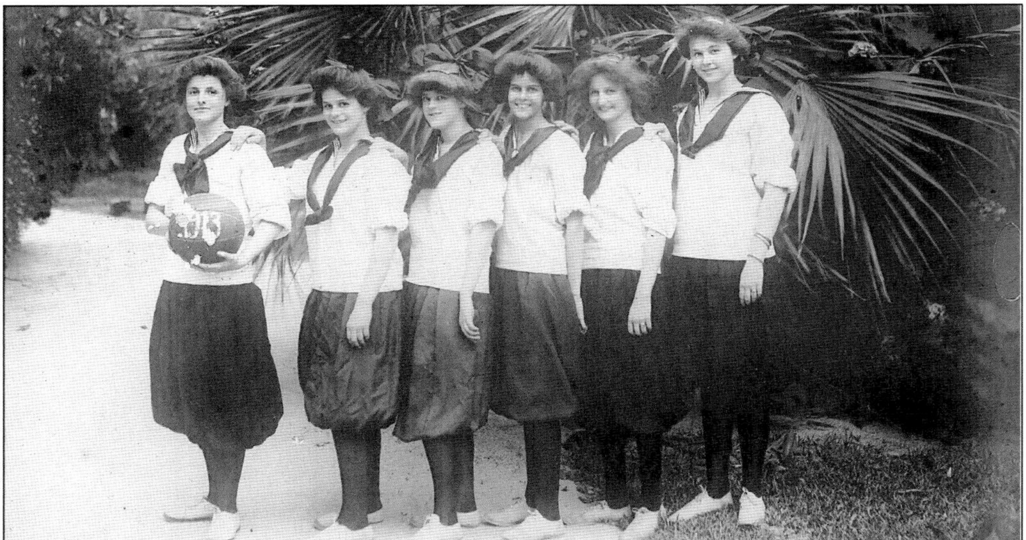

BASKETBALL, 1913. The 1914 *Cerberus* tells about an "exciting double-header played in the Gym" between the seniors and faculty at Ashley Hall. The faculty line-up consisted of Miss McBee, Ruth Harvey (a substitute student), Miss Mundorf, Miss Hazzard, Miss Dotterer, and Miss Oakman. Despite their "unique head gear" and "graceful poses," the faculty lost to the seniors 21 to 10. In the second game the juniors beat the sophomores 14 to 9. (Photo courtesy of the Ashley Hall Archives.)

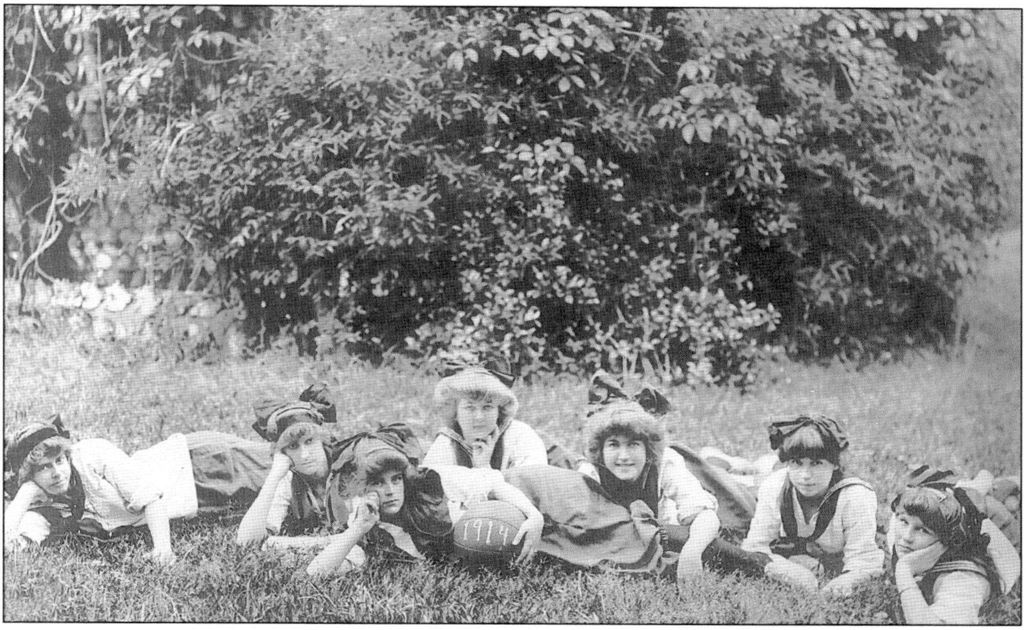

VARSITY BASKETBALL, 1914. Besides the benefit of physical activity, Miss McBee also realized the importance of camaraderie involved in team sports. The varsity basketball team was another way for girls to form close relationships with those on their teams. Because there were also intramurals, even the girls who were not excellent athletes would have a chance to participate and cheer on their teammates. (Photo courtesy of the Ashley Hall Archives.)

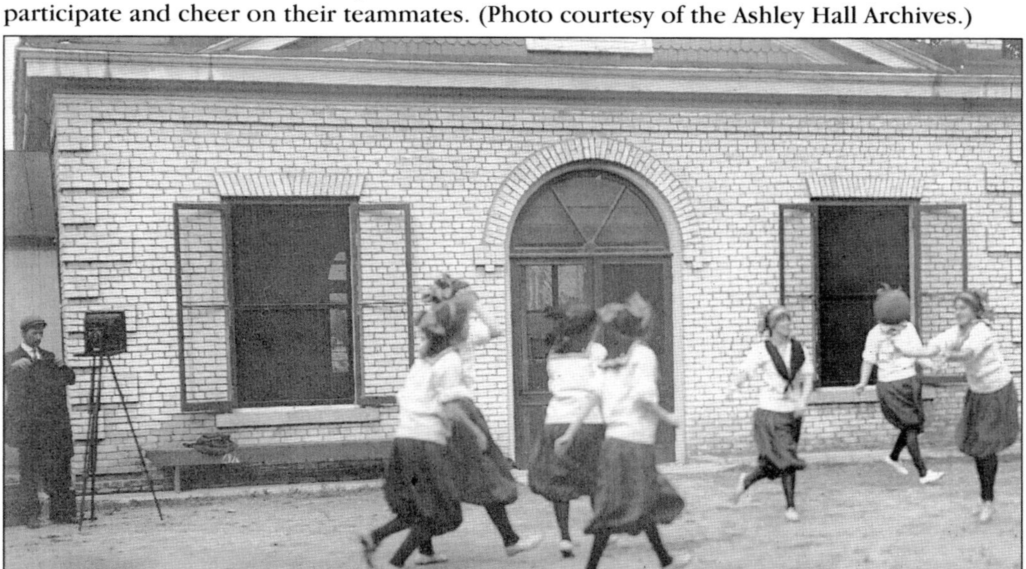

PHYSICAL EDUCATION CLASS, 1910s. The Block Ashley Hall club consisted of girls who had earned 150 points from participating in two individual sports tournaments and attaining two varsity letters. These girls were then given the privilege of officiating afternoon sports and also acting as assistants during physical education classes. Afternoon sports still continue as a weekly event through the eighth grade, and the girls get to expend all of their pent-up energy after a week of studying and classes. (Photo courtesy of the Ashley Hall Archives.)

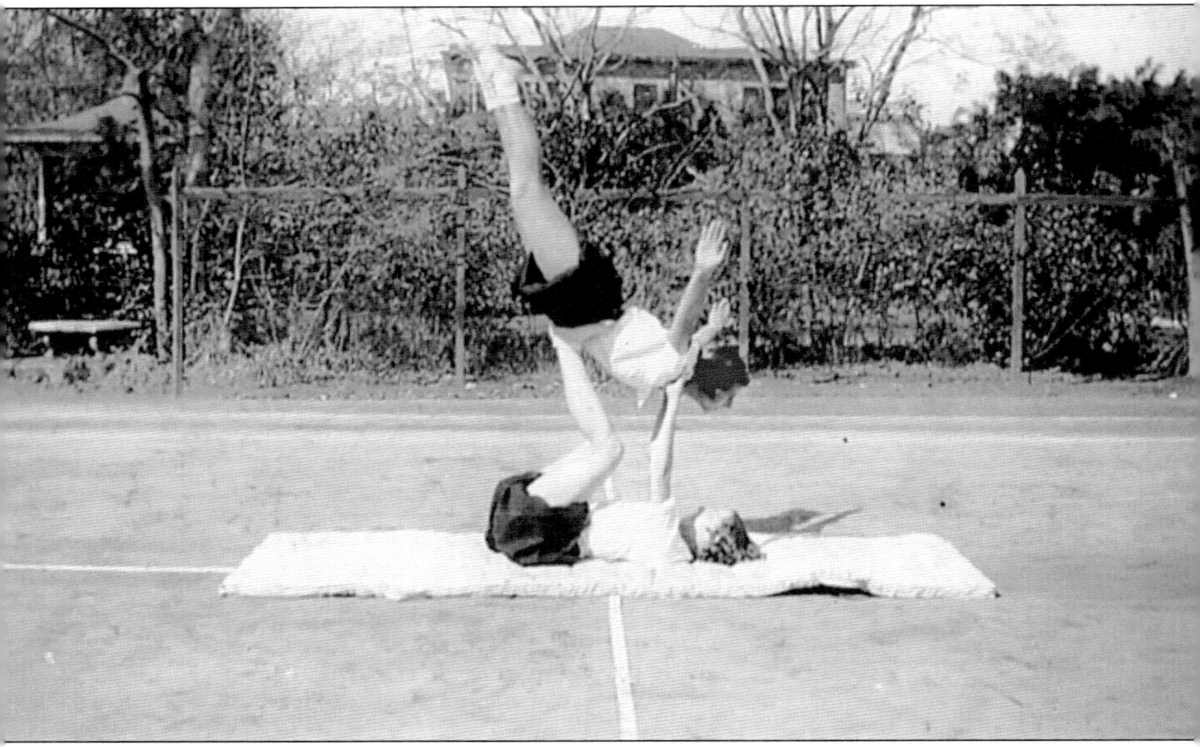

GYMNASTICS, 1930S. Besides basketball and tennis, other physically demanding teams and clubs were founded, such as the hiking and bicycling clubs. A track team and swimming team were founded in 1914, and in 1918 volleyball and rowing on Colonial Lake were added to the program. The 1933 *Cerberus* reports students participating in Deck Tennis and Shuffle Board. Also gymnastic classes were given that year by Miss Buist; prizes were awarded to the girls with the best posture. (Photo courtesy of the Ashley Hall Archives.)

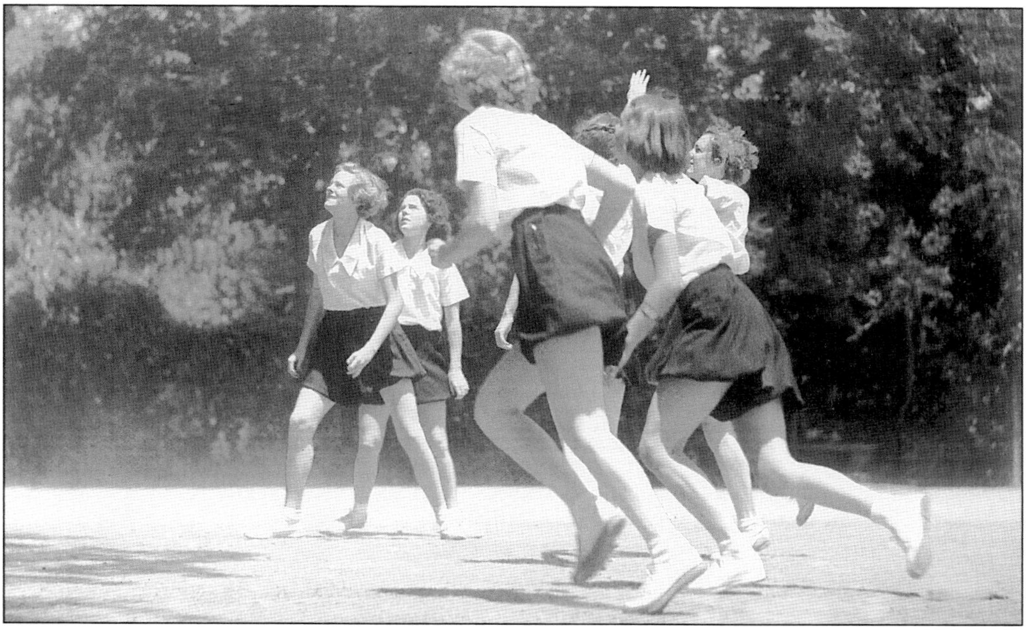

Sports, 1930s. Class Day Awards were given annually for basketball, gymnastics, and tennis. Best all-around athletics was given in memory of Rosalie McCabe to a girl on the basketball team showing the best sportsmanship. (Photo courtesy of the Ashley Hall Archives.)

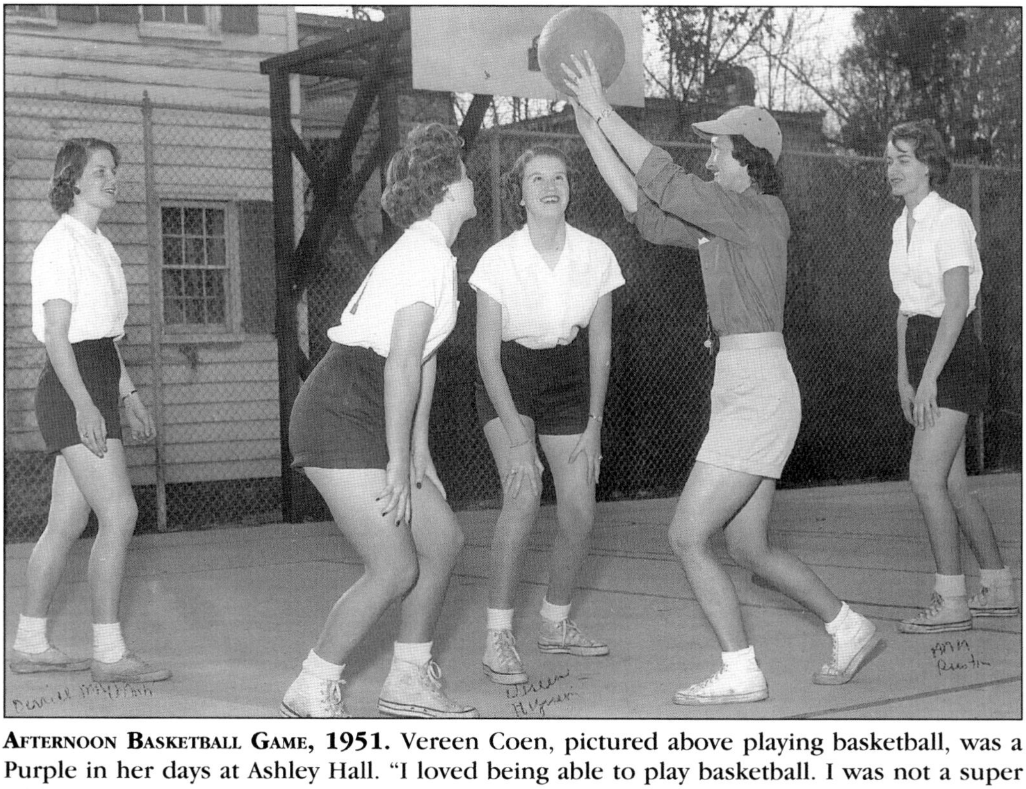

Afternoon Basketball Game, 1951. Vereen Coen, pictured above playing basketball, was a Purple in her days at Ashley Hall. "I loved being able to play basketball. I was not a super athlete, but I still had great self-esteem because my classmates would cheer me on and motivate me to improve," she remembers. (Photo courtesy of the Ashley Hall Archives.)

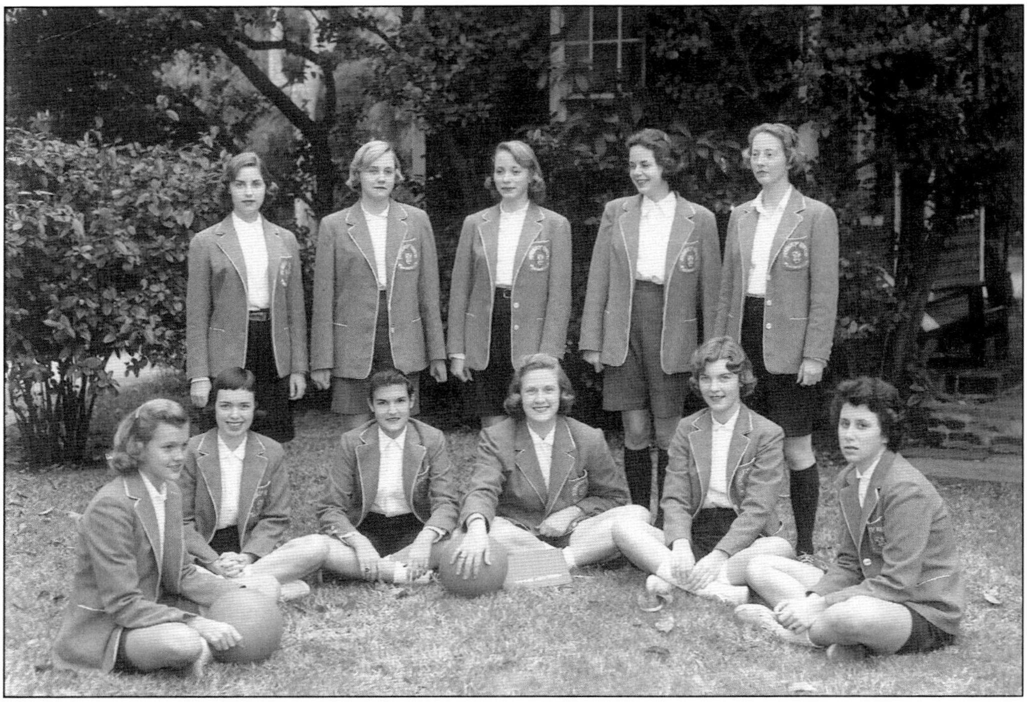

AA Board, 1958. The Athletic Association, founded in 1914 by Frances Rees, Olga Jatho, and Carla Sloan was started for the purpose of having athletics "be more on the order of 'organized labor'" (*Cerberus*, 1914). Later it was decided that the board would be composed of the Purple and White team captains and girls who played a varsity sport with the purpose of regulating sports activities and promoting interest in recreation. In the past, the board sold Ashley Hall paraphernalia, such as sweatshirts and parkas for money for the treasury. (Photo courtesy of the Ashley Hall Archives.)

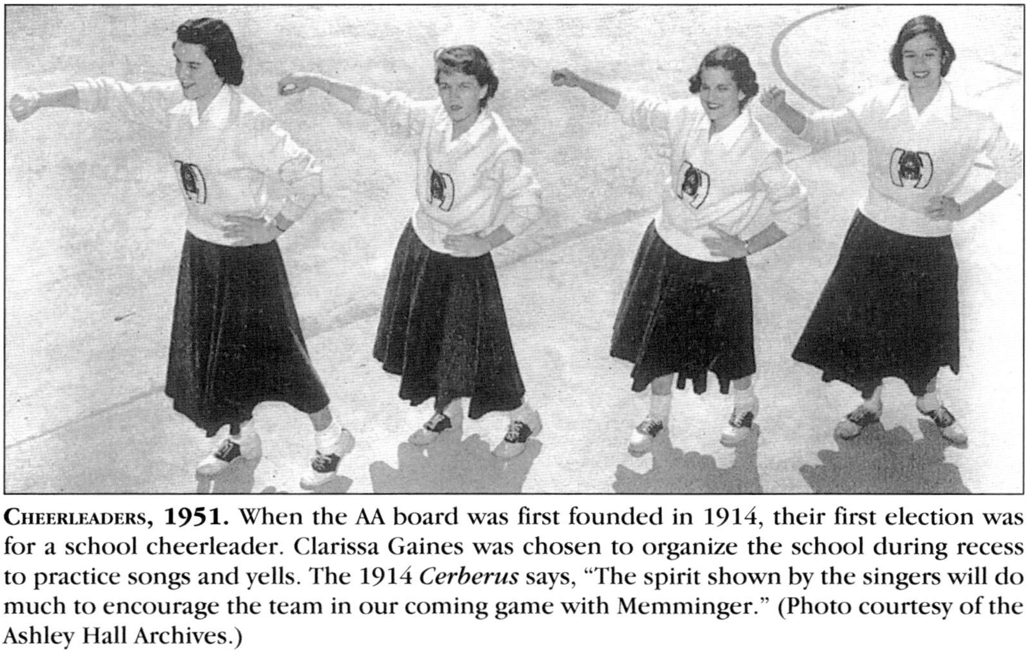

Cheerleaders, 1951. When the AA board was first founded in 1914, their first election was for a school cheerleader. Clarissa Gaines was chosen to organize the school during recess to practice songs and yells. The 1914 *Cerberus* says, "The spirit shown by the singers will do much to encourage the team in our coming game with Memminger." (Photo courtesy of the Ashley Hall Archives.)

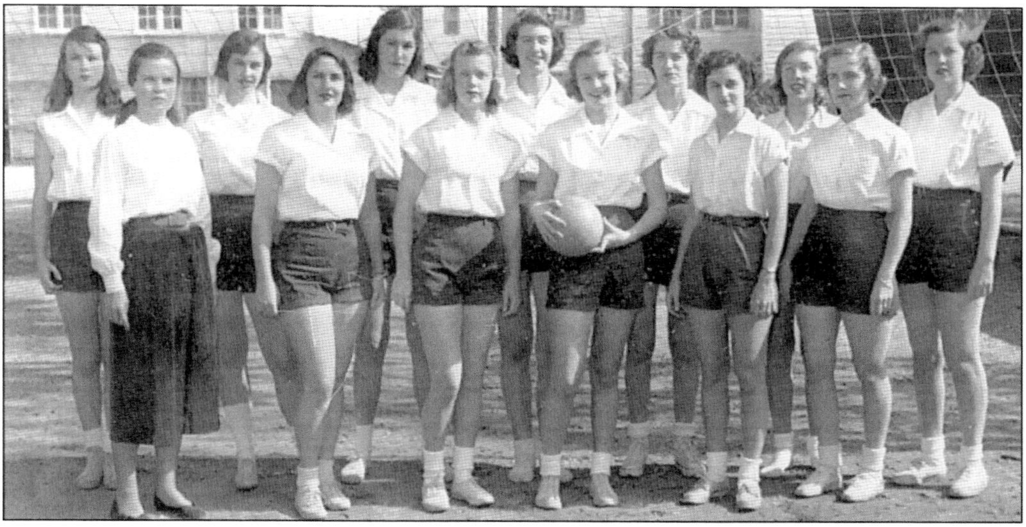

ASHLEY HALL VOLLEYBALL, 1952. Started as one of the school's first sports programs, volleyball has grown in popularity over the years. When this picture was taken, the school still did not have a gym in which the girls could practice. Members of the team recall playing on the tennis courts or various fields on the campus. There were very few other teams around to play, so the girls enjoyed intramural matches among Purples and Whites. (Photo courtesy of the Ashley Hall Archives.)

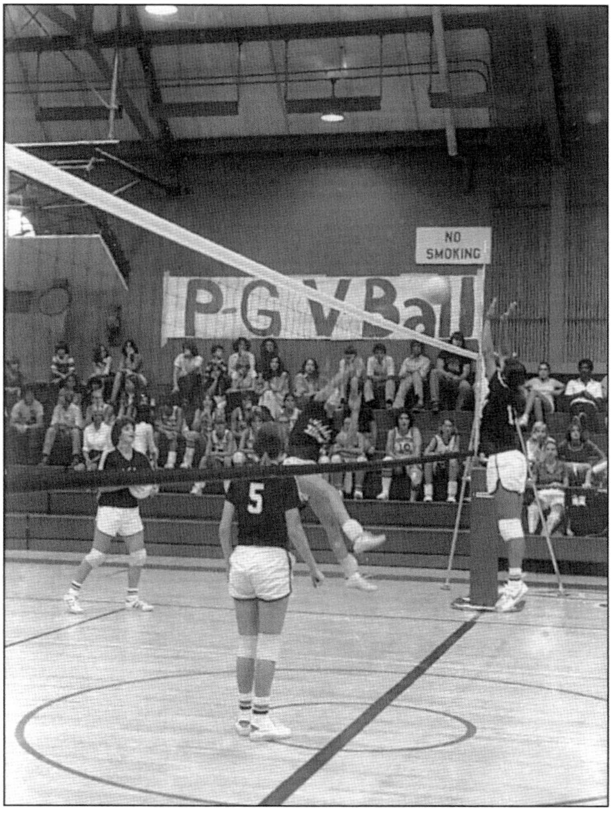

PANTHERS VS. CYCLONES, 1979. Franny Slay (née Frances Rivers, class of 1980) played setter for the varsity volleyball team and remembers the beginning of Ashley Hall's big rivalry against Porter Gaud. Now the volleyball coach for Ashley Hall, Slay recalls beating every team they played her senior year: "There were six senior starters on the team; that was the beginning of Ashley Hall's volleyball dynasty." After winning five state titles in a row, Ashley Hall still has an outstanding record. Slay says, "Playing a team sport prepares you for everyday life because you all have to learn to work together for a common goal. As a member of the team you rely on others to participate to their fullest; otherwise you will have a drop in momentum." (Photo courtesy of the Ashley Hall Archives.)

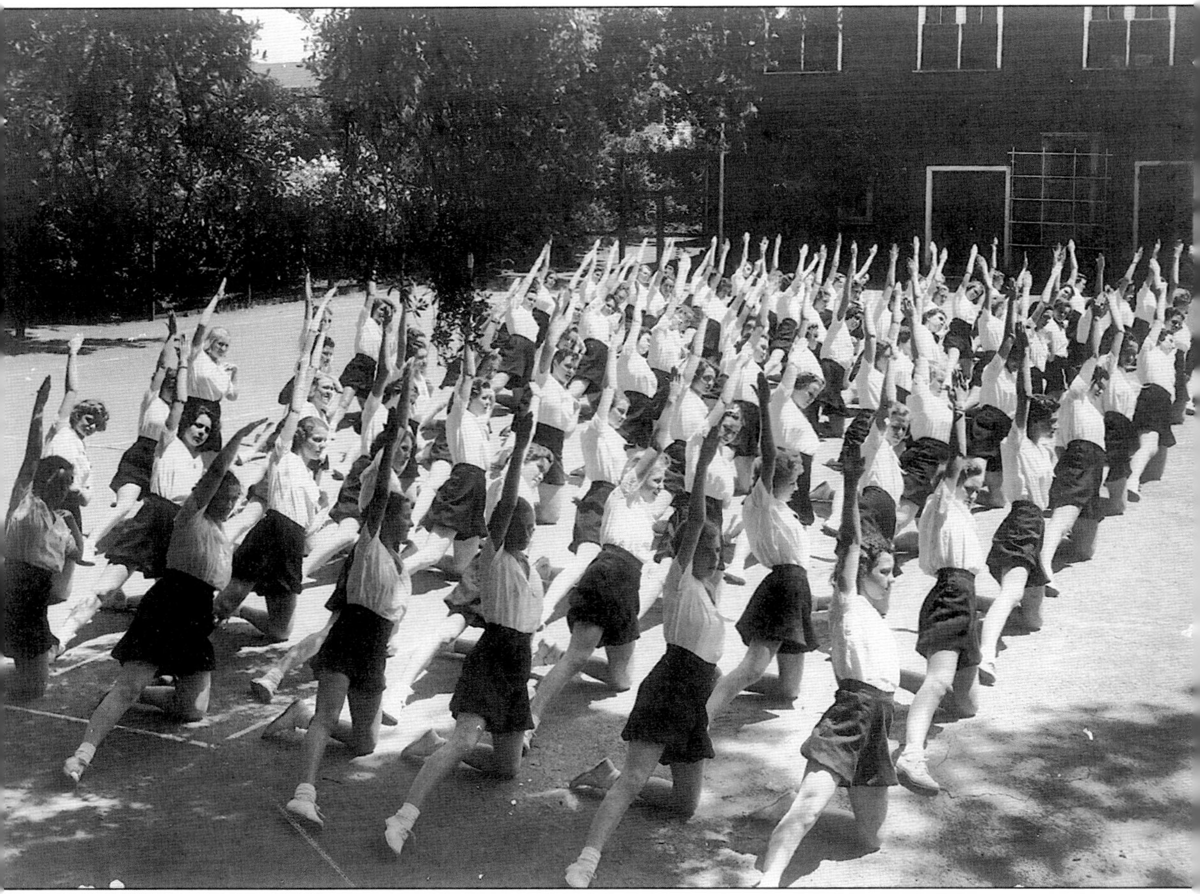

Sports, 1930s. Songs and cheers were a necessary spirit booster for winning the cup at field day. Written by Mrs. J.W. Locke, "In an Oak Shaded Garden" is listed as one of the school songs in the 1935 *Cerberus*. Its words are as follows:

In an oak-shaded garden
In a city by the sea.
There stands old Ashley Hall, so dear,
That's where I love to be.
In days of mirth and sadness, too,
She stands serene and calm,
A beacon bright to lead us on,
And keep us from all harm.
CHORUS: Oh, Ashley Hall, dear Ashley Hall,
That's where I love to be. (Photo courtesy of the Ashley Hall Archives.)

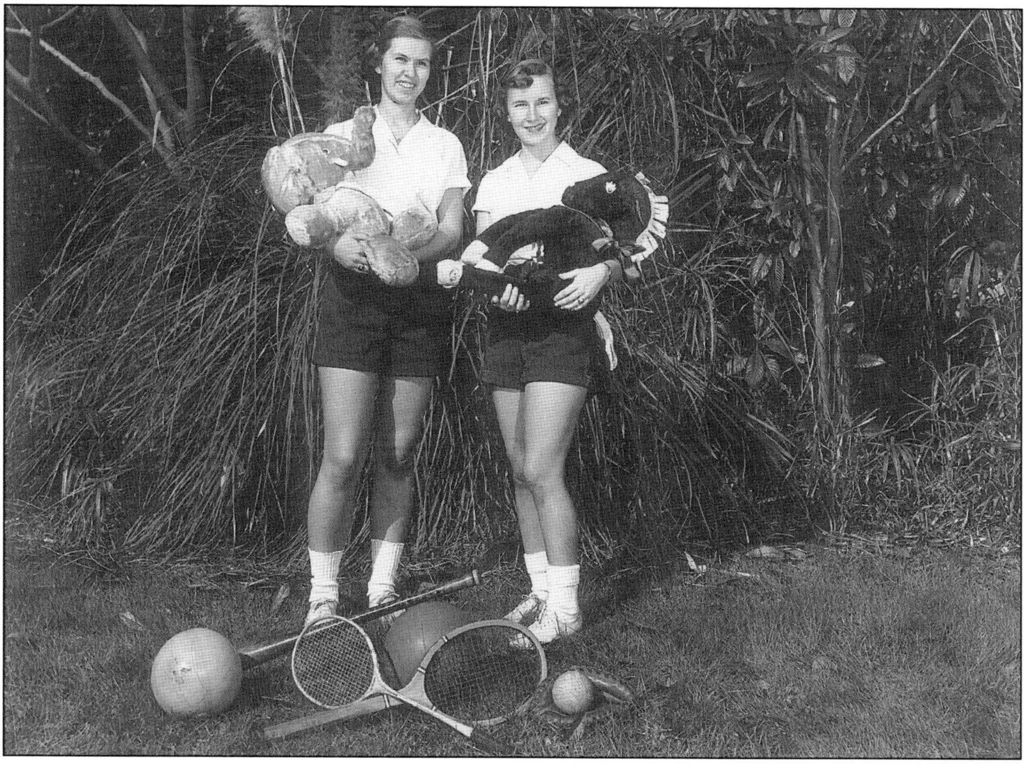

Purple and White Captains, 1954. The Purple and White teams, started by Miss McBee in the first years of the school, are representative of Ashley Hall's school colors. Captains were elected each year to try and lead each team to victory and to have bragging rights of the school cup. Besides sporting events, the two teams also compete in the fields of academic achievement and extracurricular participation. (Photo courtesy of the Ashley Hall Archives.)

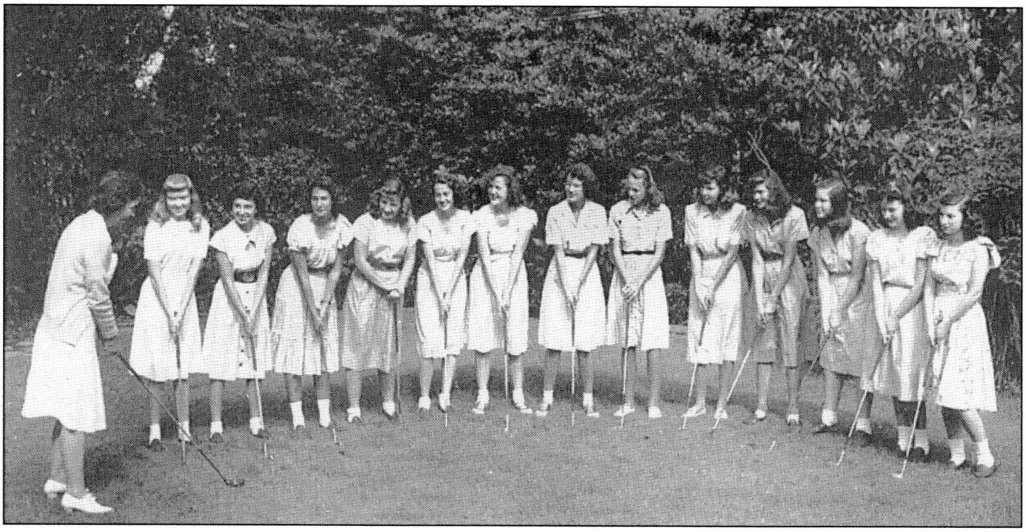

Golf Team, 1947. The first golf in America was played in Charleston, and it has been played here ever since. A 1950 Alumnae News Letter says, "Golfers among the Ashley Hall girls play on any of the three excellent club golf courses in Charleston and immediate vicinity." (Photo courtesy of the Ashley Hall Archives.)

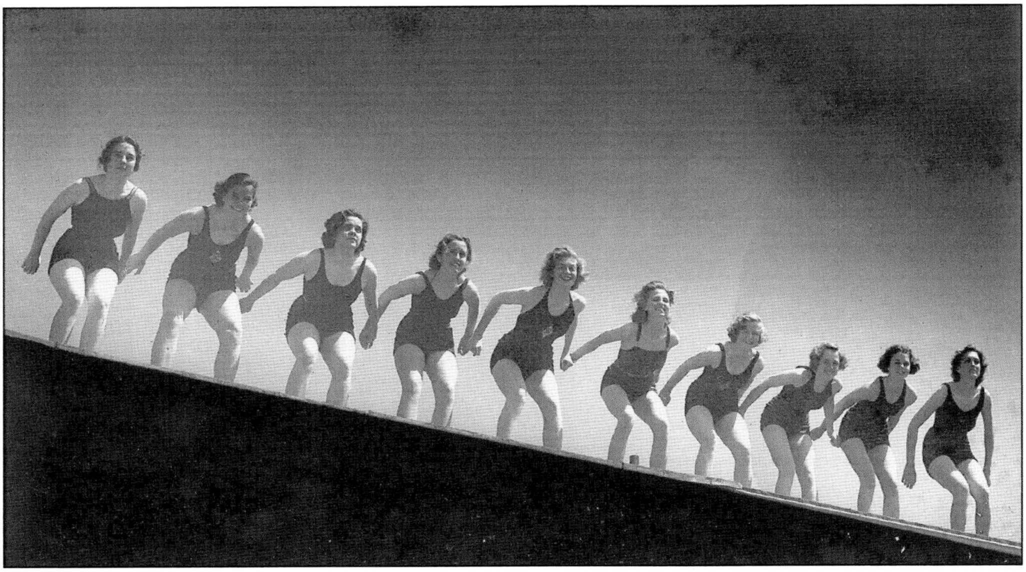

Swim Team, 1936. Having one of the first school pools in the states of North and South Carolina, it seems only fitting that there would be a swim team. Many other schools around Charleston, including the Citadel, were allowed to practice there, and annual swim meets were an exciting event. The pool was also open in the afternoon to ladies of the community who did not attend Ashley Hall. Life-saving classes were always offered to students at the school. (Photo courtesy of the Ashley Hall Archives.)

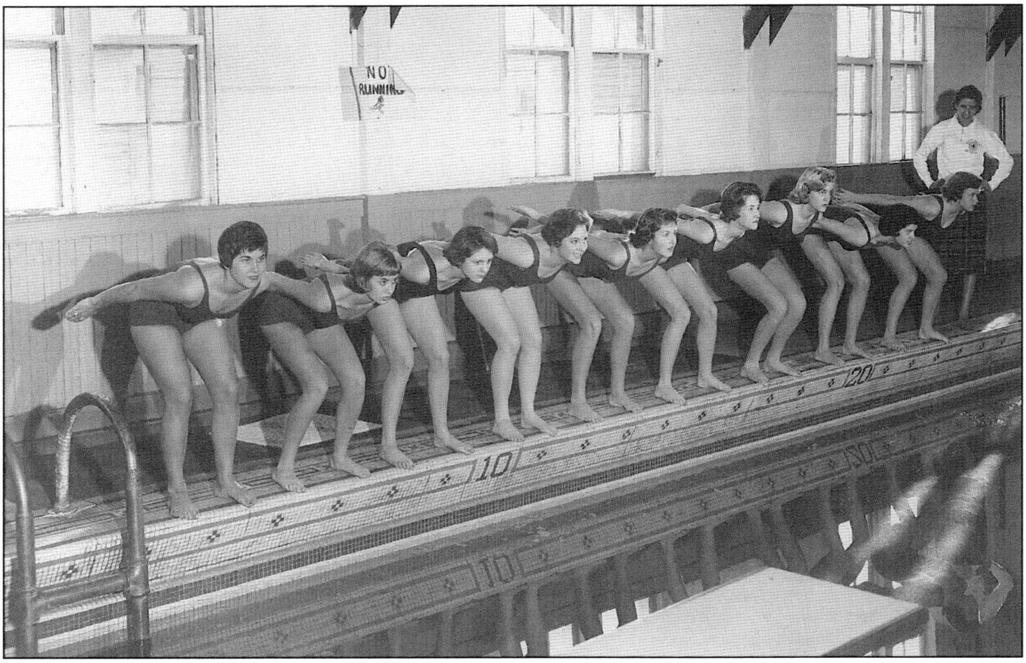

Varsity Swimming, 1960. The traditional events at the swim meets were the 50-yard backstroke, 50- and 100-yard free-style, medley swim, 50-yard breast stroke, and relay. Girls also competed in diving competitions. The big rivals of the sport were Memminger and the College of Charleston. Purples and Whites also competed against each other on a regular occasion. (Photo courtesy of the Ashley Hall Archives.)

Seven

Student Life

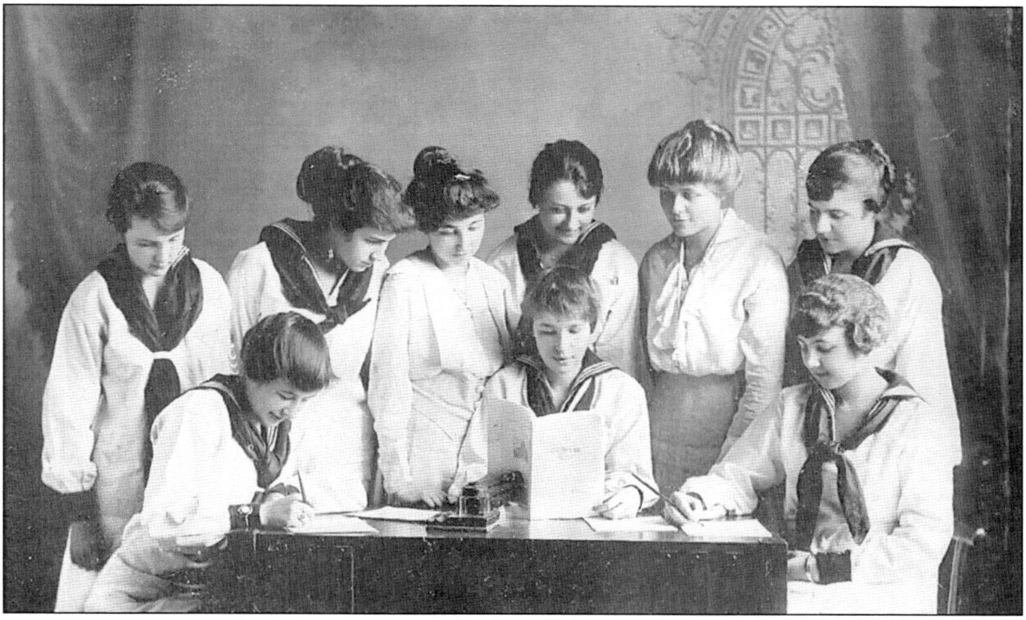

***Cerberus* Staff of 1915.** In the days before electronic media, singing was a staple of entertainment. Glee clubs would travel the country and perform at other schools. Once the Shady Side Academy club of Pittsburgh, Pennsylvania visited Ashley Hall on their annual Southern tour, performing songs like "Drink to Me Only With Thine Eyes," "Stars of the Summer Night," and "Land of Hope and Glory." The girls had the pleasure of a live performance as well as the opportunity to meet boys from other states. (Photo courtesy of the Ashley Hall Archives.)

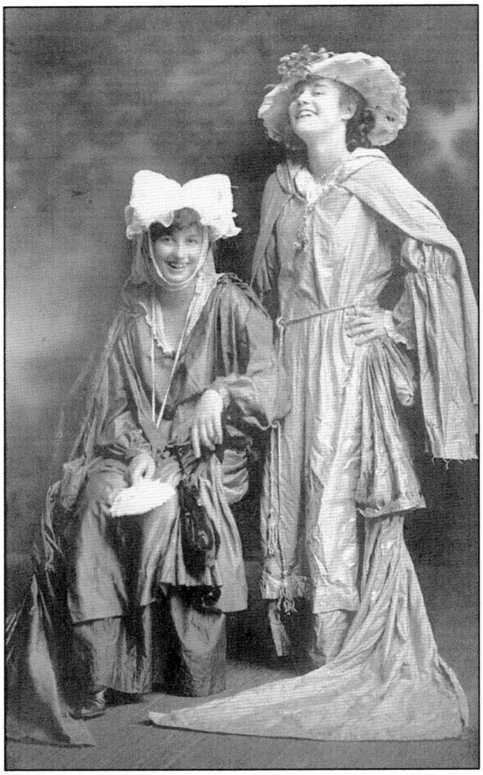

Dress Up, 1940s. The rules for boarders at Ashley Hall were very strict. Gloves and hats had to be worn if the girls were leaving the campus and a chaperone was never far behind. "They even followed us to the drugstore!" recalls Katherine Orr. (Photo courtesy of the Ashley Hall Archives.)

Around Town, 1910s. Besides school, clubs, and sports, students had the assets of the city of Charleston—the shops on King Street, plays at the Footlight Players and Dockstreet Theaters, and of course, the boys across the street at Porter Military Academy and further down the road at the Citadel. Although they were always chaperoned, the girls did get a chance to leave the campus and explore the vibrant city. In Miss McBee's day the boarders were always taken to the Episcopal church every Sunday. (Photo courtesy of the Ashley Hall Archives.)

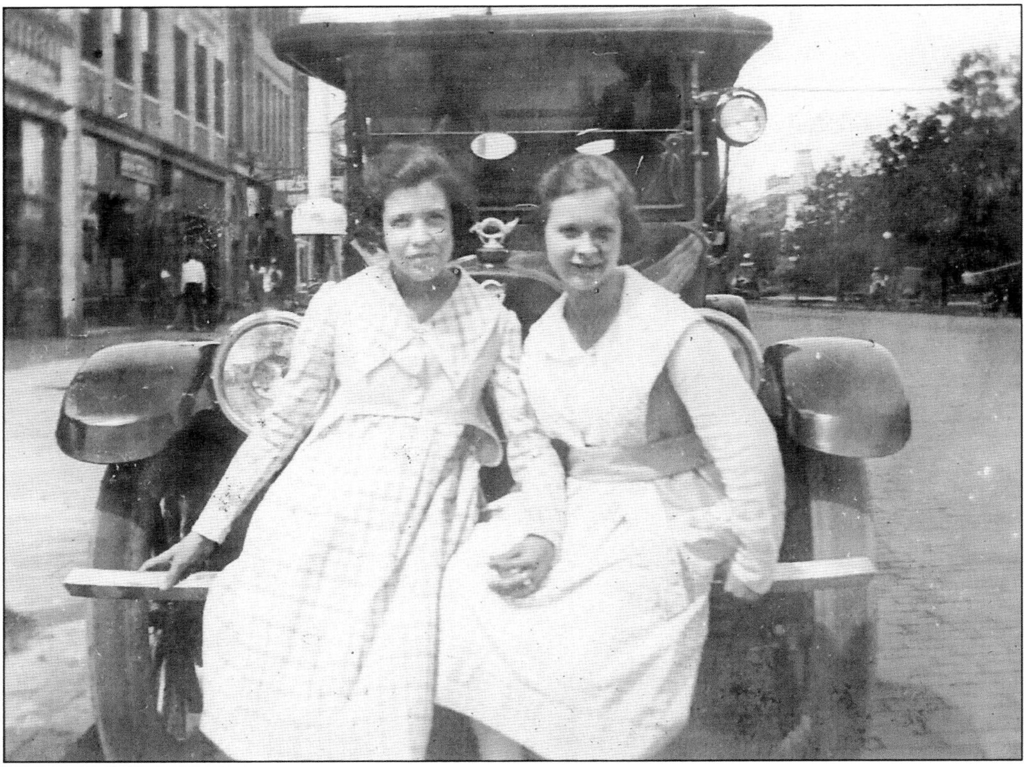

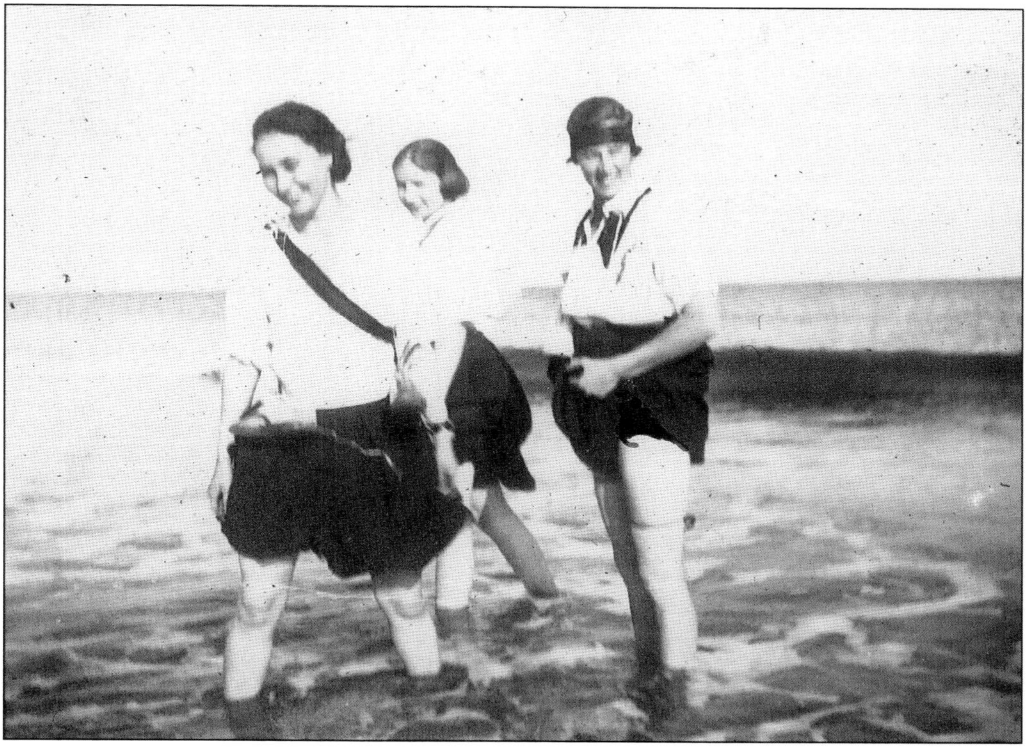

Sullivan's Island, 1910s. Here the boarders are enjoying another one of Charleston's great attractions, the beach. On long weekends or hot Saturdays, the faculty and boarders would head to Sullivan's Island to cool off and relax. The bus would go all the way down to the beach for less than 25 cents. Sullivan's Island was the more popular beach until the Hurricane of 1940 wiped it out and everyone began to go to Folly Beach. (Photo courtesy of the Ashley Hall Archives.)

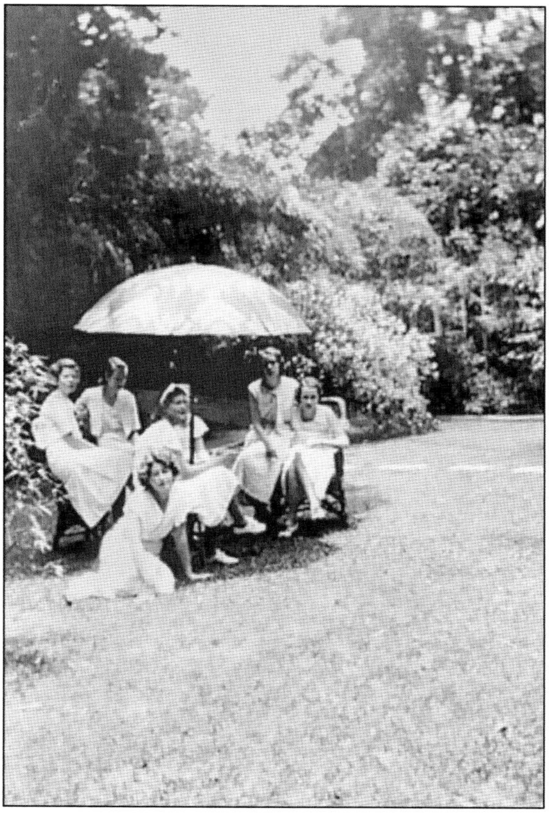

Bathing Beauties, 1920s. When the beach was too far away for the girls, the lawns and gardens on campus made perfect spots for sunning and enjoying the weather. Picnics were great excuses to sun outside, as long as the girls were careful not to expose too much skin in front of Miss McBee. It was not even proper for women to show their bare ankles during Miss McBee's reign. (Photo courtesy of the Ashley Hall Archives.)

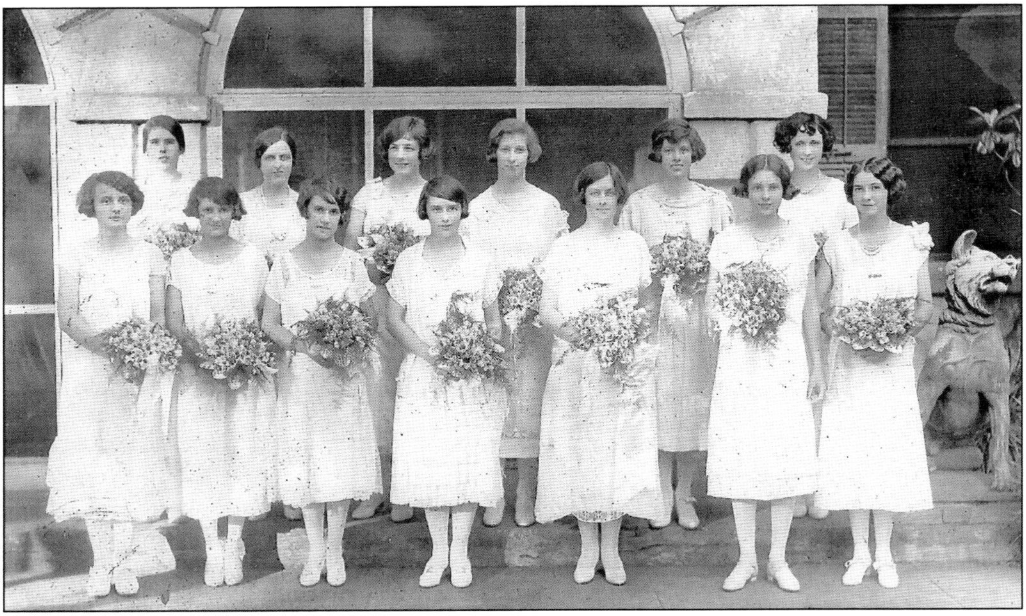

Commencement, 1925. When the high academic standards at Ashley Hall became known, the class sizes began to grow. It is hard to believe that the school started out with only 45 students and by its 25th anniversary the enrollment had increased to 230 students. This graduating class of 1925 shows the growing number of graduates. (Photo courtesy of the Ashley Hall Archives.)

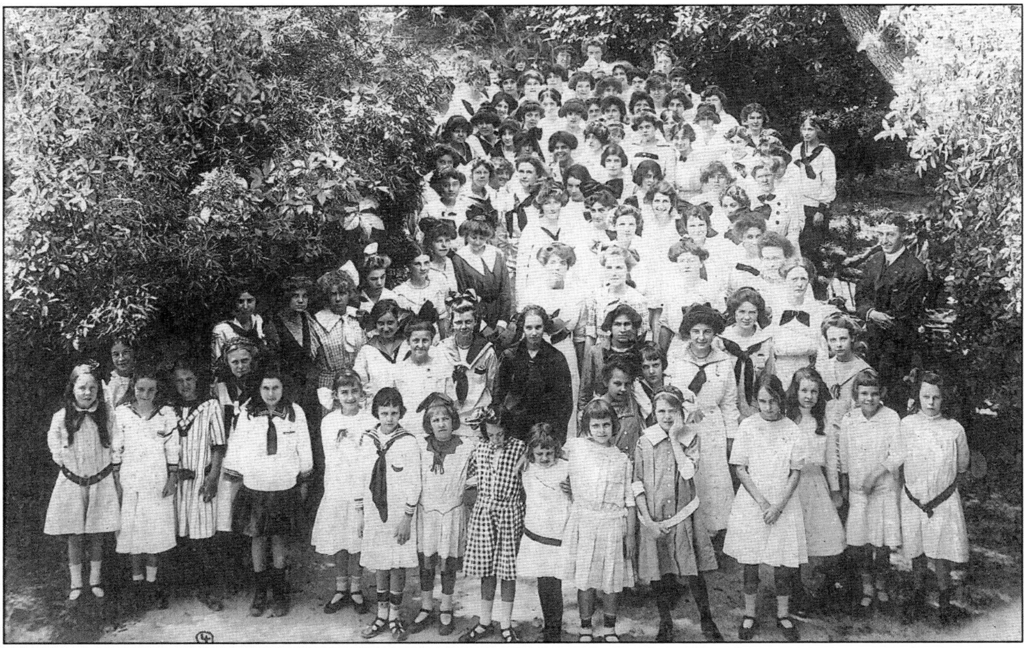

School in 1913. The old ballroom in the McBee House served as the school's assembly hall. Chapel was held there every morning at nine, elocution classes during the day, and in the evenings there were dramatics and Friday night parties. Josephine Pinckney writes in her pamphlet *Call Back Yesterday* that "most of the general bustle took place" there. (Photo courtesy of the Ashley Hall Archives.)

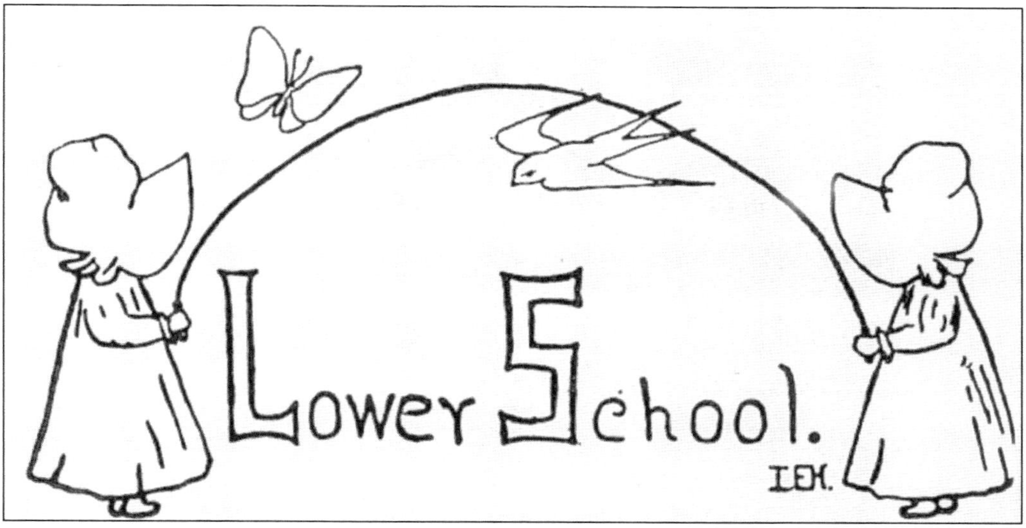

CERBERUS, **1913.** The term lower school was not used until the second school catalogue was printed in 1910. But classes and curriculum have always been provided for younger children ranging from kindergarten and up. Not known to very many, is that Ashley Hall once allowed boys to attend the school until third grade. This is no longer the case and boys must find a different school after kindergarten. (Photo courtesy of the Ashley Hall Archives.)

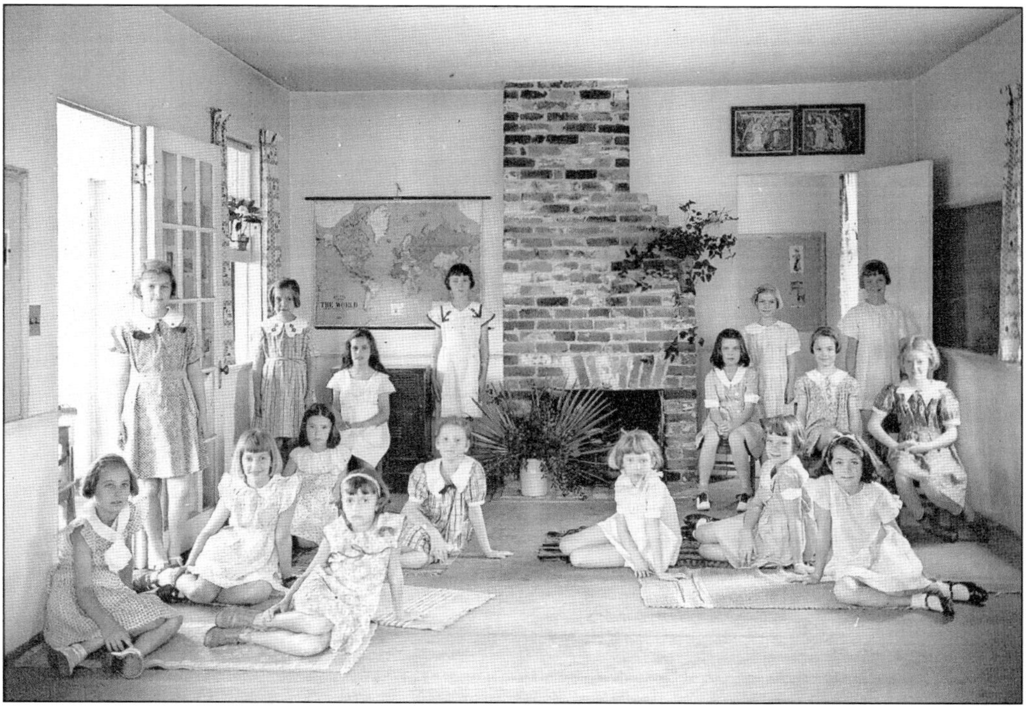

LOWER SCHOOL, 1930s. The lower school curriculum consisted of reading, English, mathematics, French, music, art, and physical training. In the sixth grade, history, geography, and sciences were also taught. Reports were sent home six times a year and parent-teacher conferences were scheduled if there were any concerns. Achievement tests of the Educational Records Bureau were given each spring ensure that students were at the same level as other students across the nation. (Photo courtesy of the Ashley Hall Archives.)

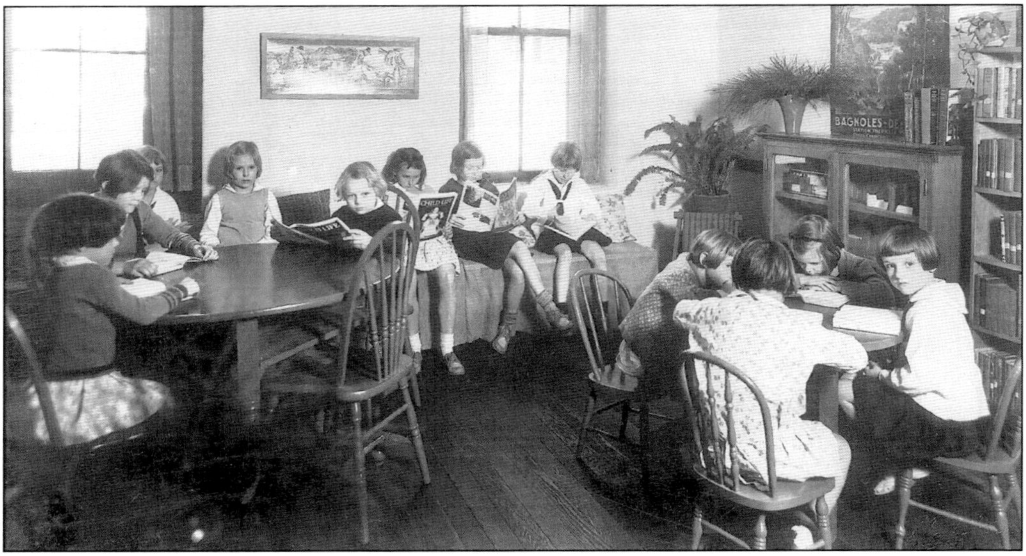

LOWER SCHOOL LIBRARY, 1930s. The lower school students were given many opportunities to participate in extra-curricular activities such as lower school glee club, student council, chapel programs, and editing of the lower school newspaper, *The Inkwell*. Laird Chisholm, of the fifth grade, published a poem in the 1935 *Cerberus* entitled "The Forty-Niners:" "In olden days when the West was won/ The parents would say, 'Go west my son.'/ And off he would go with a pick and an ax/ And dreams he would bring gold back in sacks./ At the parting the mother would weep/ And the father would ask God to keep/ Him safe from all dangers 'til the end/ And never a reckless life to spend." (Photo courtesy of the Ashley Hall Archives.)

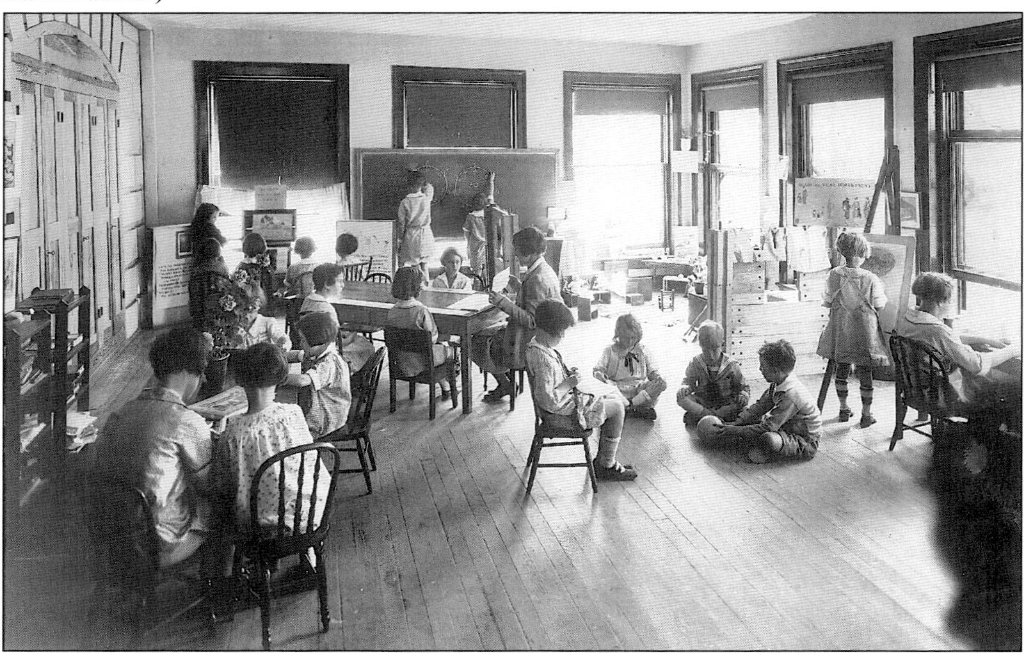

CLASS TIME, 1929. *Cerberus* joke: "Mother: 'Well, daughter, what do you have to know for Math Three?' Daughter: 'All we have to know is one thing.' Mother: 'What is that?' Daughter: 'The answer.'" (Photo courtesy of the Ashley Hall Archives.)

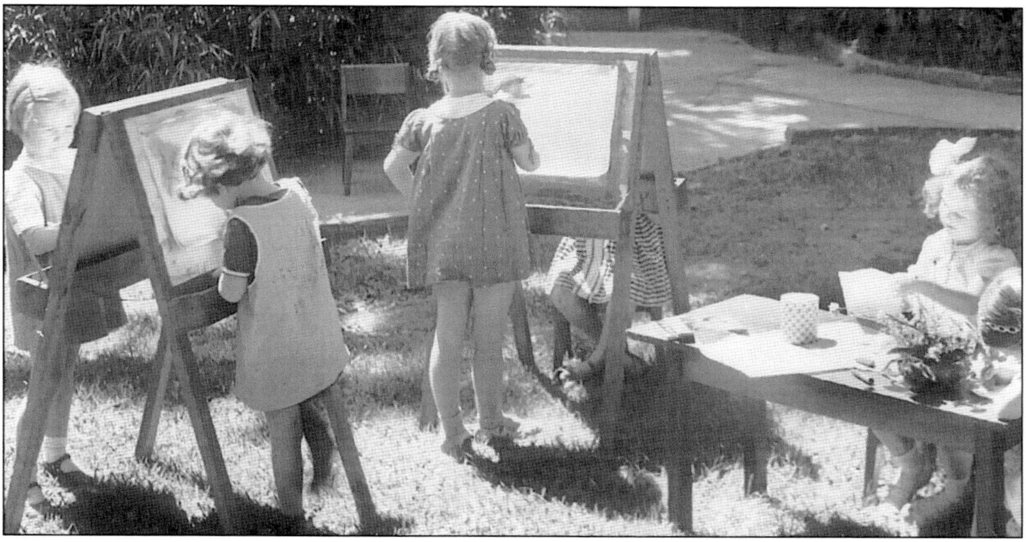

ART CLASS, 1935. Until girls were in sixth and seventh grades they were not given specific art instruction, but beginning in kindergarten there was an art class where they were encouraged to paint and draw. An early brochure states, "art classes provide stimulating experiences for all students. . . . There is a definite plan for the study of the world's masterpieces. The facilities of the Gibbes Art Gallery and the Charleston Museum contribute to the enrichment of this course." (Photo courtesy of the Ashley Hall Archives.)

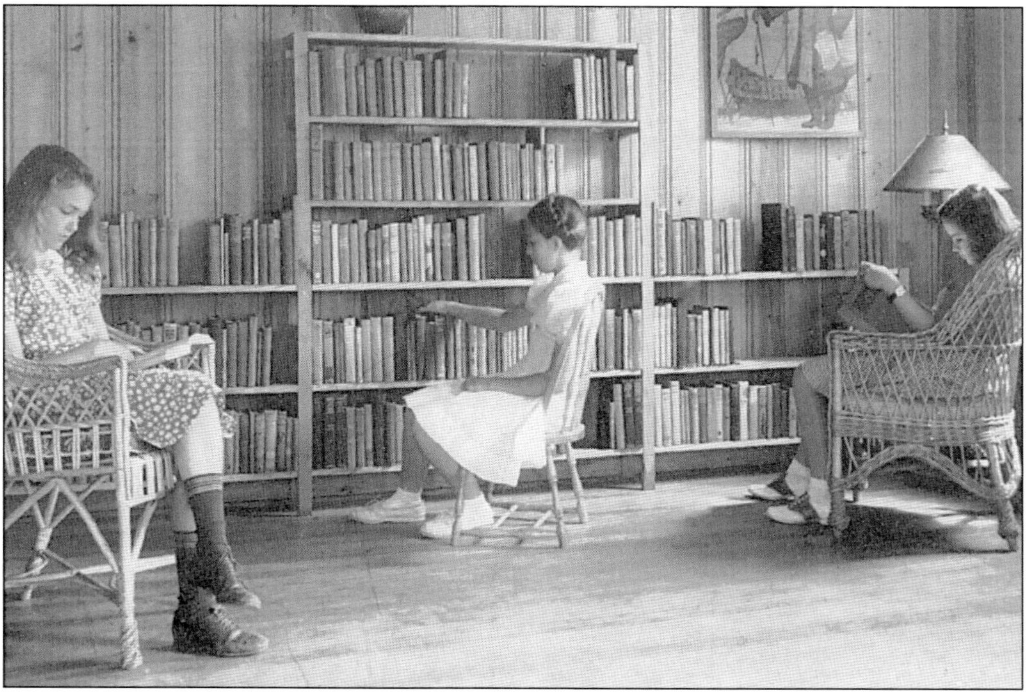

LOWER SCHOOL LIBRARY, 1930s. An early Ashley Hall brochure states that the lower school library, containing over 2,000 volumes, provides each class "with a shelf of carefully selected books for special use." The lower school had its own yearbook called *The Bannister* (from 1973 to 1977), which featured individual pictures as well as clubs and activities of the younger girls. (Photo courtesy of the Ashley Hall Archives.)

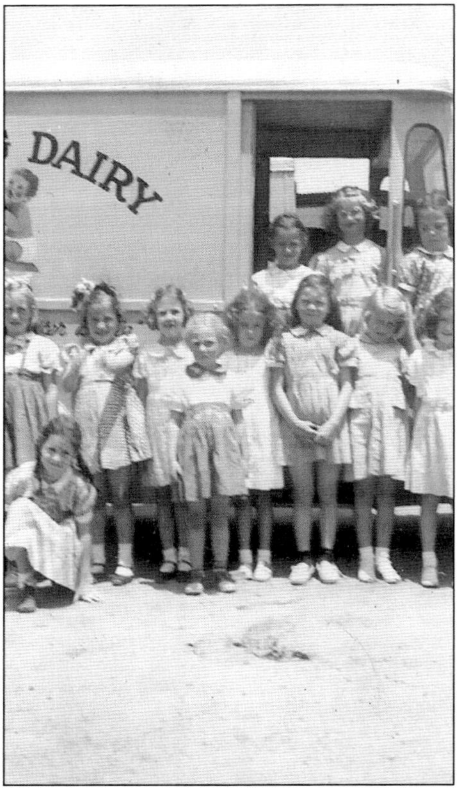

Field Trip, 1930s. "Field trips are planned according to the needs, interests and activities of the various groups," quotes an early Ashley Hall brochure. Here learning about farms and animals is made fun by taking a trip to the dairy and giving the children a way to interact as they learn. (Photo courtesy of the Ashley Hall Archives.)

Fairies Pose for a Picture, 1910s. The lower school girls at Ashley Hall enjoyed dancing classes and put on performances each year for the school. In 1925, dancing classes under Miss Sadi Innes Brown put on a ballet pantomime at the Charleston Theatre called the "Toy Shop." The production, sponsored by *Le Verre D'Eau*, made $190 for a fund to start a free kindergarten in Charleston. (Photo courtesy of the Ashley Hall Archives.)

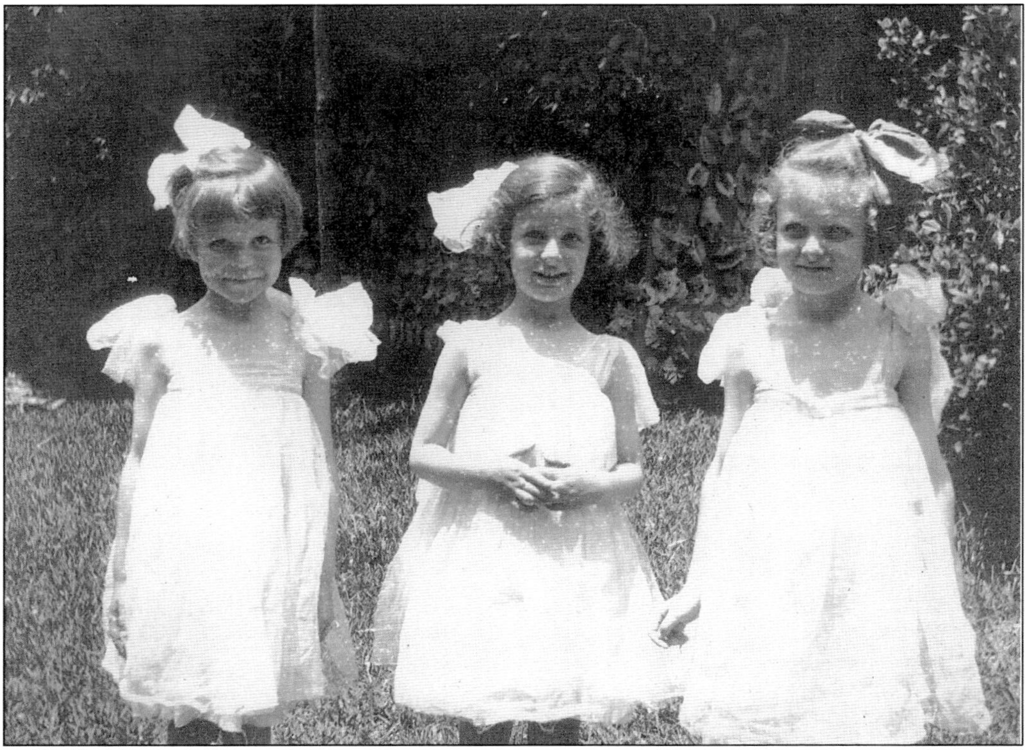

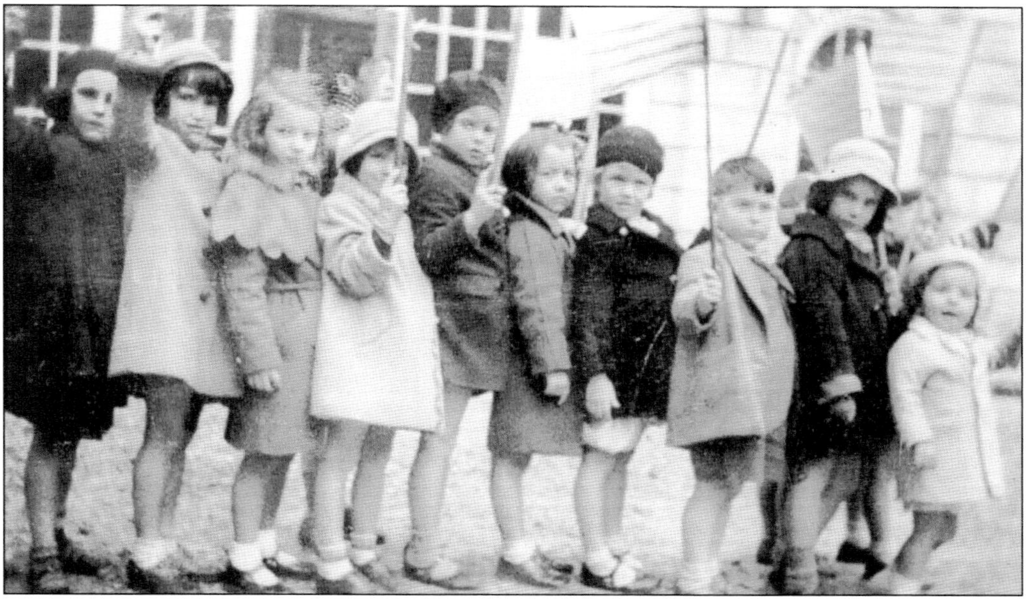

LOWER SCHOOL, 1936. An old chapel program from 1948 is titled "Piano Pupils in Recital." "Three Little Chickens," "A Giddy Girl," and "Looby Loo" were just some of the pieces performed. At that time, the lower school and kindergarten classes had very little interaction with the older girls except during these chapel presentations. (Photo courtesy of the Ashley Hall Archives.)

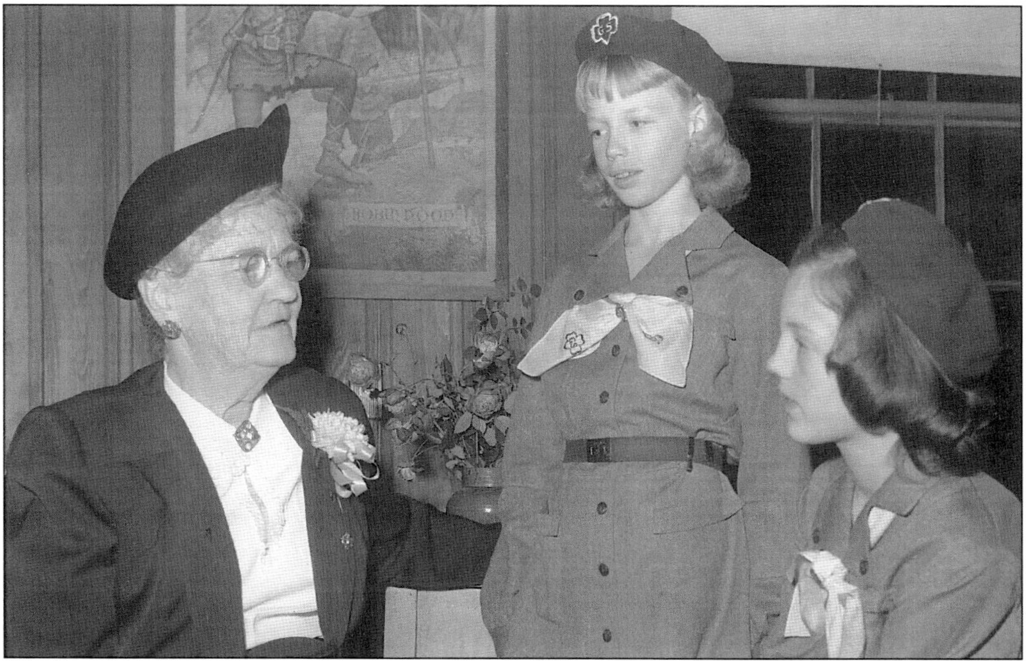

MISS MCBEE, SALLY ANN BARSH, AND MARGARET MILLER, 1924. Ashley Hall had the first Girl Scout troop in Charleston. Started in the late 1900s, Troop #1 began the custom of volunteering in the community at a young age. The Citizenship Cup was given each year to a scout who had shown the most involvement in the community. (Photo courtesy of the Ashley Hall Archives.)

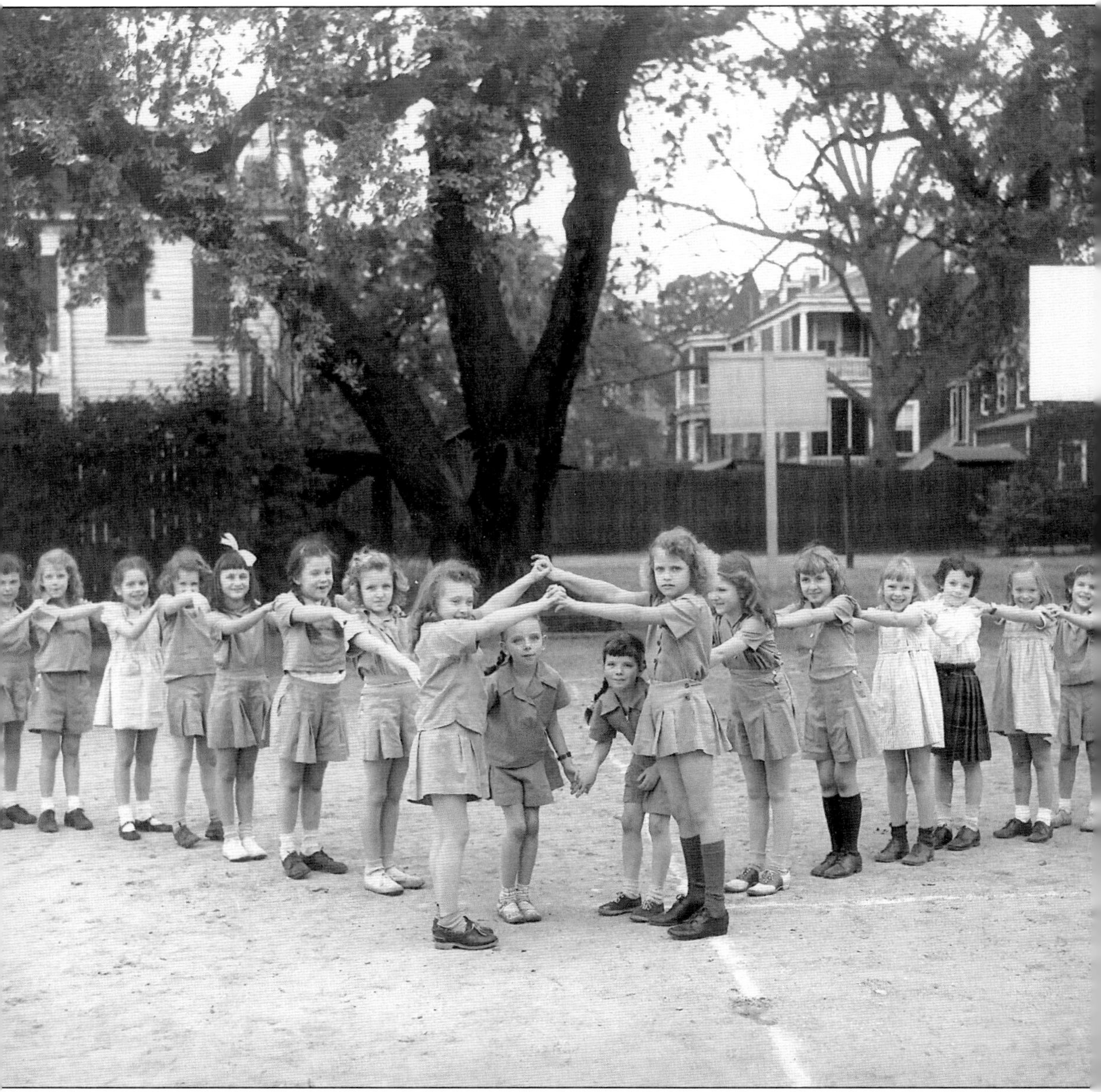

CHARLESTON TROOP #1, 1948. Shown here in the back of campus near the old tennis courts, the Girl Scouts pose for a picture. Josephine Pinckney writes in her pamphlet *Call Back Yesterday* that one Ashley Hall graduate, Alice Wagner, went on to become a National Officer for the Girl Scouts of America. (Photo courtesy of the Ashley Hall Archives.)

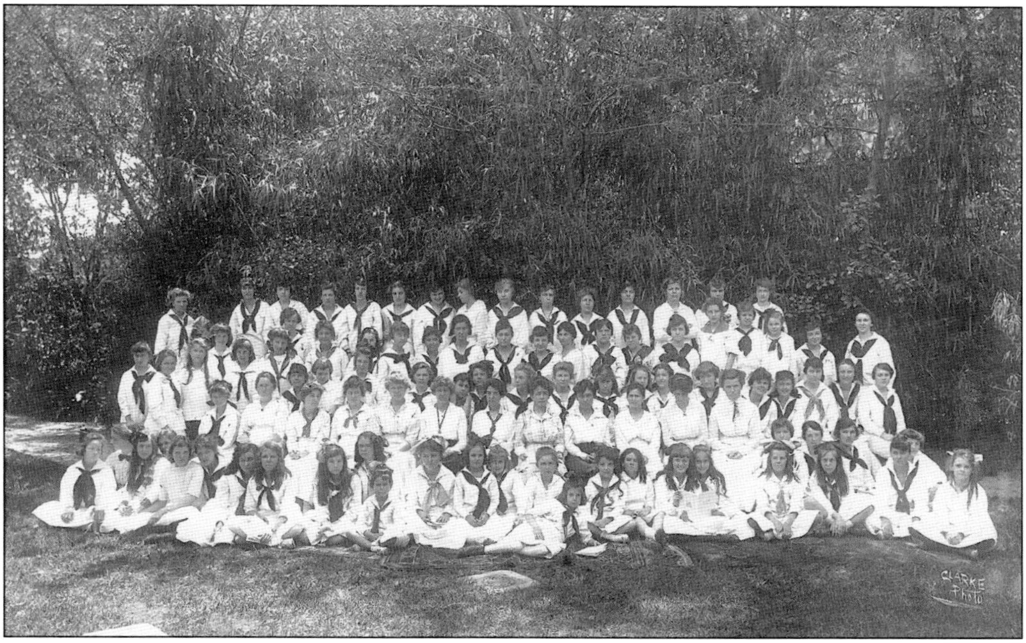

School in 1916. In April of this year, the girls participated in the Shakespeare Festival at the College of Charleston. The Shakespeare play given for the graduation week performance was *The Tempest*, and the commencement speaker was mayor Tristram T. Hyde. (Photo courtesy of the Ashley Hall Archives.)

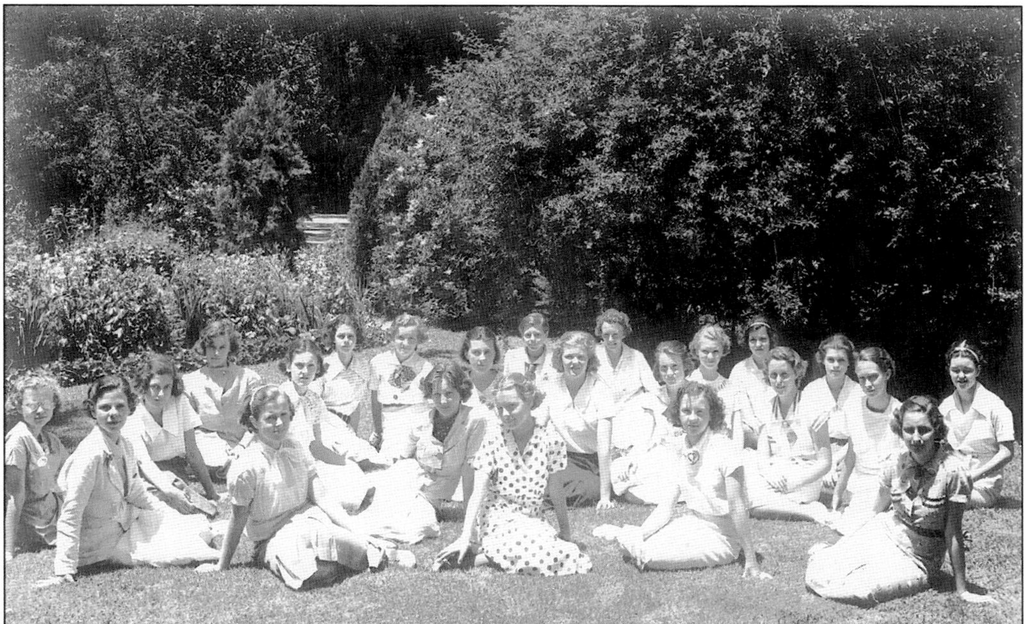

Eighth Grade Class Picture, 1936. An advertisement for the school in the late 1930s reads: "ASHLEY HALL: an accredited college preparatory school for girls in an atmosphere of southern culture and colonial tradition. The mild climate permits outdoor sports all winter. Riding, Swimming, Tennis, Basketball." (Photo courtesy of the Ashley Hall Archives.)

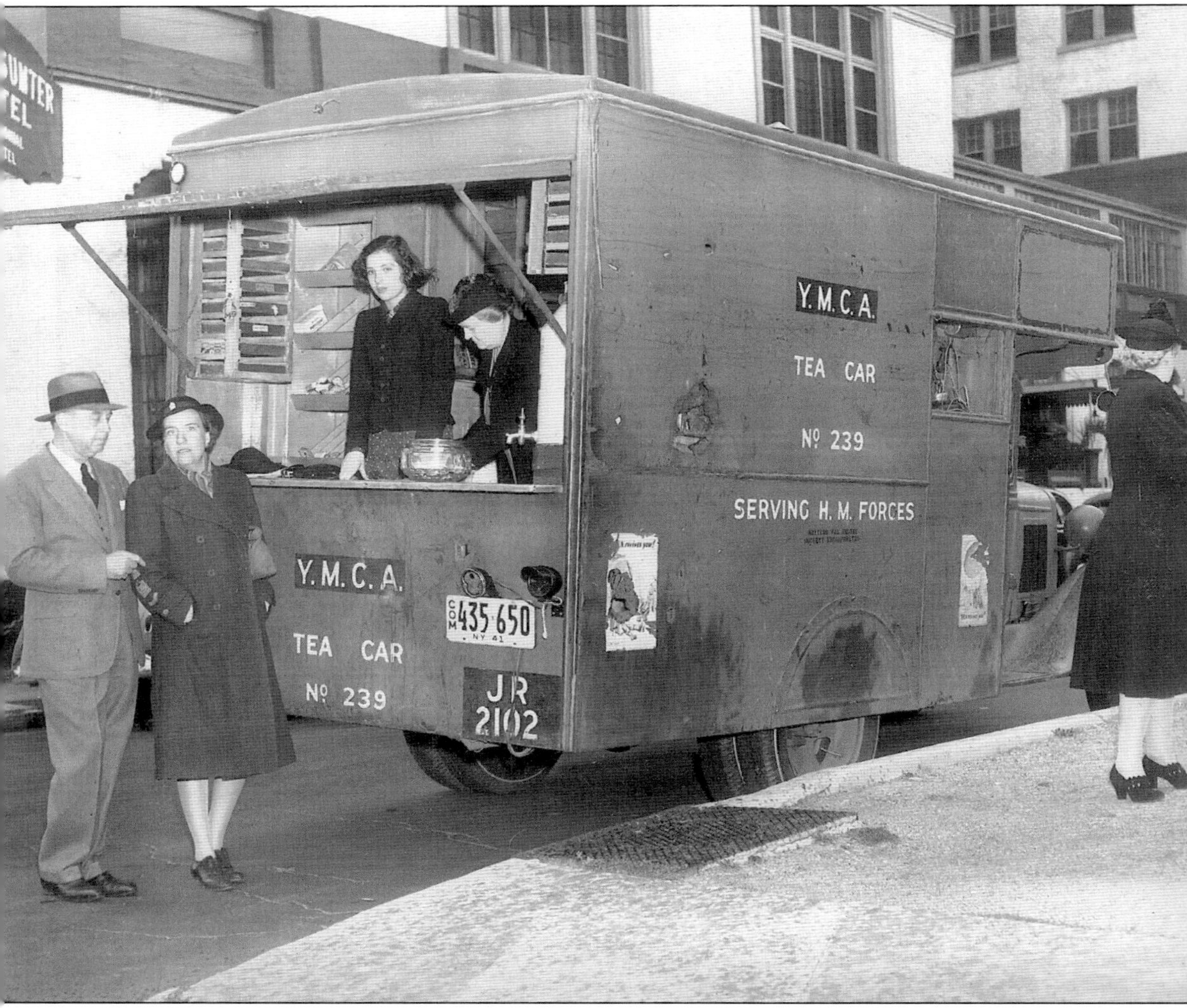

YMCA Tea Car, 1942. Usually boarding students had to be high school age (8th to 12th grade), but during World War II, they could be younger. Girls of all ages at the school contributed to the community in small but helpful ways. In 1943, the school decided not to publish a yearbook or issue of *Cerberus* in order to conserve paper. Doing their part to help out in the war effort at home, Ashley Hall girls manned a tea car outside the Fort Sumter Hotel. (Photo courtesy of the Ashley Hall Archives.)

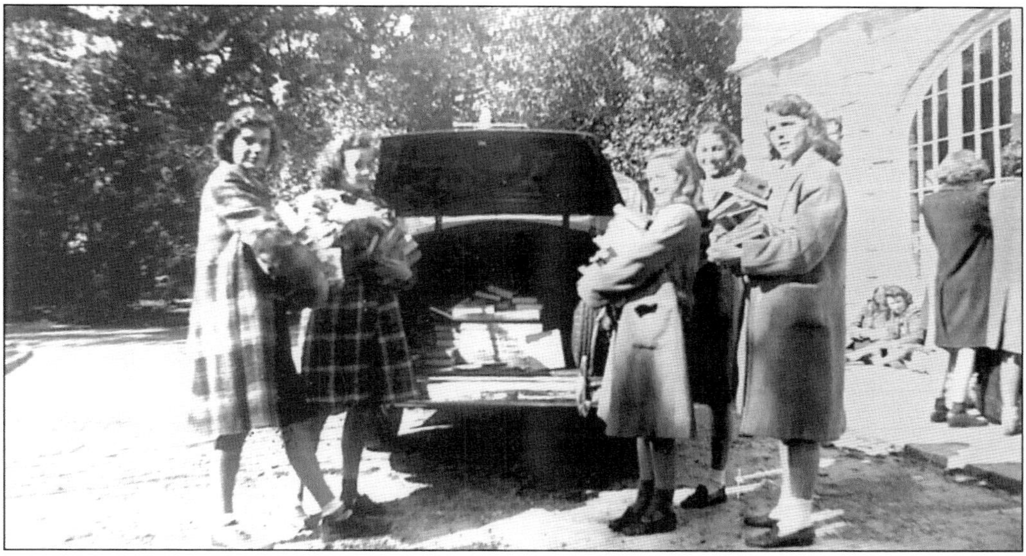

Book Donations, 1940s. Always trying to do their part for the community, girls are shown here filling a car's trunk full of books for donation. Angie LeClercq says, "Ashley Hall was a vital part of the Charleston community, and it was special because it was a place where women could compete without having to cater to the demands of men." (Photo courtesy of the Ashley Hall Archives.)

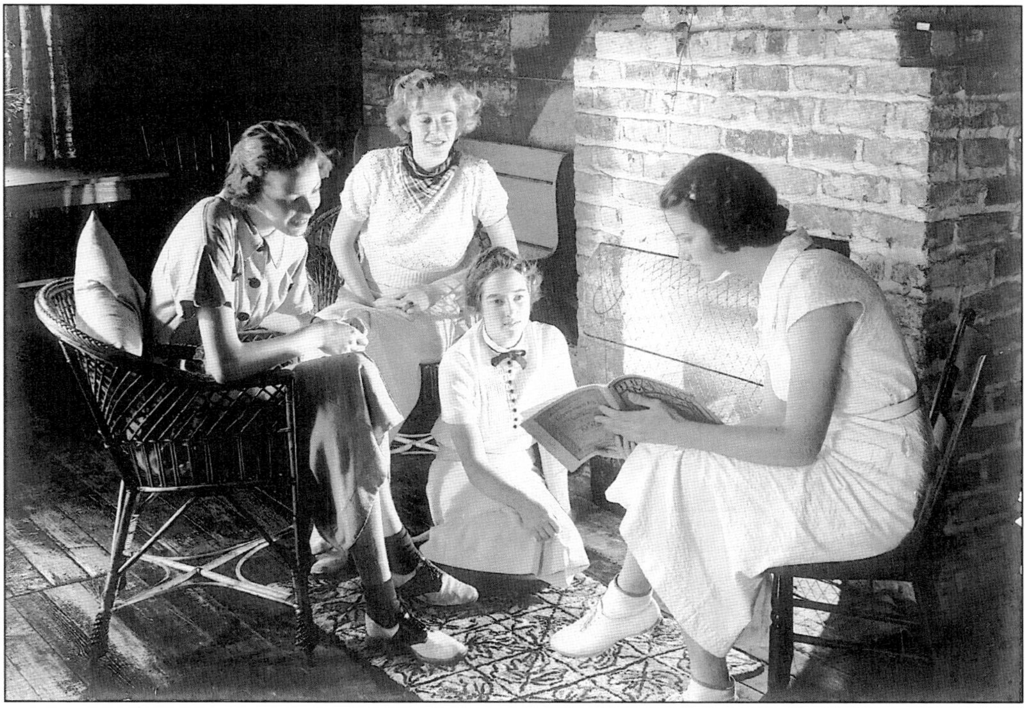

Fireside, 1936. Girls enjoy a good magazine article as they sit beside a warm fire. Caroline Haydock remembers her days as a boarder at Ashley Hall very fondly: "The top floor with the demi-balcony of McBee House was the senior floor. I was just a young school girl running around having a great time, but now I have come to realize the magnificence of the building." (Photo courtesy of the Ashley Hall Archives.)

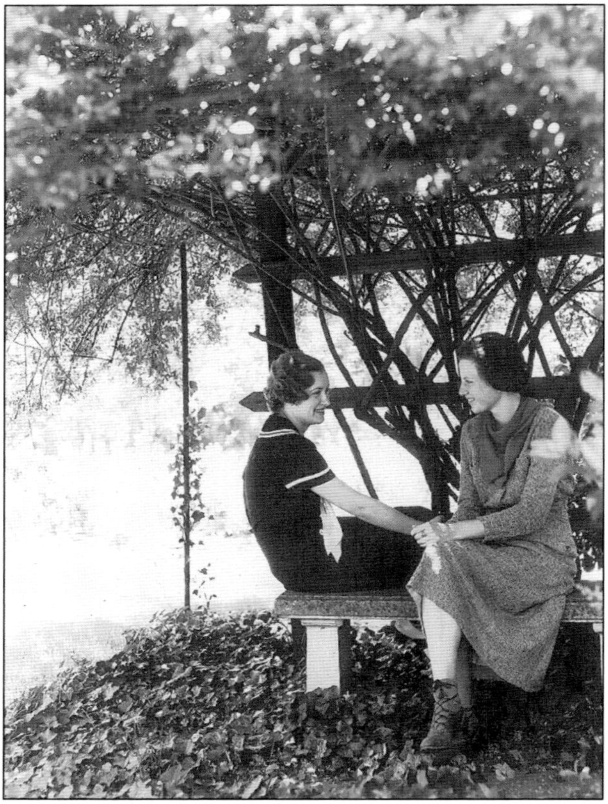

Enjoying the Outdoors, 1930s. Ashley Hall's mission is to "produce an educated woman who is independent, ethically responsible, and prepared to meet the challenges of society with confidence." (Photo courtesy of the Ashley Hall Archives.)

Chatting in the Dorms, 1930s. This photo taken from the senior residence in Lane Hall shows a more modern dorm room. Molly Gray (née Molly Hoyler, class of 1965) remembers her room with three other girls on the second floor of McBee House off of the drawing room: "The front windows faced the garden, and the side windows faced Radcliffe Street, so we were very central to things. We had house mothers on each hall, and a tiny old-fashioned bathtub where our knees came up to our chests." (Photo courtesy of the Ashley Hall Archives.)

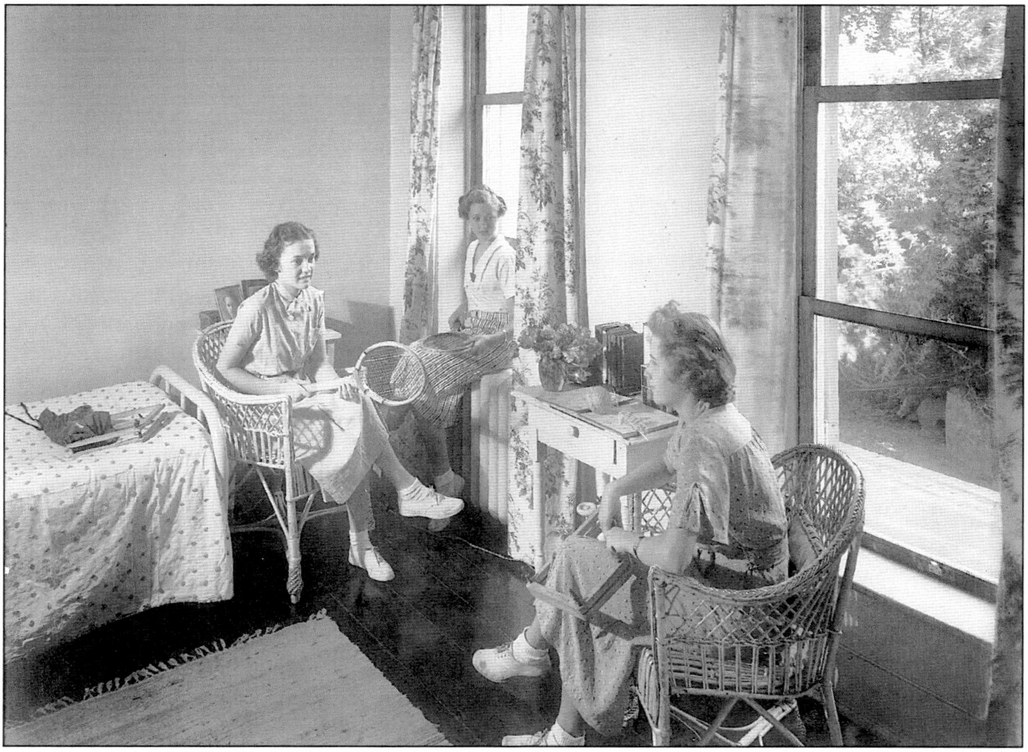

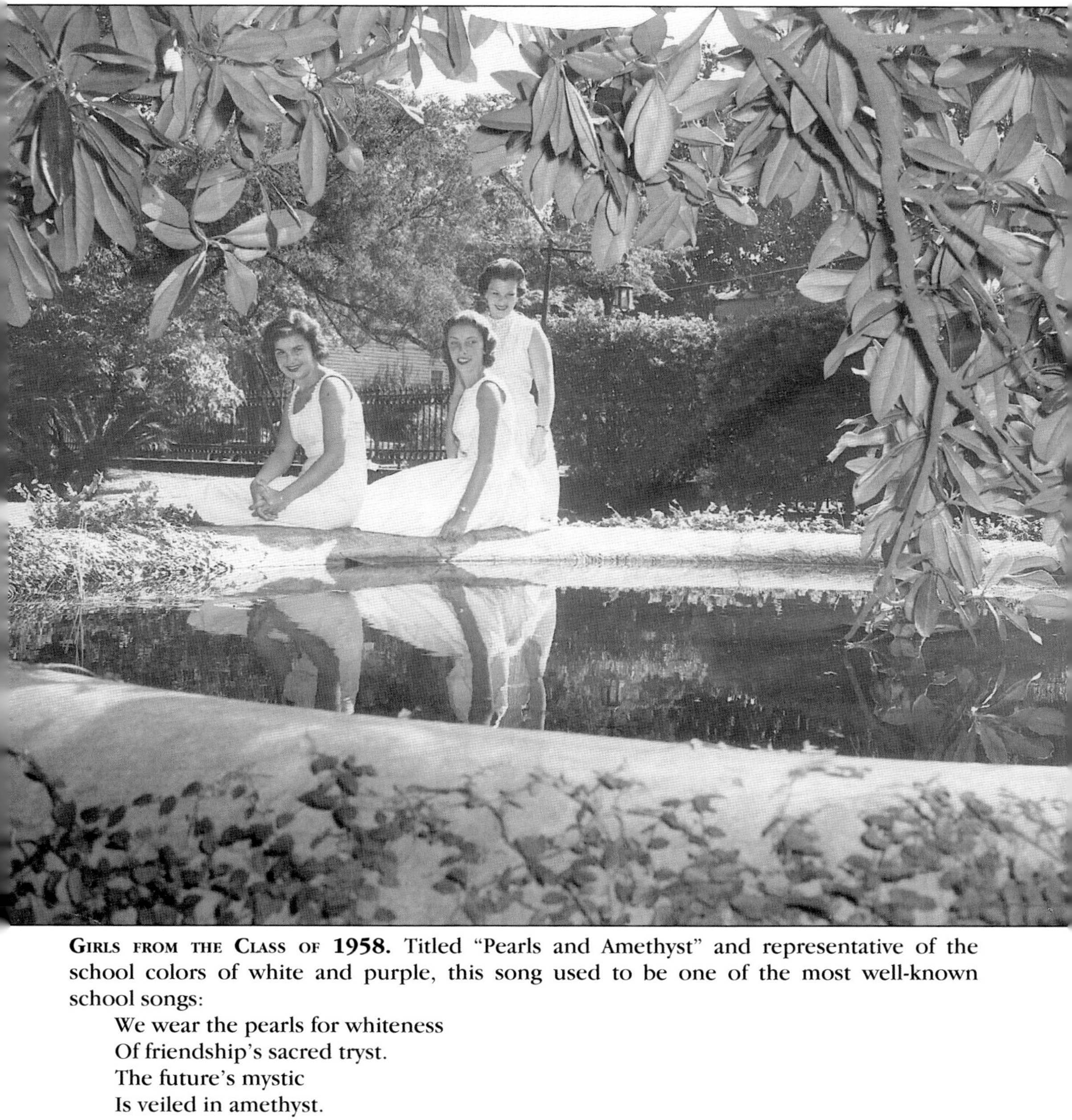

Girls from the Class of 1958. Titled "Pearls and Amethyst" and representative of the school colors of white and purple, this song used to be one of the most well-known school songs:

We wear the pearls for whiteness
Of friendship's sacred tryst.
The future's mystic
Is veiled in amethyst.
But rarer is the token
The light reveals to all—
The golden links unbroken/
Speak of Ashley Hall.
(Chorus) (Photo courtesy of the Ashley Hall Archives.)

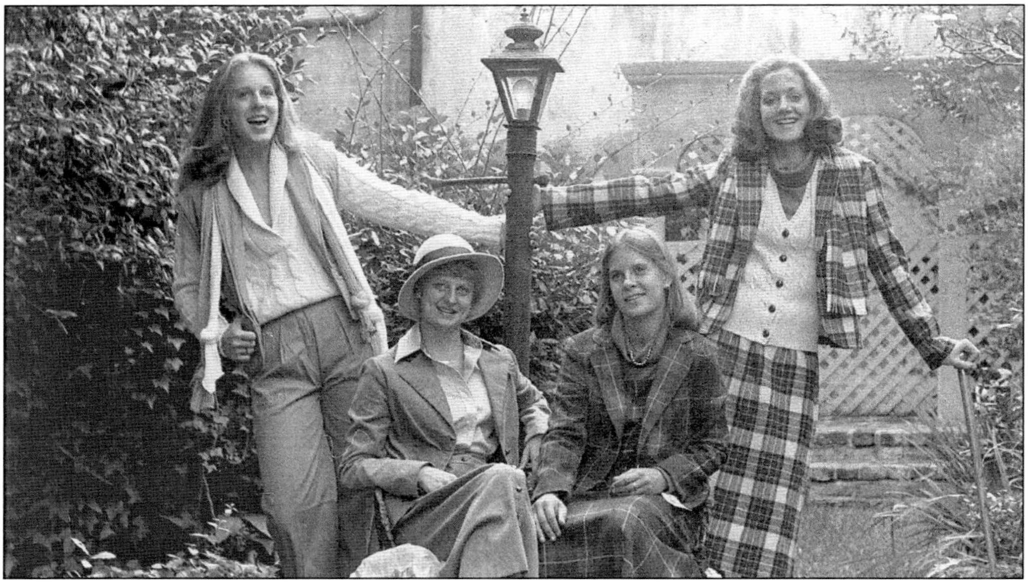

Yearbook Ad, 1979. Carolyn Swan (née Carolyn Evans, class of 1979) was the editor for the *Spiral* this year and remembers the fun and hard work that went into putting together the yearbook. "We would go door to door and ask people to buy ad space to help pay for the yearbook," she explains. Many times the advertisers would be friends or relatives of students. "We always worked together with the photography staff to make sure we had fun candids that would remind girls of the events of that year, even if they were looking at it 25 years later." (Photo courtesy of the Ashley Hall Archives.)

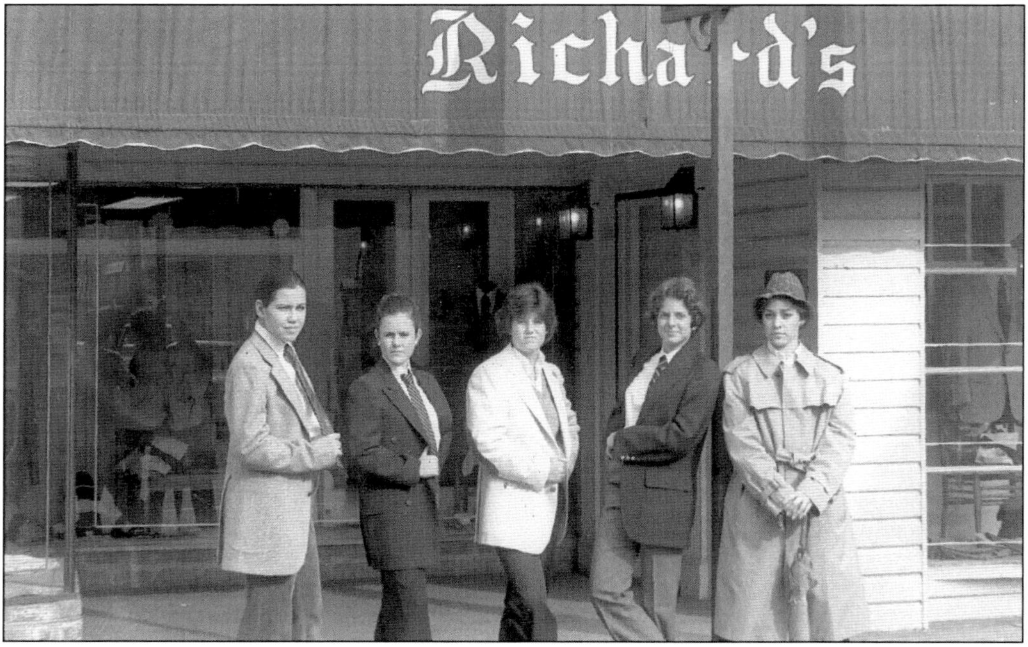

Richard's Clothing Store Ad, 1970s. Girls pose here for a clothing store ad, which is featured in the back of the *Spiral*. Dressed in men's clothing, the girls have fun making poses. A 1936 *Cerberus* joke: "Bobby waiting for the 'Courier.': 'Oh, Miss Kenley I thought you were the mail.' Miss Kenley: 'No, female.'" (Photo courtesy of the Ashley Hall Archives.)

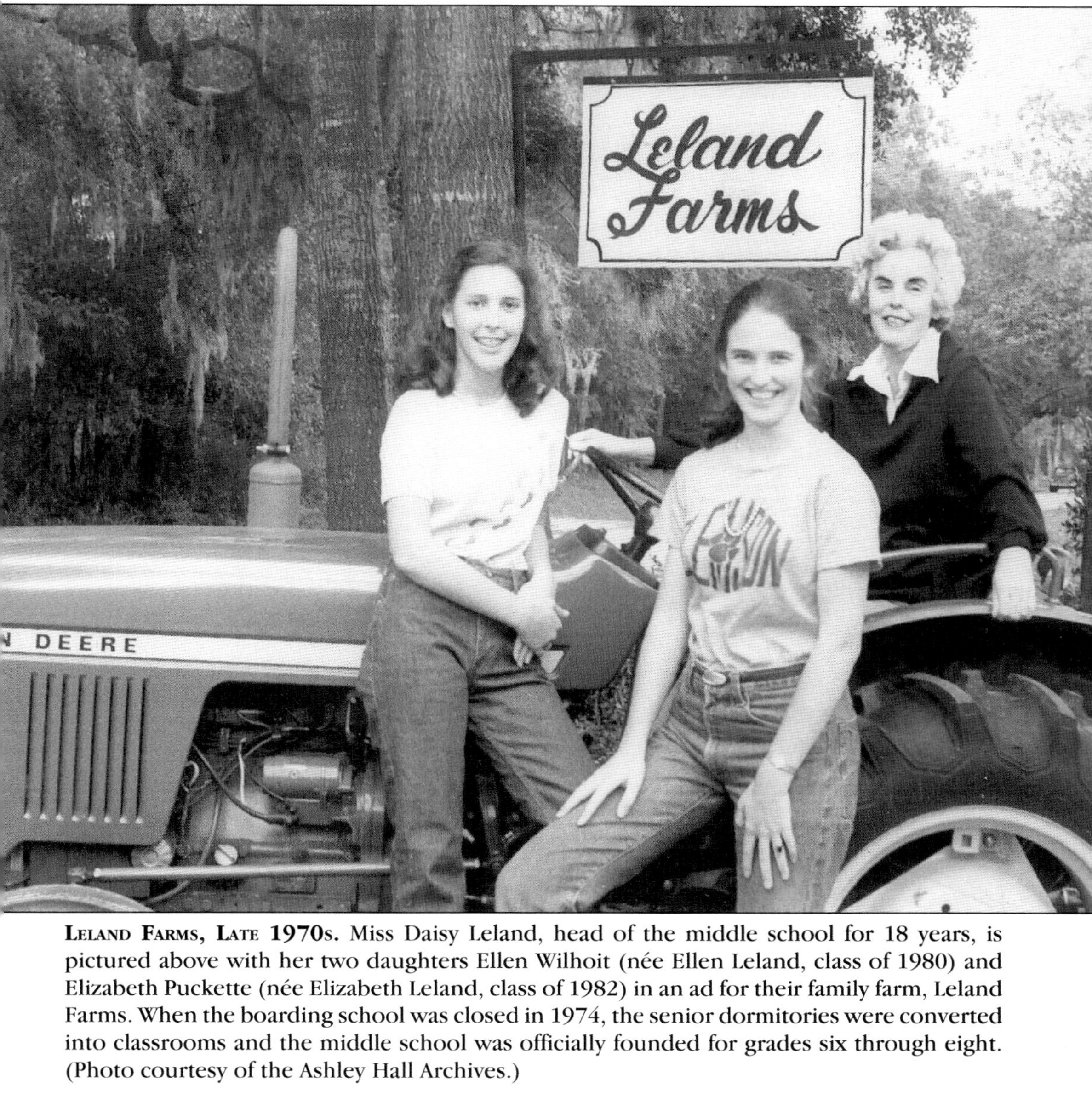

Leland Farms, Late 1970s. Miss Daisy Leland, head of the middle school for 18 years, is pictured above with her two daughters Ellen Wilhoit (née Ellen Leland, class of 1980) and Elizabeth Puckette (née Elizabeth Leland, class of 1982) in an ad for their family farm, Leland Farms. When the boarding school was closed in 1974, the senior dormitories were converted into classrooms and the middle school was officially founded for grades six through eight. (Photo courtesy of the Ashley Hall Archives.)

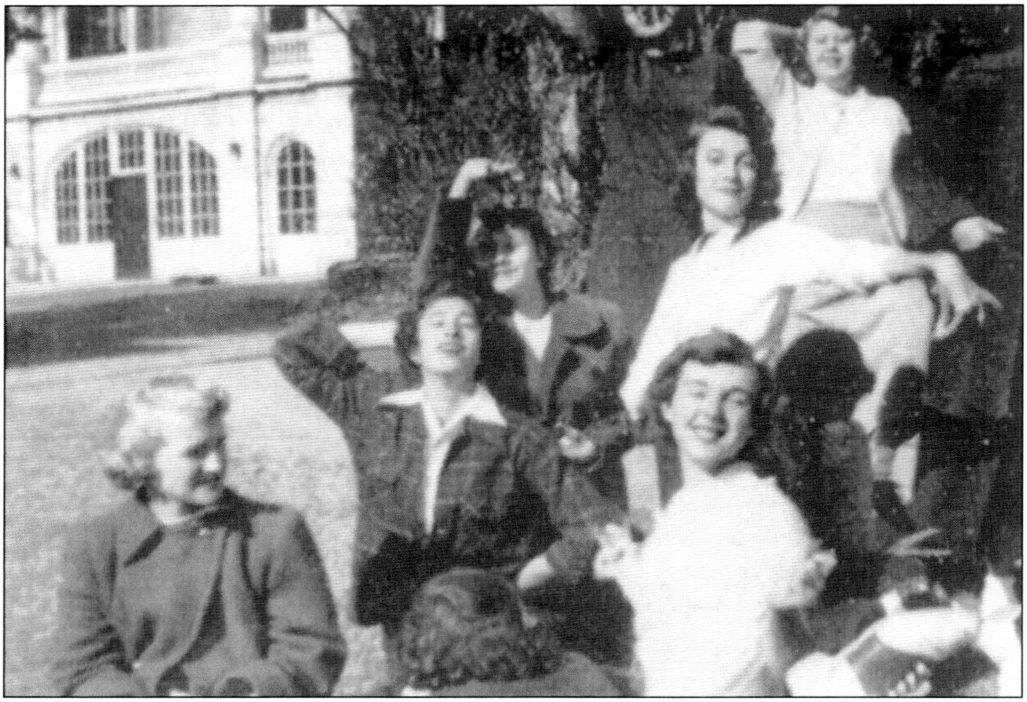

Nice Smiles Girls, 1951. Jane Thornhill recalls a friend Marietta Wade, whose father was Colonel Wade of Porter Military Academy where they lived on the campus: "Every morning the girls would rush to find Marietta to see if any boys at Porter had written them a letter." (Photo courtesy of the Ashley Hall Archives.)

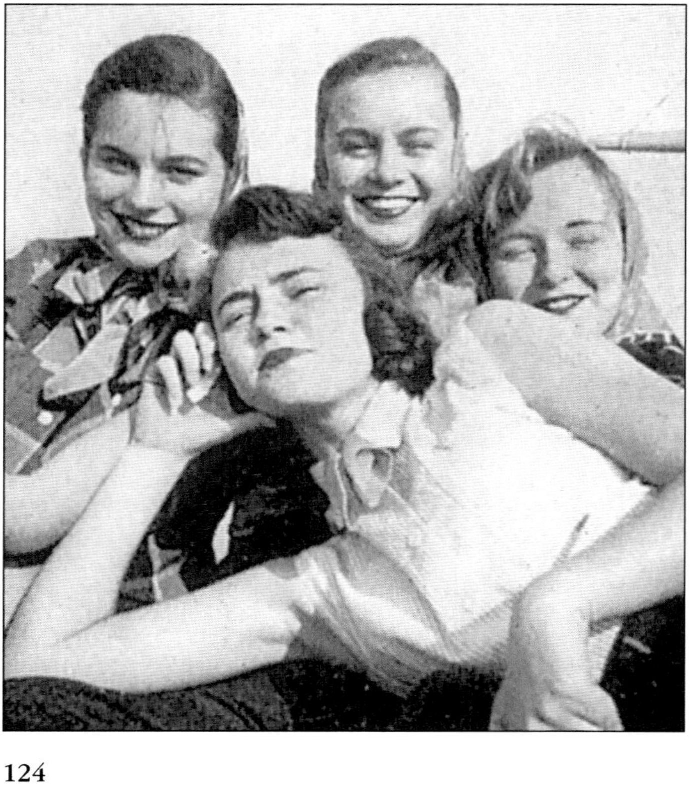

Look Pretty for the Camera, 1953. Ashley Hall attracted many girls from the North due to the inexpensive tuition, and because "Northern fathers wanted to expose their daughters to the manner of the South," claims Jane Thornhill. Little did their fathers know of some of the un-ladylike fun some of the boarders were known for. Sneaking downstairs at night with flashlights to raid the pantry and throwing water balloons on people as they walked down the street were just some of the innocent pranks pulled by the boarding students. (Photo courtesy of the Ashley Hall Archives.)

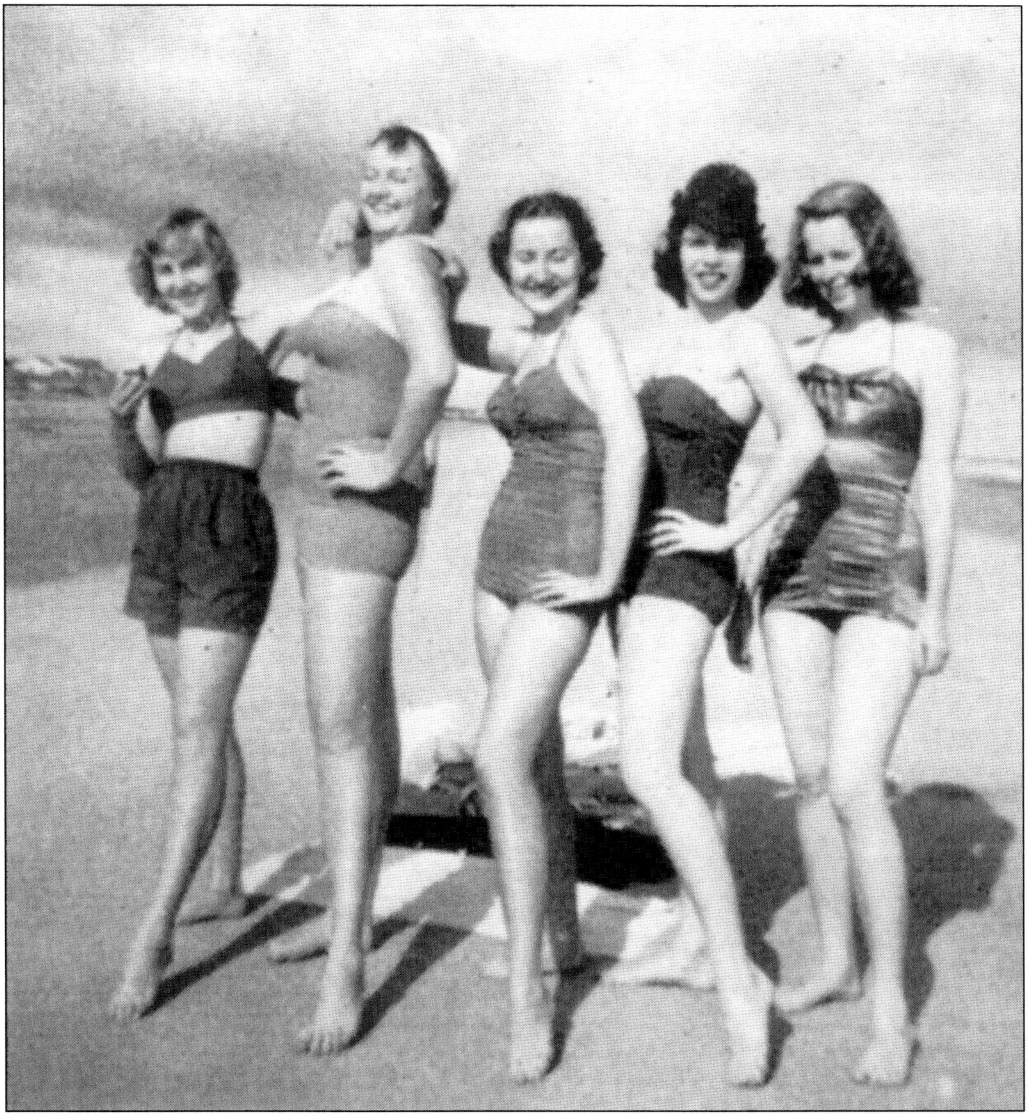

SHOWING OFF THOSE LEGS, 1953. Miss Pardue would have been appalled to see these girls showing so much of their legs. Josephine Hutcheson tells the story of her one time breaking a school rule: "I was always very good and sort of admired the girls who got in trouble. My senior year I was told to report to Miss Pardue who told me I was in violation of the dress code for not wearing stockings." Hutcheson was wearing sneakers and no socks or stockings, so she was sent home to change. The school dress code used to be very strict. It was not until the 1970s when lower school girls were allowed to wear pants; they used to have to always wear a dress, jumper, or skirt. (Photo courtesy of the Ashley Hall Archives.)

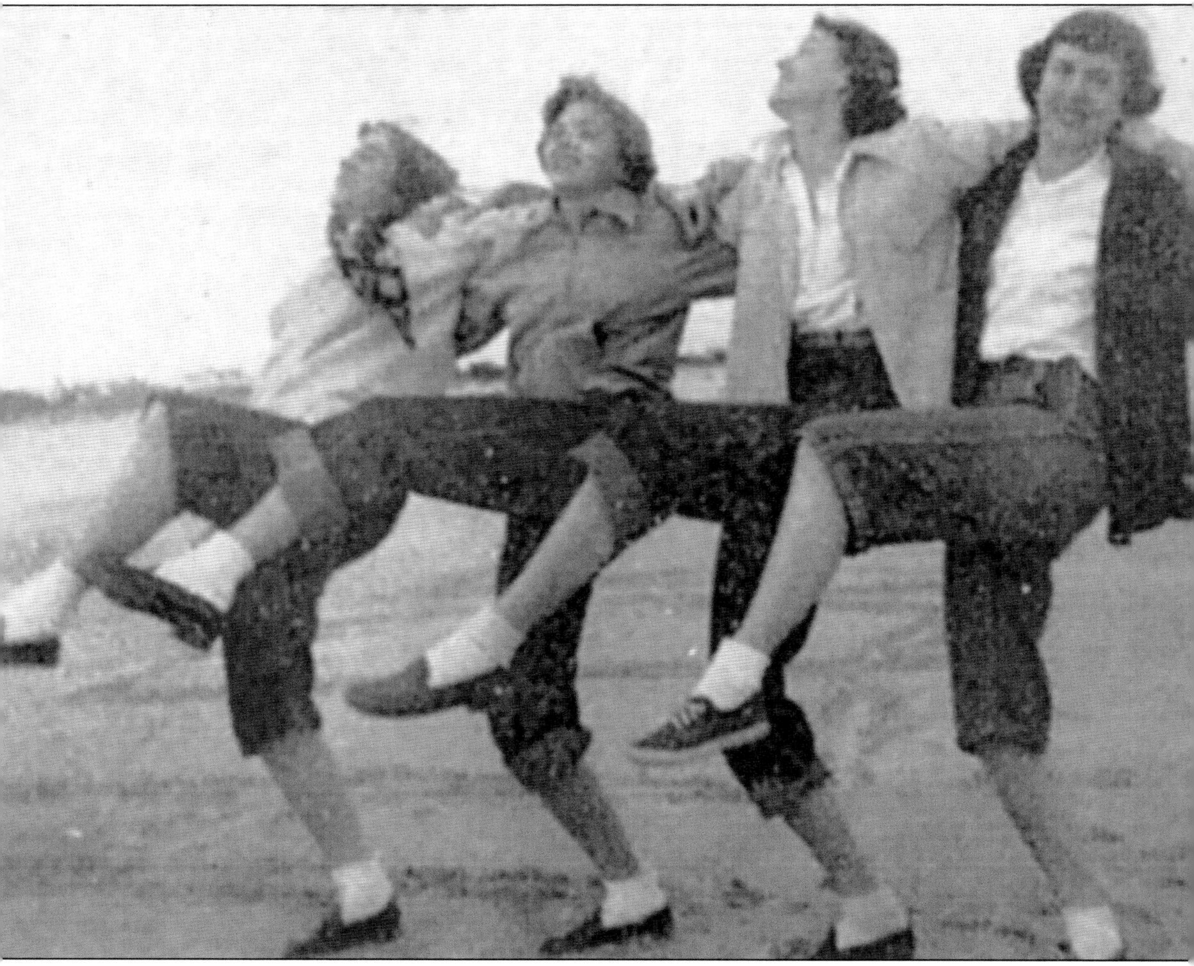

CAN YOU DO THE CAN-CAN? 1951. Besides Porter Military Academy, the girls also had regular dances with the Citadel. Weekly teas with the cadets were always fun for both parties present. One graduate recalls putting on lipstick very lightly then dusting powder over her lips so that the chaperones and teachers would not see the lipstick. Then after passing the chaperone room, the girls would lick off the powder, so the boys could see their alluring lipstick. (Photo courtesy of the Ashley Hall Archives.)

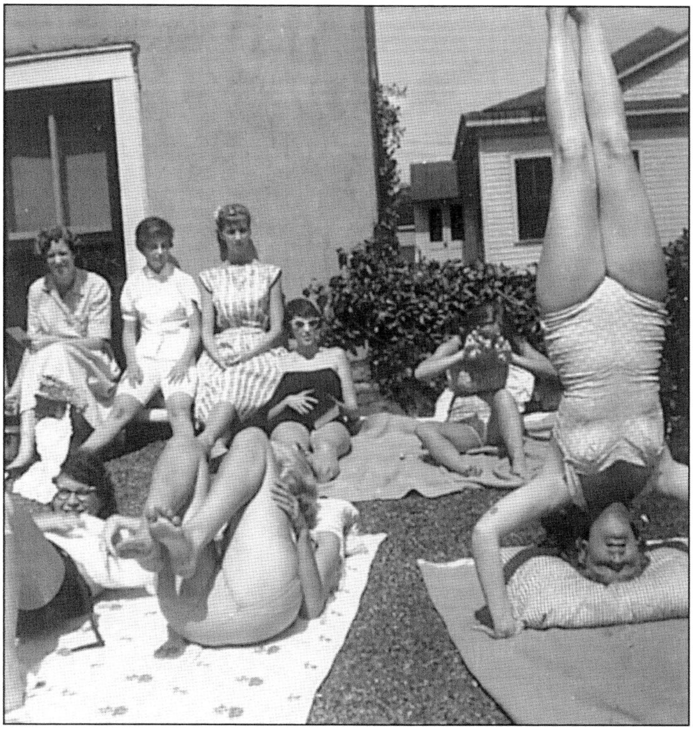

Relaxing "On the Porch," 1960s. Patti Workman (née Patti Fishburne, class of 1960) in the photo here remembers, "we [the boarders] would go up to this flat tar-paper roof on top of the sophomore and junior hall to get a tan." At the time Mrs. Brown was the head of the boarding department and she and Miss Pardue were like second mothers to the girls. "They were very tough, but very fair. We always felt we could go to them for anything." (Photo courtesy of the Ashley Hall Archives.)

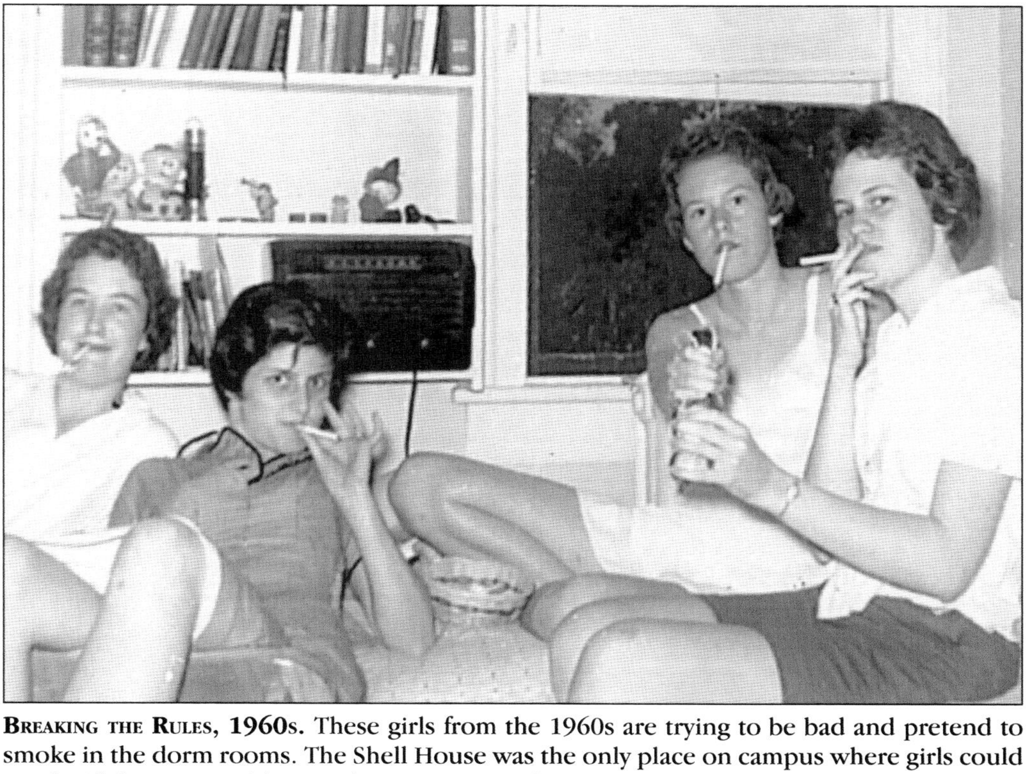

Breaking the Rules, 1960s. These girls from the 1960s are trying to be bad and pretend to smoke in the dorm rooms. The Shell House was the only place on campus where girls could smoke if they were old enough. Because smoking was so popular at the time, the Shell House was one of the campus hot spots. (Photo courtesy of the Ashley Hall Archives.)

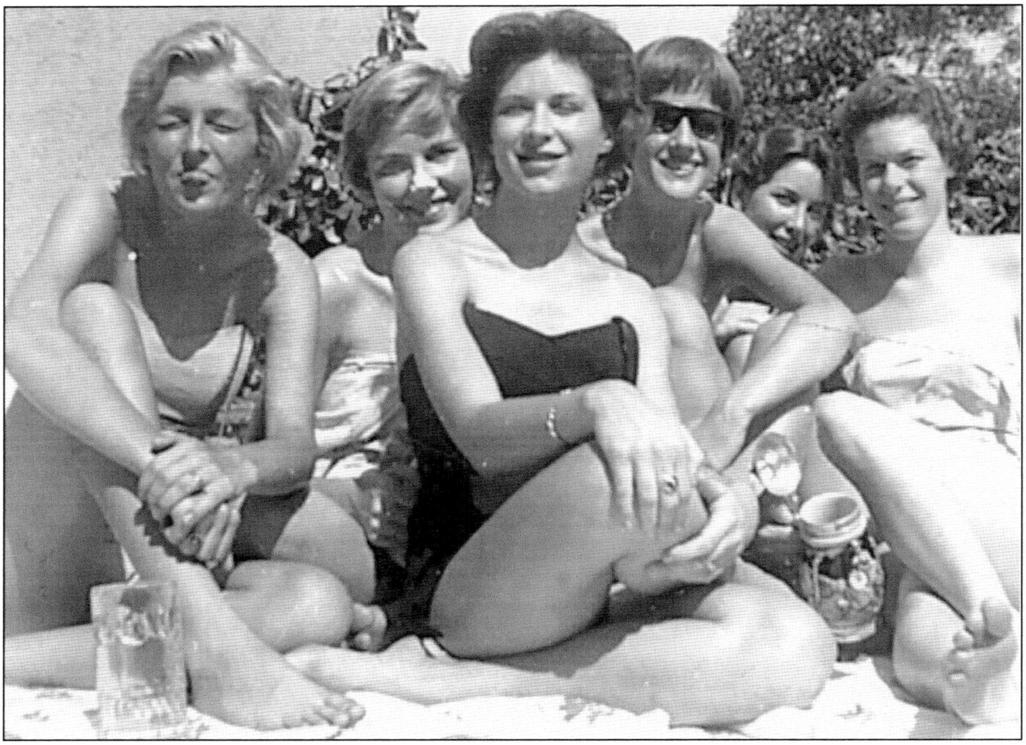

Sunbathing, 1960s. Molly Gray remembers really enjoying her days as a boarder at Ashley Hall. "Charleston was a wonderful place at that time in history; it was really beautiful," she recollects. (Photo courtesy of the Ashley Hall Archives.)

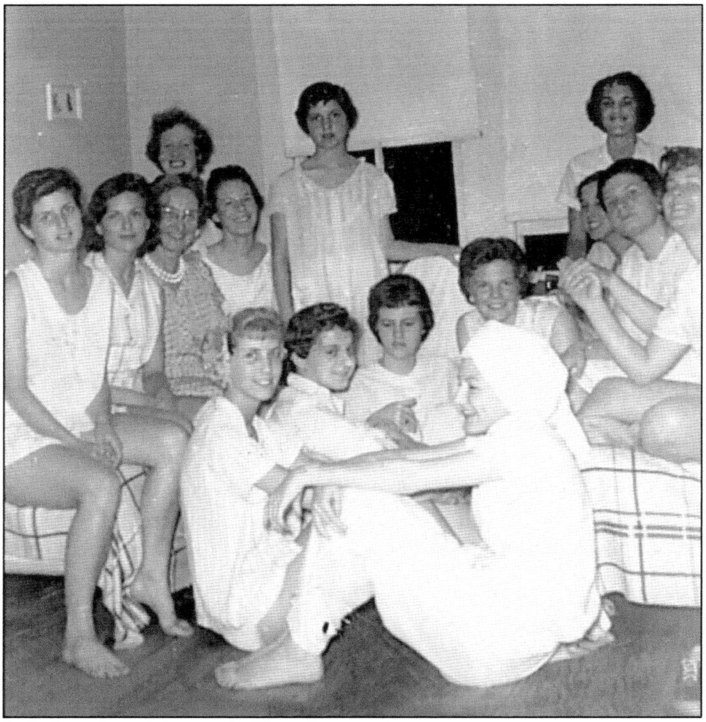

Sally Dobbins (class of 1960) recalls Ashley Hall being "great preparation for college." As a boarding student, Dobbins remembers waiting out Hurricane Hazel in the upstairs of her dorm with her friends and dorm mother as the loud thunder and wind rushed outside. "I don't remember being scared, but I do remember looking out the window the next day and seeing a motor boat going down Rutledge Avenue with a man on water-skis behind it!" (Photo courtesy of the Ashley Hall Archives.)